The Power of Professionalism

Select Endorsements for *The Power of Professionalism*

"My brain lights up when I come across a book that asks an inconvenient question we'd all prefer to ignore, like that proverbial elephant in the room. Wiersma casts a spotlight on that elephant and brilliantly shoves inconvenient truths down our throats that all of us—leaders, professionals, everyone—had better swallow. One of the few Must Reads of the Year!"

— **Warren Bennis,** the dean of leadership gurus (Forbes), Distinguished Professor of Business, University of Southern California, and author of the recently published *Still Surprised: A Memoir of a Life in Leadership*

"The most compelling business books aren't the ones that just convey knowledge or advocate doing certain things. As important as those are, the most compelling business books encourage readers to be something. *The Power of Professionalism* is destined to change the way people think about professionals and, more important, to change the way professionals view themselves."

— **Bill Roper**, President, Roper Capital Company, former CEO at VeriSign and former CFO at SAIC

"Simply put, Bill Wiersma is a genius. His new book, *The Power of Professionalism*, is revolutionary—one that will provide a much-needed renaissance of professional ideals, that speaks to the mind-sets that made America great, and that will continue to inspire us to future greatness. Thought-provoking, brilliantly stunning, *The Power of Professionalism* is crucial medicine, whether it be for a Fortune 500 company, a hard-charging entrepreneurial start-up, or for a passionate nonprofit. Please read this book—your professional life depends on learning and living these strategies."

— **Kathy Ireland**, CEO/Chief Designer, kathy ireland WorldWide

"*The Power of Professionalism* is a tour de force. Bill Wiersma has written a masterwork of nonfiction rarely seen today. It is smart, profound, and challenging. It will provoke you, engage you, and change you. It will make you think deeply about how you work, how you relate, and how you live. It will compel you to elevate your standards, raise your hopes, and lift your sights. There hasn't been a book with this kind of intensity and power in years . . . maybe decades. You really must read it and put it into practice."

— **Jim Kouzes**, award-winning coauthor of the bestselling *The Leadership Challenge*, and the Dean's Executive Professor of Leadership, Leavey School of Business, Santa Clara University

"There are books that represent such breakthroughs in ideas that they often become a generational standard and spawn thousands of imitators. *The Power of Professionalism* is one such book. Professionalism in business enterprises, non-profits and government institutions is the key to success in the modern world. In my role as an educator I've used this book for over two years with my entrepreneurial students with glowing results. *The Power of Professionalism* is hands-down the most comprehensive and well-researched book ever written on a topic of paramount importance to our global future. When it comes to thought-leaders, there are few emerging faster than Bill Wiersma. This is due largely to his unrivaled experience in the niche he gave birth to—namely using 'professionalism' as a platform to transform people and organizations. An awesome work!"

— **Raul A. Deju,** Best-selling author, Director Institute of Entrepreneurial Leadership, John F. Kennedy University and former President and Chief Operating Office of both EnergySolutions and Headwaters, Inc.

"When initially asked to review this book, my natural inclination was to decline-based on my comically busy workload. However, after reading the preface and early chapters, I was hooked. This topic couldn't be more important to America's future. The book is a great read, the ideas are fresh and insightful, the authors are the best in their fields. This is essential reading for professionals and for those who employ them."

— **Steve Kerr**, Executive Director of the Jack Welch Management Institute and former Chief Learning Officer at both General Electric and Goldman Sachs

"Bill Wiersma has rendered an incredible gift to leaders in all three sectors. Inspiring in its breadth, profound in its depth, compelling in its presentation, *The Power of Professionalism* is destined to be one of our era's most celebrated books."

— **Frances Hesselbein**, President & CEO, Leader to Leader Institute (Formerly the Peter F. Drucker Foundation for Nonprofit Management), former CEO Girl Scouts of the U.S.A.

"*The Power of Professionalism* captures a fundamental truth of life, not just business. This book takes a seemingly Victorian subject—professionalism—and shoehorns its relevance into the heart of our twenty-first century problems. Wiersma's tome is masterful; his timing superb.

— **Thomas Moran**, Chairman, President, and CEO of Mutual of America Life Insurance and Chairman of Concern Worldwide (U.S.), an international humanitarian relief organization that operates in twenty-nine of the poorest countries of the world

"For those concerned about the moral grounding of leaders in organizations, this book provides the ultimate tuning fork for professionals. As Wiersma makes clear, professionalism is neither a title nor a tactic we follow. Rather, it's about discipline and standards. In this masterful restatement of professional ideals, Wiersma recaptures timeless wisdom that which is often lost in today's culture of unhealthy competition, shortcuts, and winner-take-all mentality."

— **Carolyn Woo**, President and CEO Catholic Relief Services, former Dean of the Mendoza School of Business at the University of Notre Dame

"Prepare to be challenged, be inspired, and, ultimately, be a better professional."

— **Paul Sarvadi**, Chairman and CEO, Administaff (Insperity)

"Wow! Now that's a word that you rarely hear people use in describing a business book. But wow perfectly describes this masterful treatise on a subject—professionalism—that seemingly didn't need one. Few authors could have done justice to this topic in quite the way Wiersma has, with his penetrating insights, meticulous research, and wonderful storytelling ability. For each of us, this book marks the beginning of the journey in becoming a truly better professional."

— **Beverly Kaye**, Founder and CEO, Career Systems International, internationally recognized expert in talent management, career development, and the co-author of the classic *Love 'Em or Lose 'Em*

"Absolutely compelling! One of the finest business books I've ever read. This is one of the few select books on leadership—because of its breadth and depth—that should be a permanent addition to every professional's library. *The Power of Professionalism* is a '10' in every regard!"

— **Lewis L. "Lee" Bird III**, CEO at Garden Ridge, former Group President at Nike Inc., former COO at Gap, and former CFO at Old Navy

"Someone once remarked that Peter Drucker practiced 'the scholarship of common sense.' The same can be said of Bill Wiersma. *The Power of Professionalism* is a terrific road map for doing things right while doing the right things."

— **Rick Wartzman**, Executive Director of the Drucker Institute at Claremont Graduate University and columnist for Bloomberg Businessweek

"I've read hundreds of the best business books and had thought-provoking conversations on management and leadership with thousands of CEOs, but I was astounded to realize after reading *The Power of Professionalism* that no one had previously addressed this all-important topic. Never again will people question what it means to be a professional. For those who want to grow as individuals and as leaders, you can't help but be elevated in your thinking and be inspired by what's possible after reading this ground-breaking book."

— **Paul Witkay**, Founder & CEO, Alliance of Chief Executives

"Because professionalism is the foundation for all other organizational virtues and is essential to developing a high performance workplace, this topic will hold marquee value for savvy leaders, new and seasoned. *The Power of Professionalism* serves as a reminder to each of us how important it is to serve a purpose bigger than ourselves."

— **Tom Werner**, CEO, SunPower Corporation and Chairman, Silicon Valley Leadership Group

"Whether by design, inattention, or ignorance there's too much counterfeit professionalism being practiced today. In an age of declining standards *The Power of Professionalism* shows us true North. This important book should be required reading in every MBA program!"

— **Marc Effron**, President, The Talent Strategy Group, founder of the world's largest organization for talent management professionals. Marc's trend-setting book, *One Page Talent Management*, with coauthor Miriam Ort, was recently published by Harvard Business Press

"Revolutionary and highly persuasive. Bill Wiersma has solved one of the great conundrums of our time: why an era so focused on the training, development, and identification of leaders has produced so few who are sustainably successful. Wiersma's insight— his *Big Aha*— is that the central role of professionalism has not been fully appreciated, let alone understood well. *The Power of Professionalism* gives all of us a new frame for thinking about how we work and who we are at work. How powerful and transformational is that?"

— **Sally Helgesen**, author, *The Female Vision, The Web of Inclusion, Thriving in 24/7,* and *The Female Advantage*

"We are living and working today in the most competitive time of our lives. This powerful, practical book shows you how to develop the 'winning edge' that will enable you to survive and thrive no matter what happens."

— **Brian Tracy**, internationally renowned authority on personal and business success with more than forty years in the field and author of more than forty books, including the recently published, *Now, Build a Great Business*, with coauthor Mark Thompson

"With a constant focus on trust and personal standards, this book stands out as must-read material for anyone striving to be an improved professional in the workplace."

— **Gary Keller**, *New York Times* bestselling author of *The Millionaire Real Estate Agent* and *The Millionaire Real Estate Investor*, Cofounder and Chairman of Keller Williams Reality

"Professionalism is fundamental to a leader's ability to build a valuable company. Before now, no book has so thoughtfully illuminated the components that make up this important concept. Wiersma's seven mind-sets will prove both useful and actionable for everyone from the shop floor to the executive suite."

— **Geoff Smart**, CEO of ghSMART, a management assessment, coaching, and executive learning firm for CEO's and investors, and coauthor of the New York Times bestseller *Who: The A Method for Hiring*

"Here's a fresh and valuable insight especially for leaders and managers on the power of what it really means to be a professional. Wiersma has done it again, providing yet another *Big AHA!*"

— **James O'Toole**, Distinguished Professor of Business Ethics at the Daniels College of Business at the University of Denver and an internationally recognized authority on corporate culture and leadership and the author of fourteen books, including the classic Leading Change

"As someone who has spent my professional lifetime educating managers at a business school, I have always believed that management can be a noble profession. Invariably it is noble when trusted professionals are involved. This book makes explicit what a professional mind-set is really all about and why it's a prerequisite to being considered a trusted professional. Yes, there are profound ideas here. Yet more important, the book holds great promise in raising standards, ones that are characteristic of the most noble managers in my acquaintance."

— **Allan Cohen**, Edward A. Madden Distinguished Professor of Global Leadership at Babson College and coauthor of *Influence Without Authority and Power Up*

The Power of Professionalism

The Power of Professionalism

THE Seven Mind-Sets THAT Drive Performance AND Build Trust

BILL WIERSMA

AUTHOR OF **The Big AHA!**

Ravel Media
Los Altos, California

The Power of Professionalism

Published by Ravel Media
Ravel Media, LLC
www.ravel.tv

ISBN: 978-1-932881-04-2 (hardcover)
ISBN: 978-1-932881-05-9 (Kindle)
ISBN: 978-1-932881-13-4 (ePub)

Cover design by George Foster, Foster Covers, Fairfield, Iowa
Interior design and typesetting by Desktop Miracles Inc., Stowe, Vermont

Publisher's Cataloging-In-Publication Data
(Prepared by The Donohue Group, Inc.)

Wiersma, Bill.
The power of professionalism / Bill Wiersma.
p. : ill. ; cm.
Includes bibliographical references and index.
ISBN: 978-1-932881-04-2
ISBN: 978-1-932881-05-9
ISBN: 978-1-932881-13-4
1. Professional employees—Psychology. 2. Reliability. 3. Respect for persons. I. Title.
HF8038 .W54 2011
658.3044

Printed in the United States of America

To Martha

Contents

Acknowledgments

One name—mine—graces the cover of this book as author. However, hundreds of people in one way, shape, or form helped to make this book possible. All have proved important, whether they be a world-renowned thought leader or a research librarian. And all have been exceptionally generous, which is something for which I'm especially grateful.

As a practical matter, it's unrealistic to acknowledge here everyone involved in the creation and support of this book. But some key people warrant special mention.

I'm especially indebted to my two editors—Martha Dayley and Ed Curtis—who made significant contributions in improving the content and readability of this book. Martha, to whom this book is dedicated, died tragically in 2009. Martha and I worked together for over five years; she was the editor of my first book, *The Big AHA!* Martha helped set the foundation and tone for this book. More important, though, she was an important collaborator, a trusted confidant, and a good friend. Martha epitomized what it means to be a consummate professional.

After Martha's passing I was very fortunate to find Ed Curtis, a savvy editor with formidable skills. In addition to shaping my disjointed ideas into coherent text, Ed did great work on the content involving the Founding Fathers. His advice and perspectives have proven invaluable.

A very special thanks goes to those individuals who consented to be formal contributors to this book: John Bogle, Marshall Goldsmith, Frances Hesselbein, Kathy Ireland, Gen. Richard B. Myers, Paul Orfalea, and Dave Ulrich. Throughout my writing, they have allowed me to interview them and later consult them by phone and e-mail, and they have reviewed the chapters in which they are quoted. Their contributions to this work are invaluable, and my thanks to them is indescribable.

I would like to offer many thanks to Tony La Russa for the powerful foreword, written in Tony's forthright, compelling style.

I especially appreciated the feedback provided by Paul McKinnon (Head of Human Resources at Citigroup) on the first draft of the manuscript. Paul's feedback proved to be the catalyst that facilitated substantive changes that enhanced the book's content. Also, Allan Cohen, Edward A. Madden Distinguished Professor of Global Leadership at Babson College, provided wonderful support and insights on chapter 4, "Trust: The One Thing You Have to Get Right."

Susan Couden, Tim Stalder, Jim Earle, and Marcia Eblen provided priceless feedback on the book's final content.

Special thanks go to my proofreaders: Donna Astramecki, Jim "Gymbeaux" Brown, Jen Colosi, Curt Cournale, Ben Dreese, Paulie Fabela, Ellen Fletcher, Victoria Ghulam, Jim Gill, Lars Johansson, Chris Lukis, Kelan Raph, Heidi Stoltz, Holly Wiersma, and Natalie Wiersma.

I cannot understate my appreciation for the coordinating efforts of Elena Bicker, Gloria Fahlikman, Lyda Goldsmith, Kevin Laughlin, Kate Love, Judy Seegmiller, Emily Snyder, Ruben Torres, and Erin Voto with the book's contributors.

Thanks also should be tendered to George Foster for producing a great cover, to Barry Kerrigan and Del LeMond for producing another stellar book layout, to Peter Bowerman for his insights on the book's promotional copy, to Joshua Oram for his outstanding work on the book's graphics, and to Dottie DeHart and Rajesh Setty for their sage advice on book marketing.

Finally, inexpressible thanks goes to my wife Holly for supporting yet another book project—one that frequently competed with family priorities (that is, honey-dos). The fact that she was also willing to proofread the pages is no small testimony to her encouragement to me from start to finish of this project.

List of Contributors

John Bogle is the founder and former Senior Chairman and CEO of the Vanguard Group, the world's second largest mutual fund company. *Fortune* magazine named Bogle as one of the investment industry's four giants of the twentieth century. John is the author of eight books, including the bestsellers *The Battle for the Soul of Capitalism* and *Enough.* Bogle currently serves as Chairman Emeritus of the National Constitution Center in Philadelphia, a museum dedicated to the U.S. Constitution. John previously served as Chairman of the Board of the National Constitutional Center from 1999 through 2007.

Marshall Goldsmith is a world authority in helping successful leaders achieve positive, lasting change in behavior. He has recently been recognized by the *Times* (London) and *Forbes* as one of the world's top fifteen business thinkers. Goldsmith is the author or editor of thirty-one books, including the *New York Times* bestsellers *Mojo: How to Get It, How to Keep It, How to Get It Back If You Lost It* and *What Got You Here Won't Get You There: How Successful People Become Even More Successful* (a *Wall Street Journal* number-one business book and winner of the Harold Longman Award for Business Book of the Year). He is one of a select few executive advisors who have been asked to work with more than 120 major CEOs.

Frances Hesselbein is the President and CEO of the Leader-to-Leader Institute (formerly the Peter F. Drucker Foundation). She serves on numerous nonprofit and private sector boards and has been featured in *Business Week, Fortune,* and *Chief Executive* magazines. France was awarded the Presidential Medal of Freedom—the nation's highest civilian honor—and has served on two presidential commissions. She has also received twenty honorary doctorate degrees. She is the co-editor of twenty-seven books in thirty languages. Frances served as CEO of the Girl Scouts (USA) from 1976 to 1990. The legendary Peter Drucker called Frances the greatest executive he's ever known.

Kathy Ireland is CEO/Chief Designer of kathy ireland WorldWide (kiWW), a design and marketing enterprise with an estimated $1.5 billion in annual sales (*Forbes*). Kathy—a savvy, self-taught fashion dynamo—has quietly forged remarkable business achievements that have proven much more successful than her celebrated modeling career. Today kiWW has over forty-five thousand individual products in tens of thousands of stores in seventy countries and ranks sixteenth of all companies in licensing revenue (*License! Global Magazine*). An author of six books, Kathy is recognized as one of America's most accomplished entrepreneurial CEOs (*Forbes*).

Tony La Russa, a future Baseball Hall of Fame member, is one of only two managers to win the World Series in both leagues. He also is the first ever to win multiple pennants in both leagues. As a manager, La Russa is ranked third all-time for the total number of career wins and is a five-time recipient of Manager of the Year honors. Tony, a California resident, is cofounder of Tony La Russa's Animal Rescue Foundation (ARF).

Gen. Richard B. Myers (Ret.) is the former Chairman of the Joint Chiefs of Staff (2001–2005), the highest-ranking military officer in the United States. A former Air Force general, he was awarded the Presidential Medal of Freedom and holds the Colin Powell Chair of Leadership, Ethics and Character at National Defense University. Myers is the author of *Eyes on The Horizon* which chronicles his rise and stint as Chairman of the Joint Chiefs. In addition to being Foundation Professor of Military

History and Leadership at his alma mater, Kansas State University, Myers serves on the board of directors of Northrup Grumman Corporation, Deere and Co., United Technologies, and Aon.

Paul Orfalea is the founder and former CEO of Kinko's, the copy-center dynasty that Federal Express acquired in 2004 for $2.4 billion. His illustrious business career and the philosophies that fueled it have been covered by the nation's prominent television and print media as well as memorialized in Paul's 2005 book *Copy This!* Paul and his wife, Natalie, are founders of the Orfalea Family Foundation, a philanthropic endeavor benefiting higher education, families at risk, and autism research. California Polytechnic State University dedicated its business school in Orfalea's name.

Dave Ulrich is the world's leading human resources consultant. He has written twenty-three books, many of which are based on his consultation with over half the Fortune 200. Dave has been recognized by *HR Magazine* as the number one most influential international thought leader (2010). His book *The Why of Work: How Great Leaders Build Abundant Organizations That Work* (published in 2010 with Wendy Ulrich) was a number-one bestseller for the *Wall Street Journal* and *USA Today.* Dave was ranked as the number-two management guru by Executive Excellence (2005). He is a Partner and cofounder of the RBL Group and a Professor of Business at the Ross School of Business, University of Michigan.

Foreword

by Tony La Russa

Early on a reader notices that the contributors to *The Power of Professionalism* are well known for their expertise on the subject of this book. Once that gets your attention and you start to examine the guts of what's written, you will be impressed that the essence of this book asks and answers two critically important questions.

What does it *really* mean to be a professional? And once that is known, what are the implications to individuals and their organizations?

These are seemingly straightforward questions, but their answers are often partially or totally missed. Professionalism is used in so many ways and contexts that its meaning varies widely.

The context of my experience is professional baseball. One description of today's pro baseball environment that I agree with is that it represents potentially the *best* and *worst* of times!

The best because players have tremendous opportunities to earn significant money and security while gaining considerable public attention that can translate into potential postcareer advantages.

The worst because a player's professional and personal life is much more vulnerable to distractions and other challenges that were not significant during other baseball eras.

To reconcile these opposite consequences and pursue your career in the best manner possible, the solution is "to recognize that success depends more on your mental abilities than your physical ones!"

The most important first step a person can take is to recognize the truth of that statement! Once that priority has his or her attention, he or she can begin to learn how to acquire the "professional mind-set"!

Bill Wiersma has combined his knowledge and experience with the insights from his contributors to take professionalism to new and *personal* levels. Today's distractions are dealt with by focusing on personal motivation. It's all about how each of us measures up!

This book is important because it objectively sets standards and expectations for each of us in our journey toward our professional best. We alone control our outcome!

Part 1 explains why professionalism matters. Then part 2 presents seven mind-sets that lead you to your goal: becoming a trusted professional!

Bill Wiersma's *Power of Professionalism* is the nexus of three powerful principles that combine psychology, organizational street smarts, and consulting know-how. He presents these valuable insights by making the complex simple and understandable.

It's an approach that works. When I do it right, I'm professional and trusted. When I don't, then I go back to these basics and fix it!

Preface

Professionals, the advice goes, should never take things personally. This book is an exception. It's an appeal to the best in people and written especially for those wishing to become an even better professional. Take it personally, very personally.

The book's message is that professionalism matters—often more than any other factor—in creating a competitive advantage for individuals and, collectively, for the organizations of which they are part. This is easy to understand, but hard to do.

You may be thinking, Oh, no, here's another "secret sauce" book! Follow Wiersma's multistep formula and—viola!—guaranteed business success is yours!

Nothing could be further from the truth!

Business success is often as elusive as the holy grail. Just as elusive is understanding the path that leads to it. There's always a myriad of factors involved, and they're dynamic. Finding the right factors in the right amounts and incorporating them at just the right time are tricky maneuvers. In other words, pushing button X (better marketing) does not always produce outcome Y (higher profits). Sometimes, it produces outcome Z (flat profits).

Said another way, it's extremely difficult with any level of empirical precision to claim that cause X produced effect Y.[1] Yet many authors do just that. That said, this book advances the premise that **professional ideals, for both individuals and their organizations, have an inseparable correlation to success.** Why? Because developing a culture centered on professional ideals, by default, builds trust.

Each week we hear of yet another crash-and-burn story about some business highflyer. The cause? The highflyer failed to be found trustworthy and fell short of prescribed professional expectations. Behind nearly all of the stories are several all-too-common themes: people at the mercy of their egos, so-called leaders succumbing to the allure of power, still others being seduced by blind ambition. It's always a matter of bad judgment and a lack of trustworthiness any way you cut it. Does this only apply to rock-star CEOs? Absolutely not! For every story you hear, there are twenty you don't. These violations of trust, in varying degrees, impact every level of an organization.

To paraphrase Bill George, former chairman and CEO of Medtronic: We in business do not need more self-indulged people—whether revealed through financial shenanigans, power trips, or appeasing one's ego. And we certainly don't need more laws. **We need better professionals—and more of them—the great antidote for much of what ails business today.**

If you believe, as I do, that trust is the bedrock of personal and organizational success, then organizations should develop their people and culture with professional ideals as their cornerstone. Most organizations don't—at least not in the way advanced by this book. John Toland, the Pulitzer Prize–winning author, said, "It is human nature that repeats itself, not history."[2] And it's the unproductive aspects of human nature that produce distrust.

Consider the 2008 meltdown of the U.S. financial markets. To paraphrase a popular political catchphrase: "It was about confidence, stupid."[3] Unfortunately, stupid is as stupid does. Financial institutions took brazen risks, regulators were asleep at the wheel, and consumers bit off more than they could chew. The result? Stakeholders lost trust—that increasingly rare trait that makes everything from financial markets to executive teams work! A 2002 Watson Wyatt study showed that high-trust organizations outperformed low-trust organizations by 286 percent in total return to shareholders (that is, stock price plus dividends).[4]

Professionalism is unique; it's the ladder upon which all other organizational virtues mount. The greater the quality of professional ideals within an organization, the greater the likelihood stakeholders will have confidence in it. They'll find it trustworthy. And while our focus in this book leans toward the for-profit world, the same principles are applicable for nonprofits, nongovernmental organizations (NGOs), and higher education.

Let's be clear: as important as culture is, it is certainly not an independent agent in terms of driving success. The proper fundamentals (for example, effective strategy, quality products or services, sufficient capitalization, etc.) must also be in place to complement an organization's professional ideals. And while it is unusual, there are exceptions where an organization experiences success without a culture grounded in professional ideals. This is precisely why I used the word *correlation,* not *causality.*

So what does it mean to be a professional? What defines a professional? Do you consider yourself a professional? If so, why? Is it your title or degree that makes you a professional? Something else? What characteristics make your behavior or, more important, your thinking different? And what separates real professionals from the wannabes?

Be forewarned! I will be challenging the conventional wisdom on the subject on two levels: what defines a professional and who qualifies as a professional. I will also reveal the subtle, important ways that being a professional differs from being a leader. For these reasons, you may find parts of this book to be somewhat provocative. It's likely to challenge your thinking, perhaps even change it.

Understanding what makes professionals tick is to understand how professionals think. From hundreds of hours of research, dozens of interviews, and over two hundred references, I have discovered seven distinct and powerful mind-sets common to trusted professionals. These comprise a pattern of thinking that separates the average Joe from the trusted professional. The ideals I will speak of are outlined in great detail in chapters 6–12, the seven mind-sets that make up the title of this book.

Some might think that I'm merely talking about a group of admirable people who populate a given organization, which alone would be sufficient to jump-start performance. Oh, if only it were that simple! We've all met admirable people who, for whatever reason, (1) didn't or couldn't deliver the prescribed results, (2) delivered the wrong results, or (3) unintentionally or unknowingly delivered the right results the wrong way. The reluctant leader, the sympathetic sales representative, the unorganized assistant, the ineffective manager. Admirable? Yes. Professional? Not necessarily!

First and foremost, the mind-sets reflect who a person is, not what a person does. The mind-sets transcend temperament, social hierarchy, and intellectual prowess. They are not techniques (that is, built from best practices or admired competencies, etc.) that work in one situation but not another. Rather, they're foundational—principle-centered, if you will. However, they're just as applicable to savvy veterans as they are to brand-new hires, just as pertinent in an aggressive Wall Street firm as in a benevolent nonprofit, as helpful for the gregarious extrovert as for the reserved loner, or as insightful for the PhD boss as for the self-taught tradesman.

Gen. Richard B. Myers, a contributor to this book, personifies the seven mind-sets. He had an interesting conversation with a cadet from the U.S. Naval Academy.

"I was approached by one of our young students, a midshipman, at Annapolis. His group happened to be at the Pentagon for the day. He had camped outside my office for a really long time. My secretary made me aware that this young guy wanted to talk to me. Finally, I was able to carve out a couple minutes ahead of my next meeting, which happened to be with the other members of the Joint Chiefs. When the cadet realized I didn't have much time, he said, 'I only want to ask you one question, General Myers. What does it take to become chairman of the Joint Chiefs of Staff?' Oh boy, I muttered to myself.

"He certainly noticed my frustration as I motioned for him to come to a side hall out of earshot of everyone else. Measuring my words carefully, I said, 'Son, what we really need to do is to sit down and have about a four- or five-hour discussion about this. But right now, I've got three minutes. The way I see it, that's exactly the wrong question for you to be asking. What you should be asking is, 'How can I become the very best midshipman I can be?' Then, when you get your specialty, become the best at that. Do those things and your career will take care of itself. Careerism is the enemy of professionalism.'"

The general's experience is both instructive and revealing. The young midshipman learned an important lesson about being a professional from the nation's highest-ranking military officer. And we can glean from General Myers's advice to the young man that focusing our energy on being the best at whatever our responsibility happens to be naturally includes the virtues of integrity, honesty, and hard work, to name a few.

I've been in the business world for nearly thirty years, first as a director for a respected company and for the past eight years as principal and founder of my own organizational consulting firm. Much of what I do as a management consultant is help organizations and individuals overcome the unproductive aspects of human nature. Organizational leaders are prone to believe that the issues they face are especially unique. It's true that issues relating to one's market, industry, regulatory environment, and the like are indeed unique. The preponderance of issues, however, is far more common than different. Why? Because, in one way shape or form, issues involve people. This shouldn't be surprising. After all, organizations are run by people, and their relationships, motives, and views of one another are an integral part of the organizational stew.

I work with many accomplished executives from a wide variety of different industries, and I have observed repeatedly that most people in the business world do not view themselves as professionals, let alone understand the mind-set required to be one. This is unfortunate as, too often, style wins out over substance, and expediency wins out over principle.

My charge with this book is to stimulate your thinking and to provide clarity on what it *really* means to be a professional and why this is so vital. The point isn't to tell you *what* to think; I'm merely suggesting *how* you think about this important subject in a different way. I hope this book becomes a difference maker, a catalyst in raising the bar of professional values.

The problems you and I hear about, the ones that are personally exacerbating and organizationally debilitating, are largely remedied when people show up as professionals. However, the mind-sets are not about making people smarter—the business world is already full of really smart people. It's about using greater discretion and better judgment. And it's about wisdom, something that is too often in short supply. The mind-sets are about becoming better, not just doing better. Have we forgotten what it means to be a professional? Is it a lost art or are we rediscovering an age-old secret? Or perhaps we never truly knew it in the first place.

Consider that business schools produce professionals by bucketfuls. Yet upon graduation, these same students are not likely to understand what it *really* means to be a professional. I interviewed numerous senior business leaders for this book, and many of them could not define what it means to be a professional either. That seems odd. So many self-described professionals are still struggling to understand what it means to be one. If the business wizards don't know, then the newbies haven't a prayer.

In this book I make explicit that which is now largely implicit. Identifying unprofessional behavior and encouraging people to emulate behaviors contrary to those is certainly one way of thinking about the problem. Thus by producing a competency model, we naturally receive standards to measure against. But while pointing out departures from virtue is a popular blood sport in some organizations (otherwise known as the gotcha game), a culture based on criticism and faultfinding provides little transformational power for individuals. One never truly becomes a professional simply by avoiding bad behavior.

General Motors spends tens of millions of dollars to hype its best products as professional grade. This is no accident. People consider *professional* to be synonymous with *best.* The desire, then, to apply the term *professional* and all that goes with it to individuals (or collectively to their organization's culture) is natural. After all, who doesn't want to view him- or herself or be viewed by others in such a favorable light?

Self-images have transformational power, and viewing oneself as a professional is part of that transformational power. Showing up as a professional is the type of aspirational goal that inspires and induces passion, energy, and enthusiasm. It's personal, very personal.

In order to become the kind of professional we so admire in others, the seven mind-sets described and outlined in this book answer the all-important question, "What's required of me?" They're comprised of compelling dos, not nagging don'ts. For virtually any organization, they're not only comprehensive but complimentary and compatible with any set of values or priorities deemed by an organization to be in its best interest.

Taken in isolation, there is not a whiff of anything revolutionary in the underlying principles of each of the seven mind-sets. Taken collectively, however, they form the basis for a powerful framework of thought processes held by the most revered professionals among us. French historian Alexis de Tocqueville observed, "The knowledge to combine is the key to all other knowledge." The collective framework for the mind-sets and their application to an organization is, indeed, an attempt to connect several important dots, the result of which can have far-reaching impacts.

You will notice the contrast between how the mind-sets may appear when compared to the norms of the greater culture. For instance, contrast Mind-Set 2 (Professionals realize and act like they're part of something greater than themselves) with the clarion call of the so-called millennial generation (What are you going to do for me?). The contrast couldn't be greater! Examples of this difference are almost limitless. We live in what some have called a "world of distrust" that is largely driven, I believe, by this generation's declining standards. Declining standards degrade values. The by-product of this noxious cocktail? Fewer professionals—at the precise time they're most needed. Our understanding these trends in the greater culture becomes imperative, because they are dragged into the workplace.

The Center for Public Leadership (CPL) at Harvard annually publishes *A National Study of Confidence in Leadership.*[5] The findings from the 2009 study are disturbing. In short, America is alarmed by the quality of its leadership. The leadership crisis—first identified in CPL's 2005 report—remains a problem, with 69 percent of those surveyed believing there is indeed such a crisis, 45 percent of Americans believing the country is moving in a negative direction, and 67 percent believing the United States will decline as a nation unless we get better leaders—leaders we can trust to do something besides just looking out for themselves!

Count me among the 67 percent. Personally, I'm alarmed at the deteriorating standards and frightening complacency that U.S. culture has grown to accept. Whether it's ethical decline, lack of fiscal discipline, or moral[6] relativism—declining standards have occurred in virtually every facet of society, and they impact the workplace in varying degrees. Personal responsibility, once an American cornerstone for a can-do nation (and essential for an effective democracy), is in short supply because people are shielded from the consequences of their poor decisions or unfortunate errors in judgment. Certainly, there's been an unmistakable shift in values. Warren Bennis has noted, "America has never been less interested in achievement or more interested in success."[7] At the risk of generalizing pop culture—namely its celebrity obsession, seduction by style, and water-cooler sitcoms—we have been shown to be shamefully superficial at times. At best, we've gotten sloppy; at worst, we're apathetic.

Many, especially older Americans, cannot readily recognize this country. The legendary actor Paul Newman at age seventy commented, "What's difficult about getting old is remembering the way things used to be. There were such things as loyalty. The community hadn't disintegrated. The individual had not been deified at the expense of everything around him. I don't think that's just an old codger, you know, wishing for the old days. Goddam, [things] were better."[8] With titles such as *Sissy Nation, The Death of the Grown-Up,* and *The Dumbest Generation*[9] donning bookshelves, it's clear that cultural norms and standards have shifted. For many thirty-somethings, it isn't the life they expected.

Peter G. Peterson is the son of a Greek immigrant who came to the United States as a teenager without a penny, not knowing a word of English, and holding only a third-grade education. One short generation later, Peterson is a billionaire. He co-founded the Blackstone Group, a New York investment banking powerhouse.

Peterson believes that the opportunities he had—kids having it better than their parents—are at serious risk. He is so concerned about the nation's well-being that he has placed the majority of his wealth into a billion-dollar foundation designed to bring solutions to the nation's most vexing long-term fiscal challenges. What was the primary cause for Peterson's concerns? Faulty leadership! Peterson is hardly alone. According to the Center for Public Leadership, an astounding 63 percent of us believe our current leaders are not as good as our past leaders.

The legal, fiscal, and political structure of this country, which were largely defined by the Founding Fathers, allow us to conduct our much-envied method of commerce (free enterprise capitalism) today wherein a humble Greek immigrant's son became a billionaire. The Founding Fathers possessed mind-sets that are emblematic of those I describe in part 2 of this book. Each of us in business today is a beneficiary of those mind-sets, and I believe the Founding Fathers have even more to teach us—especially now! Thus each chapter in part 2 elaborates on one of the seven mind-sets and contains not only business content but an illustrative story from one of the Founding Fathers.

From the Center for Public Leadership, we see little confidence in leadership in many sectors (from religion to business). Americans are particularly disenchanted with their politicians—especially their representatives in Congress—and the mainstream media. Not surprisingly, particularly in light of the 2008 economic downturn, Wall Street receives the lowest ratings of all.

What can we conclude from all this? We're long on me-first leaders but short on professionals. But it's professional leadership that holds the key to stemming the tide of deteriorating standards and reestablishing tried and true professional ideals.

We have knowingly violated the three cardinal rules followed by many publishers (and their authors) in the quest to make their books into commercial successes—meaning selling as many books as possible.

- **The no reader left behind rule.** This directive encourages authors to write to the lowest common denominator in their audience. Respectful by nature, this advice, unfortunately has the unintended consequence of dumbing down content and ultimately readers. Authors should try to raise people's sights, not lower them.
- **The fifth grade rule.** A cousin to the "no reader left behind" rule, this recommendation suggests that an author should write to the equivalent of a fifth-grade reading level. While I appreciate the intent behind the advice—namely, to make a book into an easy read—it has the unintended consequence of valuing entertainment over substance.
- **The how-to rule.** Notice how many business bestsellers are how-to's. This book is not one of them, nor does it offer a recipe or a prescriptive formula for success. This book is written for and

addresses an intelligent audience. Only an engaged reader can take full advantage of this content. That said, I expect you'll find many substantive and practical applications in these pages.

If I sell fewer books because I am trying to raise your sights a notch, that's a trade-off I'll gladly make.

In developing this book, I've collected wisdom from a myriad of respected sources, foremost among them are those I've listed as contributors. I believe I've borrowed wisely. Lawrence Summers, former president of Harvard, has observed that "academic freedom includes the 'right to be wrong.'" Thus I reserve the right to be wrong, because the conclusions here are my sole responsibility. Likewise, the fine people who served as contributors bear no responsibility for any errors I may have added.

Professionals are an increasingly rare breed, often taking the proverbial road less traveled. They are not only smart; they are also wise. Their ability to exercise good judgments stands above the rest. They willingly invest discretionary effort—more than what the proverbial service handbook requires.[10] They keep their wits under tough conditions and focus on winning contests in the marketplace, not popularity contests. They refuse to respond in kind when they're wronged. Their work is not necessarily about what they do, but rather how they do it. It takes discipline, energy, and gumption not to succumb to the easy way out. Regardless of what a professional's responsibilities entail, it's never about him or her. Simply put, they are the first player you would pick for your team.

Greatness, while sometimes hard to define, is easy to recognize. Think of great athletes, great dramatic performances, and great statesmen. Now think of the great professionals you've worked with or admired from afar. Images of a few special people will likely emerge. Because we are moved by greatness, we want to be more like the people who demonstrate it. It's emulation of the person in her or his best and highest form—not of what they do or what they might have (for example, status, position, wealth), but rather who they've become. People recognize greatness. We admire it. We gravitate toward it. And most important, we trust those professionals who have proven themselves over and over worthy of our trust.

English essayist Samuel Johnson wrote, "People need to be reminded more than they need to be instructed." For some, this book will validate what you have always known but simply needed someone to point out. For others, it's an Aha! and destined to change your thinking in many important ways. For me, this is not just a book but a movement, an appeal to bring out the very best in people, to put professionals and professional ideals front and center in an organization.

My hope is that this book will act as a catalyst. Our application of the seven mind-sets will change us, one professional at a time. The good will become better, and the better will become the best. See for yourself. Apply the seven mind-sets to your work and life. Validate them against your life experience and watch the results unfold. Let me know what happens.

In a Nutshell

This book is broken into three distinct parts:

Part 1: Why Professionalism Matters (chapters 1–5) covers the premise behind professionalism as the catalyst for individual growth and team development. This material is foundational. For some, it is destined to change the way they think about what it means to be a professional.

Part 2: The Seven Mind-Sets (chapters 6–12) provides a comprehensive view of each mind-set. Contributors also share their varied experiences in for-profit and nonprofit enterprises.

Part 3: Upgrading the Culture (chapters 13–15) explores the upside of organizations that center their culture around professional ideals. It enables leaders to assess the degree to which their culture reflects the professional ideals embodied by the mind-sets.

Honoring Your Time: The Fast Break

Since time is our most important resource, I have provided several methods for reading this book. Reading the entire book is not a requirement for getting benefit from it. Chapter summaries will aid those who want a quick synopsis of any given chapter. Chapters 6 through 12 can also be read as stand-alone chapters, making it easy to reread or brush up at a later date. Part 1, however, is foundational, and speed-reading or skipping part 1 in its entirety will dilute the depth of your understanding of the seven mind-sets.

If you are a professional who happens to be an individual contributor: Read chapters 2 and 4. Consider chapters 3 and 5 optional. If you happen to be a psychology junkie, you'll find chapter 3 particularly interesting. Chapter 5 is about the big picture, illustrating how the mind-sets were integral in establishing our nation's freedoms and our much-envied system of commerce and why they're so integral now in stemming our country's current tide of distrust. Read all of part 2 (chapters 6–12). If you have an interest in organizational development or an interest in enhancing your organization's culture, consider reading part 3 (chapters 13–15). Chapter 13 particularly provides one of the more coherent and understandable explanations of culture; one that demystifies a subject that many see as ethereal.

If you are a professional who happens to have leadership responsibilities, which includes organizational development (that is, executives, senior leaders, partners, human resource executives, managers, team leaders, etc.), follow the same advice offered to the individual professional contributors above, except you should be sure to include all of part 3 (chapters 13–15) in your reading.

PART I

Why Professionalism Matters

CHAPTER **ONE**

The Power Within

The premise of this book is simple yet powerful. The priorities that are of utmost importance to the leaders of virtually any organization—namely productivity, accountability, organizational cohesiveness, commitment to organizational initiatives, etc.—are all driven by the degree of professionalism achieved by its leaders, managers, and employees. The higher the degree of professionalism, the better the attainment of priorities, all of which drives better results.

Simply put, organizations whose members view themselves as professionals outperform, outsmart, and outlast organizations that don't. Professionalism is the grease that lubricates an organization's functional gears. Of course, professionalism alone is inadequate to ensure business success. It must be accompanied by the leadership's compelling vision for the business and the execution of a well thought-out strategic plan. Assuming these exist, the organization's people will make the difference in the end.

Our self-view (which I cover in chapter 3) is a powerful driver in influencing our future actions. Seeing oneself as a professional makes it easier to engage in those unpleasant, yet inevitable tasks, such as going the extra mile when we're already fatigued, approaching a colleague on an unpleasant topic, supporting our boss on a position with which we don't agree, or taking a necessary action that is destined to be unpopular. Most important, it also enables us to do our very best work. Consider the following story from the music business.

The world-renowned Dave Matthews Band (DMB) produces an eclectic mix of jazz, soul, classical, rock, and bluegrass music. The group began performing together in 1991, but in late 1999 Dave Matthews, the band's namesake, had turned melancholic. For Matthews, being unsettled and despondent was as dispiriting as it could get. He said, "I felt like I was failing everyone."[1]

He was not alone in his feelings; something just wasn't quite right with the band. Their studio sessions were not going well, and despite the group's strong work ethic, their sessions were too free form, even undisciplined. There was a feeling of discontent among the band members. Still, the music was good, and the band was still tight, but something was amiss. Each band member knew it, but Matthews did not know what to do about it.

This funk was so out of character after eight blockbuster albums, tremendous international acclaim, and nearly ten years together as a band. By all accounts, the DMB was still a rising star. Fortunately, the band's troubles were evident only within the group. Whether the problem was merely a growing pain or an emotional slump was not clear. Ahead of them, however, was their next studio album. They decided to change producers, which proved to be a tough but necessary decision.

Enter Glen Ballard, a multi-Grammy-winning producer and protégé of the legendary Quincy Jones. Ballard worked with the band for ten days, and during that time they produced an unheard-of nine new pieces of music!

The DMB has a reputation as a premier live band, characterized by long rifts by some extremely talented musicians. Ballard felt, however, that a studio recording required something different: shorter, tighter songs. He brought both discipline and a supportive environment to the process.

The resulting album—*Everyday*—opened at number one with 755,000 copies sold during the first week, and it stayed at number one for two weeks. After twenty-five weeks of sales, this album sold a remarkable 2.5 million copies.[2] The experience with Ballard rejuvenated and energized the band.

In speaking of *Everyday* a short time after its release, violinist Boyd Tinsley said, "These songs . . . have been the best songs we've ever recorded." Drummer Carter Beauford echoed those sentiments and praised Ballard. He said, "We not only are treated as a good band, but we're being treated as good musicians. And I think that's probably the most important thing for us, because for so long, we'd been playing stuff by ear." Beauford added, "Now we've got charts," referring to the intricate sheet music Ballard developed.

When asked how that made him feel, Beauford summarized his outlook in one word: "Professional." He elaborated: "It makes me feel like a professional musician, and that makes us want to continue to move forward and write professional-sounding tunes and not this sophomoric kind of stuff that we started out with—the garage-sounding sound that we had in the early, early days." Beauford spoke reverently about the term *professional,* all that it meant and all that it implied.

When you consider the resounding success the DMB had achieved prior to working with Ballard, Carter Beauford's thoughts are profound. Said another way, it was nearly ten years after the band's inception before Carter *felt* like a professional in quite that way. Coincidently, this is precisely when he and the band did their best work. Suddenly, Beauford saw himself as a professional musician. Once he saw himself in this way, along with the pride he took in generating his best work, he wanted more of it.

Ballard was able to not only advise the band technically and relentlessly prepare it to perform, but what is most important, he was able to bring out the band's best performances. Ballard proved to be just the ticket for the DMB. Because he placed uncompromising standards on himself, Ballard helped the band to reach down deep to find a new level of artistry that they previously could only dream about.

Ballard treated every member of the band like a professional; they then responded like professionals. The experience was transformative. The band members were able to *feel* what it was like to be *professional* musicians doing their very best work, and then they demanded the same from themselves.

This story speaks to an important point that I made in the preface, namely how most people don't view themselves as professionals. Even talented people, such as drummer Carter Beauford, who had experience and past success fail to take this crucial step. Surely if anyone should have viewed himself as a professional in such a deeply felt way, Carter Beauford should have.[3]

The views we hold, whether of others or of ourselves, are often the single greatest influence in establishing our effectiveness. My first book, *The Big AHA!* was about the views we hold of others; this book is about the views we hold of ourselves. Because it's personal, because it's about who we are, viewing yourself as a professional turns out to be a big deal.

Professionals: A Matter of How to Be

In the end, professionals stand out because they're doing their best work. They are able to win the battle with their own emotions when things get dicey. They stick to their convictions on the things that matter most. Those hard-fought victories are often the by-product of the view they hold of themselves as professionals.

Many leaders have never been taught this concept, and many organizations are oblivious to it—something I'll cover in chapter 4. If leaders, managers, and individual professional contributors (a term coined by Peter Drucker[4]) are to soar, they must view themselves as professionals within their sphere of influence, no matter how ordinary or mundane that position may be.

The beauty of the premise behind this book is that the vast majority of an organization's members want to view themselves as professionals, as opposed to having their organization foist this standard upon them.

Frances Hesselbein, president of the renowned Leader-to-Leader Institute, refers to leadership as "a matter of how to *be*, not how to *do*." Chapters 6 through 12 outline the seven key mind-sets of consummate professionals. The mind-sets become a scorecard to measure your progress toward identifying and raising your level of professionalism. The mind-sets teach and reinforce invaluable life lessons about personal leadership.

The concepts in this book can be applied to anyone who aspires to be a professional, regardless of rank or title. As I'll advocate in chapter 2, **our view of a professional transcends the traditional and outdated stereotype of who qualifies as a professional and who doesn't.** Professionals are found in multinational corporations, regional non-profits, and prestigious professional services firm. They can hold PhDs from distinguished universities or hold degrees from the school of hard knocks. Anyone who aspires to be a professional can become a professional in her or his chosen field by understanding the premise of this book.

Be a Professional

How many times have you said this to yourself or heard it from a colleague? Certainly, it's hard to argue with advice that evokes standards of excellence. This was the advice I advocated to readers in my earlier book *The Big AHA!* It deals with the need to be right, which is a subversive and dangerous phenomenon that derails people both personally and professionally. Most reasonable people agree that the compelling need to be right is unprofessional. Thus, the advice to conduct ourselves as professionals as an antidote to this and a myriad of other problems is well founded, but what does it mean to be a "professional"? I thought I knew, but I quickly learned that I didn't. I also found I had a lot of company.

In searching for the answer to this question with clients and readers, I did not immediately or easily discover a clear-cut answer. People frequently use the term *professional* in countless ways and contexts. Surprisingly, a literature search did not provide much substantial help either. So many people identify themselves as professionals, yet so few could confidently explain what the term meant. So I approached senior executives and asked them, "What does it mean to be a professional?"

These senior executives (the big-title, gray-hair crowd) appreciated the question and saw it as important, but it was clear that they had not thought much about the answer, perhaps because of their own understanding of the term. Professionalism is a part of our everyday vernacular, and these senior executives had their own ideas. But what seemingly appeared as a no-brainer turned into a brain-freeze. Not a freeze in terms of ideas on the subject of professionalism—there were certainly plenty of those—but a freeze in terms of being able to define what professionalism means to them personally, as well as what the implications were regarding their conduct.

Among their affirming examples were these:

- Professionalism is associated with the mastery of one's given trade/ expertise.
- Professionalism is closely linked to integrity.
- Professionalism is staying cool when the heat is on.

However, for every description of what a professional *is,* I heard a half dozen descriptions of what it *isn't.* In other words, it is far easier to identify the antithesis of professionalism than to define it. This observation was driven by a seemingly unlimited number of examples of perceived unprofessional conduct. For these senior leaders, explaining the antithesis of professionalism was like shooting ducks in a barrel, and they recalled example after example of conduct unbecoming of a professional—and a surprising number of examples were years removed. Among the unaffirming examples were these:

- The lack of candor in meetings. (The real meeting occurs in the hallway.)
- Reluctantly sharing information and resources while making yourself look good in the process.
- Sabotaging an important initiative by withholding your support.

Warren G. Bennis and Robert J. Thomas in the seminal *Geeks and Geezers* stated, "One of the best ways to define good leadership is to study bad leaders."[5] Sally Kellerman discovered essentially the same thing in her bestseller *Bad Leadership.* In my research on professionalism, part of what I did was to reverse engineer the process. I identified and defined several desirable qualities (and ultimately the mind-set) of respected professionals by studying those who exhibited bad qualities.

Yet I didn't want professionalism to be defined simply as the antithesis of bad qualities; I also documented and analyzed these positive behaviors—something I'll address in chapters 6 through 12.

Most insightful of all were the following anecdotal comments:

> "Honestly, I'm a little chagrined. I don't know (with the type of depth I expect) what it *really* means to be a professional."
>
> "At first, I thought that 'What is a professional?' was a dumb question. After I was stumped and couldn't answer it myself, I thought it was a trick question. Finally, I realized how profound the question really is."
>
> "In my nearly forty years of business experience (twenty-five as a senior executive), I've attended every conceivable type of professional development program out there. I can't remember once where this subject was addressed—and that includes all my graduate business experience, in-house corporate programs, and university-based executive education."

The Right Question

Ultimately, here's what I learned from asking, "What does it mean to be a professional?"

1. It is indeed an important, yet underaddressed question.
2. Senior leaders, surprisingly, could not confidently answer it.
3. I was asking the wrong question!

Okay, perhaps I'm being a little harsh here. The question is important, but it became particularly insightful only after it was clear that most people had such trouble with it. In hindsight, the question should have been, "What does it mean to be a *trusted* professional?" You may be thinking, Why *trusted* professional?

What made unprofessional conduct consistently easy to spot and easy to remember? A perceived violation of trust! Certainly the age-old axiom "Trust is the coin of the realm" applies here.

If a violation of trust is inseparably linked with unprofessional behavior, then developing trust is imperative to building and maintaining professionalism. Warren Buffett said, "You only have to do a very few things right in your life so long as you don't do too many things wrong."[6] For organizations to be truly effective, trust is like bedrock: everything depends on it. **Trust is to human capital what money is to financial capital.** Of those few things to get right, building trust is at the top of the list.

Being able to accelerate trust organizationally in a tangible, practical way is a big deal. Intellectually, people understand the importance of trust, but translating that concept into reality is an entirely different matter. Leaders and managers struggle with it especially. They often find it maddening knowing that building trust is essential but not knowing exactly how to build trust within their organization. Part 3 of this book (chapters 13–15) addresses the organizational (or cultural) aspects of professionalism and how that translates into a competitive advantage for those who are willing to embrace it.

Ultimately, the essence of this book is based on two important and related questions:

1. What does it mean to be a *trusted* professional?
2. What are the implications for individuals and for the organizations of which they are a part?

In analyzing the answers to the first question, we are not interested in developing a behaviorally based competency model. There are plenty of competency models available, and they can be helpful in varying degrees. But when senior leaders try to identify a competency model from within one's own corporation, they are often unable to do so. This occurs "because the competencies are generic and similar,"[7] reported Dave Ulrich and Norm Smallwood of the RBL group, a world-renowned leadership development firm. Edgar Schein, a pioneer in the field of organizational behavior, added that most competency models are "too psychological"[8] because they're defined almost exclusively by behaviors.

Behaviors are funny things—sometimes driven by intrinsic needs, other times extrinsic needs, and also by moral imperatives. Putting undue emphasis on competency models is analogous to the risky practice of blindly embracing best-practices in companies.

Robert Sutton, professor of management science and engineering at Stanford University, has written extensively about the risks and failure rates of the well-intended transference of best practices.[9] Sutton suggests that leaders first understand and then embrace the thinking, assumptions, and intent *behind* best-practice behaviors rather than just blindly copying them. This is analogous to my warning about blindly embracing competency models and the behaviors they represent.

Robert E. Quinn, a professor at the University of Michigan's Ross School of Business, observed: "Nearly all corporate training programs and books on leadership are grouped in the assumption that we should study the behaviors of those who have been successful and teach people to emulate them. But my colleagues and I have found that when leaders do their best work, *they don't copy anyone*. Instead, they draw on their own fundamental values and capabilities."[10] The same is true for any professional—leader or not.

The Seven Mind-Sets

Professional behaviors, while important to identify, are ultimately driven by something much more important, namely, by a person's mind-set. For the purposes of this book, consider a mind-set to be *attitude with purpose*. It isn't just how an individual sees the world (as important as that is); it's how an individual chooses to interact with the world.

Conventional wisdom suggests, for instance, that football championships are won with defense. Thus many coaches instill a defensive mind-set in their players. The seven mind-sets of the trusted professional have as their common purpose *being a professional*. It's about aspiring to *be* something: someone praiseworthy, someone credible, someone honorable.

It is your mind-set that puts in motion specific behaviors, similar to the effect the moon has on the tides. In other words, internal mind-sets drive external behaviors. Thus my objective was to identify the mind-sets of successful professionals. For context, success was *not* defined as getting ahead (although that frequently occurs). Rather, success was simply defined as being "happily engaged in meaningful work that reinforces one's capabilities and values."

I went about identifying the resulting mind-sets in three ways: first, through an informal study with clients and workshop participants; second, through extensive literature research, and third, through interviews with top thought leaders, many of whom came from the business community.

First, I conducted my own informal study with clients and workshop participants based on the question, "When you think of someone you consider to be a consummate professional, what did they *do* that makes you think so highly of them?" The responses (which we'll cover in chapter 2) were overwhelmingly focused on how the individuals conducted themselves. This was consistent with the sage advice given to business leaders by Dee Hock, former CEO of Visa, who advocated investing the biggest portion of your time (at least 40 percent) to managing *yourself.*

Second, I conducted extensive literature research principally, but not exclusively, centering on leadership literature or books and articles and blogs written by well-known, successful thought leaders. The business literature proved rich due to (1) the sheer volume and quality of material available, (2) the many ideas and diverse perspectives covered, and (3) the exemplary quality of profiled professionals. Not surprisingly, the business literature included far more examples of broken trust than the contrary.

I also believed there was much to learn on this topic from nonbusiness sources. Consider management guru Peter Drucker's observations that the world's best leadership development program does not reside in the business sector—that distinction belongs to the U.S. Army, and one is likely to find the best leaders in America leading major religious congregations! Thus, despite thousands of business books on leadership, many fundamental lessons about leadership are not limited to the domain of business.

I was far less interested in lessons learned by leading others and much more focused on how professionals lead themselves. I studied many of the best business practitioners, consultants, and educators. My group of practitioners included respected CEOs like Jack Welch, Bill George, and Larry Bossidy. My consultants included Jim Collins, Ram Charan, and David Maister. And my educators included Warren Bennis, James O'Toole, Jim Kouzes, Rosabeth Moss-Kanter, and Joseph Badaracco.

I sought out lessons learned about trust from both their victories and their defeats. These lessons covered every conceivable aspect of their business experience—from negotiating a blockbuster deal to putting together a first-class staff. The resoundingly consistent responses I received from my initial question gave me great confidence regarding the link between professionalism and leadership.

Third, I interviewed a number of world-class thought leaders and business icons, some of whom became formal contributors to this book.

The results of my research revealed numerous behaviors, competencies, and traits. Some were affirming, others were not. With hundreds of examples in hand, I grouped, categorized, and eventually identified seven different mind-sets from which these behaviors and competencies emanated. The resulting mind-sets are prevalent among the most successful *trusted* professionals. The seven bubbled up because they were foundational to building or losing trust in organizations large or small, simple or sophisticated. They are:

1. Professionals have a bias for results.
2. Professionals realize (and act like) they're part of something bigger than themselves.
3. Professionals know *things* get better when *they* get better.
4. Professionals have personal standards that often transcend organizational ones.
5. Professionals know that personal integrity is all they have.
6. Professionals aspire to be masters of their emotions, not enslaved by them.
7. Professionals aspire to reveal value in others.

Collectively, the mind-sets reveal not only what others expect of the professional, but also what professionals expect of themselves. For almost all successful professionals, **personal growth precedes professional success.**

My most important conclusion was that **to be a trusted professional is to master life's lessons in personal leadership.** That's leadership with a little *l*, as Kim Clark, former dean of the Harvard Business School, is fond of saying. And it's an aspect of leadership that impacts every facet of our lives, not just business. Each of the seven mind-sets requires varying levels of competency, discipline, and conviction—all of which are inseparably related to successfully leading oneself.

Other key findings in my research include:

1. Technical skills, while important, play far less a role than you might think.
2. Defining moments reveal our true level of commitment and professionalism.
3. Professionalism, despite its inherent price, is worth it in the eyes of most.
4. Professionalism, when embraced as part of a company's culture, has positive and far-reaching implications.

Answering our first question, "What does it mean to be a trusted professional?" was both insightful and fulfilling, but the personal and professional implications of achieving a high level of trust within a company are even more exciting. Imagine the following scenarios:

Individuals whose Achilles heel is their:

- lack of courage in appropriately confronting fellow employees
- willingness to support decisions with which they don't agree
- commitment to being right, rather than doing right

A leadership team whose Achilles heel is its:

- inability to hold one another accountable
- apathetic attitude toward others outside of their own silo
- complacency: a willingness to settle rather than soar

An organization whose Achilles heel is its:

- undisciplined approach in taking the organization to the next level
- culture of appeasement
- incessant internal contention while being oblivious to market threats

In your own workplace environment, you may be experiencing one of these conditions right now. It may also be difficult to imagine how to successfully address these situations with positive and lasting results. **Each of the individuals, teams, or organizations identified above overcame their Achilles heels by putting a renewed emphasis on professional conduct in shaping desired character traits, competencies, behaviors, and, ultimately, their organization's culture.** In short, embracing professionalism company-wide advances the well-being and performance of individuals, teams, and organizations alike.

Consider the following:

> A business development specialist who struggled with confronting her colleagues: "When I obsessed about my weaknesses, I continued to fail by not effectively communicating what I needed from my colleagues. Seeing myself as a professional, despite the discomfort and the price involved, was exactly what I needed for getting over the hump. It stretched me in ways that I didn't realize were possible."
>
> An operations manager whose organization struggled with accountability: "Our people were being insular, not being a part of our larger team. Commitment was low and apathy was high. That's why Mind-Set 2 really helped shake up our team—all for the good! To our pleasant surprise, our employees welcomed the clarity and expectations that each of the mind-sets brought. The motivational aspects cannot be overemphasized."
>
> A managing partner in a professional services firm whose organization had become complacent: "By the numbers, we looked like a success. But somehow, staff members had lost their professional edge with each other. It was as though we constantly had sand in our gears—increasingly allowing pettiness, self-interest, and personal agendas to undermine our effectiveness. The mind-sets enabled us to recommit ourselves to conduct worthy of a first-class professional services firm. No more sand in the gears!"

The implications of working within a culture of professionalism are profound, and they impact every level and facet of an organization. The benefits, outlined below, are significant:

Employees will welcome it. I'll cover this in great detail in chapter 3, but both desiring to be viewed as a professional and viewing oneself as a professional is a wonderful self-motivator. Despite the obligations that comprise the price of being a professional, employees long for it. Why? In a word: *respect.*

It's part of a great retention and attraction strategy. Never before has the war for talent been so prevalent. Employees increasingly view themselves as free agents who have decreasing levels of loyalty to their employers and increasing levels of their own self-interests. Treating employees as professionals (that is, respectfully) mitigates many of these factors. In addition, it builds up your reputation as being a great place to work, thus attracting top talent.

It builds leadership bench strength—big time! Successfully driving leadership bench strength has become a competitive advantage for some of the world's most successful companies: General Electric, Honeywell, Allied Signal, etc. The mind-set materials develop and reinforce those all-important and too often underemphasized characteristics of personal leadership that make or break those who successfully hold positions of formal leadership, whether they are senior executives or frontline supervisors.

It builds trust, thus accelerating speed to market. As Rupert Murdoch, chairman and CEO of News Corporation, noted, "The world is changing very fast. Big will not beat small anymore. It will be the fast beating the slow." Decreased development cycles mean increased competitiveness.

It makes any organization more adept at managing change. The only constant in today's business environment is change. And the mark of many professionals is to successfully work outside their comfort zone. Change naturally takes people out of their comfort zone, but professionals handle it much more adeptly due in part to the high standards they hold for themselves.

It naturally facilitates learning at both the individual and organizational level. This occurs primarily because of the commitment individual professionals make to get better and because information hoarding becomes less prevalent. The ever-critical practice of information sharing becomes a cultural norm.

It accelerates a self-managed model of management. More than ever, companies are moving toward a self-managed model of management. In short, this means more individual responsibility and accountability and less influence from traditional management over many of the day-to-day aspects of running a business. Developing higher levels of personal leadership through the seven mind-sets advances the goal of achieving greater degrees of self-management.

Professionalism at Its Best

Three horrific days after an explosion at a plant had killed two and caused hundreds of thousands of dollars of damage, the team reassembled at headquarters.

Everyone was surprised to see Steve taking the lead at the press conference. Recent events had been particularly bittersweet for him. His well-deserved promotion to division head had been announced only a few days before the accident, and the scheduled start for Steve's new assignment, several states away, was imminent. But Andre, Steve's best friend, had been killed in the explosion. Rumors surfaced that a gas leak was behind the explosion. Predictably, the aggressive construction schedule associated with the plant's expansion work came into question.

How could Steve face the media?

The press conference started out innocently enough, with the usual suspects asking the usual questions. Then one reporter dropped a bombshell, asking if Steve would like to comment on the impending grand jury investigation that had been announced just hours earlier. The company's team had not been apprised of the investigation, which in and of itself was a bad omen. The grand jury would be investigating possible criminal negligence on the company's part along with probable malfeasance by company officials.

Steve had flawlessly and carefully addressed each reporter's questions. He listened intently and was particularly respectful, even giving the benefit of the doubt to the inexperienced reporters who asked less-than-pertinent questions. He shined when the reporters probed for more information about the victims. How Steve managed to hold it together under such difficult circumstances was a wonder to the entire staff. The latest question, however, was like a poke in his eye. Not only would the grand jury investigation challenge the actions and character of the exceptionally talented and dedicated staff, it would also threaten the future of the company that had been a town fixture for over forty years.

Without wavering, Steve responded, "Clearly, many questions remain. But I do know that, as professionals, our people hold themselves to incredibly high standards. They would never knowingly compromise plant safety. In order to get to the bottom of this, I will personally be heading up our company's internal investigation."

Everyone's jaw dropped. Certainly Steve, as operations manager, was the most qualified to head up the investigation. But what about his promotion?

Despite the company advancement, Steve saw this unfortunate incident as a vitally important unfinished business. It was something he could not walk away from. Steve postponed indefinitely his long-awaited promotion. His bosses understood and reluctantly supported his decision and admired him even more than they had before.

As you might imagine, everyone marveled at the way Steve conducted himself. He distinguished himself and rose above the fray in a critical time of crisis. The business unit's vice president later addressed to the headquarters staff. "Never forget what you witnessed today," he said. "When you look up the word *professional* in the dictionary, Steve's picture will be there." Certainly the impression Steve left will be felt for years.

Hopefully, you've benefited by associating with people like Steve—people who conduct themselves as consummate professionals. They do what Michael Jordan did on the basketball court: they make everyone around them better. When your career is in its twilight, you'll look back fondly at the Steves you have known as having made the biggest difference.

What can we learn about what makes professionals such as Steve tick? What enables them to perform so well under such difficult circumstances? How do they make that which is so difficult look so easy? These and other questions are answered in this book. There are, of course, no magic bullets, but there are patterns of thinking that emerge which are common among professionals of this stature. In the end, a professional's mastery of life's lessons in personal leadership sets him or her apart from the crowd and helps ensure their success. Whether you're just starting your career or if you've been around the block a few times, whether you work within a bureaucracy, on the front lines serving customers, or whether you're a technical wizard or a generalist, there is something essential for you in this book. Let's get right to it.

CHAPTER **TWO**

It's a Bigger Tent than You Realize

Age does not make you an adult any more than
a vocation makes you a professional.
—Bill Wiersma

Any individual desiring to hold the lofty mantle of professional can do so, regardless of circumstances or background. Of course, this distinction must be earned. Yet realizing this distinction is a compelling objective for individuals (which is discussed in chapter 3). This is also crucial in organizations because many, for various reasons or circumstances, do not see themselves as professionals.

This chapter will also look at how professionals define themselves and how society defines them as well. Just as important, the key barriers, stereotypes, and biases that prevent others from seeing nontraditional candidates as professionals will be examined.

Perhaps this story sounds familiar. Patricia's and Robert's families were gathering at their parents' home to celebrate Patricia's first sale of a million-dollar home. Their long-retired parents looked for any reason to bring the family together. But at the last family gathering, Patricia and Robert got into a knock-down, drag-out fight when Robert insisted that Patricia, a Realtor, didn't rate as a "real" professional. Robert, a CPA, tenaciously held the view that advanced education and training were prerequisites to being considered a professional. All others (including Realtors) were mere pretenders.

When the two greeted each other that night, Robert's ego and Patricia's sensitivities quickly emerged. After some forced pleasantries, Patricia pointed out that their mother had prepared his favorite dinner.

"I know," Robert said, laughing. "I talked her into it. I didn't think you'd mind sharing your big night! Anyway, you always come around to my way of thinking." He winked.

Patricia felt herself bristling. He was baiting her, and she knew she should let the comment pass. "You know," she said, "as much as you like the idea, I *don't* always think the way you do. In fact, I'm even more confident of my position on professionalism now than I was last month. I am as much a professional as you are, whether you want to recognize it or not!"

"Do we have to go over *that* again? Okay, yes, you work hard. You make good money and wear a suit and have clients and whatever. Being in real estate is a good fit for you. I'm happy for you. Really. But the years I spent in school and all the studying I did to pass the CPA exam were excruciating—nothing like the so-called test you had to take to get your license! You haven't paid your dues. So don't insult me by insisting you're a professional like me!"

Patricia took a breath to calm down. This was no way to act at a family gathering, especially one being held in her honor, but his stubborn attitude irked her. She looked him square in the eye and said, "Some day, I hope you'll come to your senses and realize there's more than one way to look at this." She left the room before he could respond, and they avoided saying more than a few words to each other the rest of the evening.

Situations like these reveal the dicey and often emotional association many people have with the word *professional.* Is the title earned or is it bestowed? Is it dependent upon education? one's vocation? seniority? pedigree from an elite institution? job sector? An architect makes $90,000 a year in Kansas City, and an electrician makes $130,000 in Los Angeles. Is one a professional and not the other? Is there a definitive authority on the matter, or will this question forever remain a touchy subject driven by subjective opinion?

Consider this example of professionalism. It was nearly 2 a.m., seven hours after the plane's scheduled arrival at Spokane. Barbara closed her eyes for a second and breathed a sigh of relief as the airplane and its tired, angry passengers came to a stop at the gate. She and the other flight attendants had done everything they could to make the passengers comfortable and to relieve mounting anxieties. A severe regional snowstorm delayed their flight and created a series of cascading problems with air traffic nationally. What should have been a short delay turned into hours.

Barbara was proud of her colleagues. They had been flying together for a number of years, and there was almost no emergency they couldn't handle. But as passengers began leaving, Barbara was thinking about Mrs. Sullivan, an older passenger, kind and frail with a gentle nature and an almost apologetic attitude.

I wonder if anyone will be waiting for her inside. Barbara smiled at the deplaning passengers. "Thanks for your patience." "Get some rest." "Have a good night." Mrs. Sullivan waited until the others had left the plane.

"I'm so sorry to bother you, dear, but would you mind getting my coat down from the overhead?" What Mrs. Sullivan asked for wasn't unusual, but the way she said it reminded Barbara of her own grandmother, a small determined woman who lived alone and was reluctant to ask others for assistance.

Barbara helped Mrs. Sullivan with her coat, and then moved slowly with her into the Jetway with her walker. The plane was empty now except for John—a hardened, stoic pilot with over thirty years at the helm.

"G'night, Barbara. See you tomorrow," the other attendants called as they walked past her, pulling their flight luggage behind them.

Halfway through the Jetway, Mrs. Sullivan suddenly staggered and collapsed. Barbara reached for her as she crumpled to the floor, her walker knocked sideways. Barbara dropped to her knees and pressed her ear to the unconscious woman's mouth. Mrs. Sullivan's breathing was labored. Barbara looked back toward the plane.

John, the last one off the plane, was exhausted. His was not the only plane that had been delayed. The tension between pilots and air-traffic controllers had been intense. As John walked from the plane into the

Jetway, he stared in disbelief at yet another "event" unfolding before him—the type that made his skin crawl.

"John, please get the oxygen from the plane right away! She's in bad shape!"

He stopped. "You know, the Jetway isn't our jurisdiction . . . Shouldn't we—"

Barbara immediately flashed John one of those "Oh, please" looks, the kind that could kill under other circumstances. When she realized John would be of little help, she took charge. "Stay with Mrs. Sullivan while I get the oxygen," she said and then hurried back into the airplane.

Moments later, Barbara successfully revived and stabilized Mrs. Sullivan and dispatched the pilot to the terminal to call for the paramedics. Mrs. Sullivan was taken to a hospital for observation. She was released to her family the next day.

In this scenario, who showed up as the professional: the highly trained pilot or the empathetic flight attendant?

Who Are You, Really?

The characteristics attributable to professionals, whose occupations society attaches the professional label, are analyzed in the article "Who Is a Professional?" by Harvard Business School professor Ashish Nanda.[1] His article is representative of the broader trends within academic literature.

Nanda references the "rich and detailed sociological literature that is concerned with defining professionals" and readily acknowledges that there are many who might define the term *professional* differently than he does. However, it's important to note that virtually all of the literature on the topic of professionalism has strong academic leanings. Also, there are many opinions as to the "correct" definition of *professional,* but there is little consensus among the academics who have written on the topic.

Nanda attributes skill levels, complexity of diagnosis, degree of impact, perceived level of value, and degree of judgment required in determining where the professional label fits. Examples of professionals consistent with his definition include accountants, architects, clergy, doctors, lawyers, investment bankers, professors, and management consultants. Judy the orthodontist, to adopt Nanda's example, is considered a professional merely by her association with an occupation that gives rise to her career.

Nanda acknowledges that "any definition of the word 'professional' is bound to evoke criticism, in part because the word has become, in Eliot Friedson's words, 'evaluative as well as descriptive.'" In this instance, consider "subjective" to be analogous with "evaluative."

Groups aspiring to achieve professional status but failing (due to noncompliance with this or that definition) often see themselves as unworthy relative to their so-called professional colleagues. For instance, in reference to medical professionals, Nanda noted, "If society considers that nursing requires mastery over a relatively simpler abstract knowledge base, then a nurse, even if as important to patients as a doctor, *is characterized as less of a professional than a doctor*" (italics added). If you have a visceral reaction to this statement—as I did—I'm confident you're not alone. I certainly wouldn't suggest that a nurse is any less of a professional than a doctor.

It doesn't take much imagination to see how this example and many others like it create animosity and jealousy across the professions and tear down the self-esteem of many dedicated individuals. Nanda's and others' well-intended attempts to define professionals[2] using strictly hierarchal or educational criteria has the unintended consequence of being contentious and counterproductive. I hope to broaden the context surrounding the use of the word professional by creating less association with the word as a title and more emphasis on its characteristics.

It's interesting that business practitioners—with perhaps the exception of David Maister, a renowned consultant to the professional service sector—have been ominously quiet on the subject of defining professionals. In the article "How Business Schools Lost Their Way,"[3] Warren Bennis and James O'Toole quote former University of Dallas provost Thomas Lindsay: "Business education in this country is devoted overwhelmingly to technical training." Lindsay argued, along with the article's authors, that this technical emphasis is out of balance and distorts business students' views of what is required to succeed in the post-MBA world. "Even before Enron, studies showed that executives who fail—financially as well as morally—rarely do so from lack of expertise." Bennis and O'Toole believe that technical training in MBA programs has been emphasized at the expense of practical knowledge, not in conjunction with it.

Lindsay suggested that to correct this imbalance—bringing greater relevance and meaning to business education—more emphasis needs to be placed on individual accountability and moral leadership. All of this is an attempt to have business students look beyond the simply technical aspects of "learning how to calculate with a view to maximizing wealth." And it transcends the oft-required ethics courses. In other words, these professors are telling both their colleagues and their students to take in the bigger picture.

I believe that this narrow view of business education is analogous to the problem behind any attempt to define who is a professional through an occupational and technical lens. Technical myopia of this sort has sunk many a ship.

For example, as defined by Nanda's criteria, Judy the orthodontist will always be viewed as a professional when she is associated exclusively with her highly respected professional occupation. However, the orthodontist's professional status may be at risk with her patients should her technical competence slip or should she fail to manage her patient relationships appropriately. Thus there are many important factors to consider that transcend occupation for Judy to be automatically considered a professional.

Aspiring to Emulate

Recall the question in chapter 1 that was posed as part of my informal research: "When you think of someone you consider to be the consummate professional, someone you'd aspire to emulate, what did they *do* that makes you think so highly of them?

I posed this question to hundreds of people—clients, friends, workshop participants, colleagues, etc. Perhaps one quarter was not in the business world. Among the business crowd, they worked on the shop floor and in the executive suites. They were bright-eyed MBA students from prestigious business schools and older, cynical, frontline employees. They ran the gamut from every walk of life, gender, and ethnic background.

- How would you answer that question?
- What did they *do* that makes you think so highly of them?

The results I received were remarkably consistent. When asked about *who* were the consummate professionals and what types of occupations or fields were represented, few fit into the strict occupationally based definition advanced by Nanda and others, such as doctors, lawyers, etc. Rather, the participants gave descriptions such as sports coaches, family friends, business mentors, teachers, clergy, etc. Although I did see some representation from that traditionally based group, there was some crossover between the two groups. The trend was distinct and unmistakable: at least 80 percent would *not* have fit Nanda's occupationally based criteria.

When asked *what* the consummate professional did, the responses were dominated by how people went about their business. The behavioral examples included:

1. An incredible listener.
2. Extremely ethical.
3. Always took the high road, even when it wasn't to his or her immediate advantage.
4. Held demanding standards for themselves.
5. Put their clients' interests ahead of their own.
6. Made perceived sacrifices for others.

Your responses were probably similar. Now consider the following that fail to meet the title of professional advanced by Nanda and others:

- Colleen Barrett is president emeritus of Southwest Airlines. She was trained as a legal secretary and became the right-hand person to former CEO Herb Kelleher. Colleen is the architect of Southwest Airlines' break-the-mold culture that remains one of the carrier's

hallmarks and has contributed mightily to Southwest's industry preeminence.
- Charlie Trotter's restaurant, a Chicago landmark, is regarded as one of the finest restaurants in the world. Founder and owner Charlie Trotter never attended culinary school, but he receives the type of international acclaim normally reserved for Europe's finest chefs.
- Anita Roddick is the founder and owner of The Body Shop. Anita is an entrepreneur, visionary, and foundation leader. A former teacher and industry outsider, Roddick built her company from scratch into one of the cosmetic industry's most powerful brands while aggressively supporting social and environmental causes.

There are endless other examples. As previously noted, my informal research was nonstatistically based and admittedly subject to variation. If validated academically, it would have been subject to a whole host of tried-and-true academic research methodologies. As practitioners, however, I was looking for unmistakable macro trends. And I believe I found them.

Approximately 85 percent of my responses referred to *how* individuals conducted themselves; the remaining 15 percent involved various technical aspects about *what* they did in the course of practicing their given occupation. Two important points were detected.

1. When people think *professional,* they think "worthy individuals" not "worthy occupations" or "worthy professions." A worthy individual may, in fact, come from a worthy occupation, but to assume that such is always the case would be a mistake. Regardless of how frequently the term *professional* is used, people ultimately grant the much-coveted label of professional on an individual basis based on merit. In other words, it is not automatically bequeathed to a certain occupation or industry by association, regardless of its preferential pedigree or perceived prestige.
2. Professionals consistently demonstrate:
    - Technical competence: Professionals know what they're doing, and they do it in a way that builds confidence.

- Personal character: Professionals consistently conduct themselves in a manner that engenders trust.

Know-How

Professionals know what they're doing, both technically and in other intangible ways. However, as important as technical competence is, **professionals are not typically defined by their competence.** Technical competency is the *minimum* requirement when considering whether someone is a professional or not.

Tammy Farris, Director of Corporate Outreach at the University of Arizona's Eller School of Management MBA program, characterized it perfectly: "Education and training (that is, technical competence) are just paying one's green fees—they enable you to get in the game."

Once they are in the game, professional competence enables individuals to demonstrate that they technically know what they're doing. If you can do that, people will trust your technical competence, and they'll have confidence in you. For example, a surgeon with an ability to bring relief to a suffering patient will be regarded as a professional more readily than a colleague who possesses the same training but lacks the skill to apply that knowledge effectively.

Too often, however, people automatically equate *expert* with *professional.* That's a natural but often inappropriate conclusion. Being an expert isn't necessarily synonymous with being professional. Returning to the medical professional example, a surgeon's lack of a bedside manner or alienation of the surgical nursing staff will undoubtedly diminish the degree of professionalism with which the doctor is viewed by others.

So to focus only on narrow technical qualifications is to miss the broader and more important view. Defining who is or who isn't a professional strictly by decree or academic pedigree is like the winning of an envied award based solely on the number of years on the job. It's like being bestowed an honorific title.

Interestingly, few participants in my study consciously differentiated the degree of technical competence required for one to be considered a professional. This was an unmistakable pattern among the respondents.

For instance, on their list of consummate professionals, participants consistently named two or more people with quite dissimilar occupations, along with dissimilar vocational backgrounds.

One respondent, for example, identified both a former high school teacher and his firm's senior attorney as consummate professionals. Another saw a clergy member and an IT director as true professionals. The level of required training and complexity involved in any of these jobs is vastly different. Yet my experience showed that the vast majority of respondents did not eliminate individuals from their list based merely on an assumed educational or vocational threshold. There was more to it than that.

After the Greens Fees

It is likely that few of my respondents had heard of the ongoing academic arguments concerning who is and who isn't a professional. I believe that most people simply do not subscribe to the somewhat strict definition of *professional* advanced by Ashish Nanda and others. My experience suggests that professionals are not defined by *what* they do but *how* they do it. Said another way, a mastery of knowledge and skill are assumed, but mastery over one's conduct is not. Being a professional has everything to do with who you are and a lot less with what you do.

Recall the story of the pilot and the flight attendant with the vulnerable passenger. Who showed up as the professional? Given the level or training, overall responsibility, and rate of compensation, one might argue that the pilot should be viewed as an admired professional. In comparison, the empathetic flight attendant rarely receives such credit. Both were responsible for passenger safety, and both wore the company uniform. Still, most people cannot help but view the flight attendant, not the pilot, as the professional in the scenario with the ailing passenger. In the story, the flight attendant took charge—accepting personal responsibility for single-handedly reviving the collapsed passenger, even though they were, as the pilot put it, beyond their jurisdiction. The flight attendant conducted herself in a manner that engendered trust.

This story and many others suggest we should take a harder look at the term *professional* and how it applies to each of us, regardless of title or academic degree. You don't need to have a traditional profession in order to be a professional. Because of the inferred and elevated status associated with the term *professional,* many groups protectively cleave to this title, frequently objecting when others seek to join the club. Typically, those who meet Ashish Nanda's definition of professional are the ones who resist the inclusion of others who do not meet the same standards.

Looking back to Patricia and Robert's story at the beginning of this chapter, discussions surrounding who is and who is not a professional loom like an eight-hundred-pound gorilla, triggering powerful emotions. The requirements for being considered a professional frequently emanate from people who already qualify for inclusion in the club. They have paid their dues, and they are not going to let anyone else share their title unless there has been a similar dues-paying experience. Sadly, there was a time when I was right there with the jealous protectors of the professional title.

A Defining Moment

Completing a hard-fought undergraduate engineering degree was, at the time, the most significant education-related accomplishment of my life. There were times when I struggled mightily, as the course load was both voluminous and difficult. The fact that I also worked twenty hours a week (in hindsight, not a good idea) did not help the situation. But in the end, I prevailed. I was proud of that degree, and soon after graduation, I was offered a position with a well-known West Coast engineering and construction company. In my department there were engineers and nonengineers. In my mind, there was a big difference between the two.

The job functions of my particular position did not require an engineering degree. I felt that my education set me apart from my nonengineer colleagues. I was oblivious to the fact that many of them had impressive credentials in business, the liberal arts, and other fields. What resonated with me was that *I* was an engineer and *they* were not. My professional identity centered on my being an engineer. I did not know it then, but I still had a lot to learn.

From the start, I was thrust into a very busy department. Most of what I was learning had little to do with my engineering background, but rather how the company operated. Surprisingly, it was a steep learning curve. During the first three months, I felt as if I were swimming in turbulent water in the deep end of the pool.

During my second month, my boss unexpectedly asked me to cover the desk of a nonengineer colleague for two weeks while he would be in another division. I was surprised at the request and instinctively said no. It wasn't an in-your-face no. I did it with some level of tact, but it was a no nonetheless, something my boss was unaccustomed to hearing.

Two factors influenced my knee-jerk reaction to his request. First, I was struggling at my own desk. Taking on another busy desk would be a disaster, or so I thought. Second, as an engineer, I recoiled at the thought of working a desk that required no engineering expertise. I was hired as an engineer, and to work at anything less than that would feel like a demotion.

Suffice it to say, my decision was not well received by my boss. When my company hired me, they hired an engineer. At least, that's how I saw it. Regardless of the functional reasons behind my response to my boss's request, politically, saying no was an exceptionally foolish move. My naiveté was exceeded only by my pride.

I wasn't at the top of the food chain, but I believed my degree put me ahead of many others in that regard. My identity, driven largely by ego needs, was that of an engineer. Because of that closely held self-view, I failed to recognize the value that my colleagues brought to the table. I had automatically classified many of them as nonprofessionals and therefore less valuable. Simply put: they were "less than."

In addition, by declining my boss's very reasonable request, I failed to live up to my responsibilities as a professional (engineer or not) as well as a team player. What happened?

First, I held an erroneous self-view. I saw myself in terms of my title—a stereotypical and ego-driven way to look at myself. This was based on my status as an engineer, not on what I brought to the company. I had unconsciously bought in to the premise that pedigree equals professional. This view, of course, is very limiting.

Second, I held an erroneous view of my colleagues. Because I defined myself by my title, I defined them by their lack of titles. This attitude greatly decreased my ability to appreciate their contributions, which on many levels also affected the give-and-take of our highly interdependent relationships.

Third, these views got me into trouble. My outright rejection of the boss's request set me at odds with him and suggested that I had my own agenda. Luckily, my boss was able to overlook my inexperience and naiveté.

In time, I realized that it was far more important to be a professional who happened to be an engineer than to simply be an engineer. I realized that by changing the views I held of my colleagues and myself, I vastly improved the situation for all of us. Working in my co-worker's shoes for a couple of weeks would have helped to identify myself as a professional first and an engineer second, not to mention the additional perspective I would have gained. In addition, my boss would have viewed me as a team player. My experience, although innocent, was typical of the all-too-human condition of making inappropriate comparisons.

One Coin, Two Sides

Recall Ashish Nanda's observation that nurses were lesser professionals than doctors. My own experience in seeing my colleagues as "less than" is consistent (although for different reasons) with those who make unfortunate comparisons among professionals. Being "less than" or "more than" are two sides of the same coin. This issue is particularly pertinent within the legal professions.

The practice of law is clearly viewed by most in society as a professional vocation, but there is a clear cultural distinction between attorneys and paralegals. The highly interdependent relationship between attorneys and paralegals is an incredibly important one. It's true that (1) the training each receives is different, because their roles are different and (2) attorneys, literally, are the ones practicing law. They oversee the work of paralegals. In other words, they are the ones on the hook.

Ask litigation attorneys and they'll acknowledge how much critical pretrial work is done by their paralegals. Yet law schools do not include the training of paralegals within their programs. Seemingly, there would not be a better environment than a law school in which to train paralegals, but the American Bar Association (ABA) actually forbids law schools from training paralegals in conjunction with their programs. Why? Because the ABA considers the work that paralegals do as a vocation, not a profession. Some states, however, recognize paralegals as a profession.

For paralegals, the distinction begins with their training (which is segregated) and escalates to the second-class treatment they receive when they practice their craft. Kathryn Lively, a professor at Dartmouth, addressed such workplace distinctions in "Occupational Claims to Professionalism: The Case of Paralegals."[4] The article, based on fifty-one in-depth interviews with paralegals, was prompted by the desire of paralegals to be recognized and respected as professionals after enduring many perceived hardships at the hands of their attorney colleagues. Despite being extremely competent and conducting themselves in a way that engendered trust, these paralegals had not been afforded the same type of respect and consideration afforded the attorneys.

Let's be clear about the motivation for this study. It wasn't an attempt on the part of the paralegals to put themselves on a par with attorneys, nor were they trying to take the lawyers down a peg. The paralegals value and appreciate the unique skill sets that the attorneys possess. Many emulated the attorneys, considering them professional role models. But the paralegals also saw themselves as professionals and wanted to be recognized and appreciated as such. In the end, because paralegals are typically viewed as nonattorneys who haven't paid the price the attorneys have, they experience tremendous difficulty in being recognized as professionals.

No doubt, the unfortunate cultural distinctions between attorney and nonattorneys are analogous to my own shortsighted experience in viewing my colleagues as nonengineers. Viewing paralegals as nonattorneys automatically makes them less than an attorney. And when the highest life form in the firm is an attorney, by definition a professional, then any nonattorney is unlikely to be considered a professional. Viewing others in this manner creates unproductive distinctions that are centered far more on status and class distinctions than on actually practicing the law.

Such distinctions are artificial and counterproductive. The examples from the legal professions are effective because they are particularly illustrative of this phenomenon. Numerous other examples exist. Hierarchal or class distinctions are rampant in the medical and dental professions, accounting firms, and almost anywhere you look. For individuals engaging in such practices, it's unflattering; for organizations, it's shortsighted and costly. Think your firm or company is immune? Think again! Is the:

- string virtuoso (with arguably more technical skill) more of a professional than the percussionist?
- wide receiver (considered a skill player in the NFL) more of a professional than the lineman?
- traffic reporter (the star of the show) more of a professional than the helicopter mechanic?

Making less-than and more-than distinctions between trades and occupations makes for interesting although seemingly endless academic debates. But practically speaking, these differences, however rendered, entirely miss the point! My experience tells me that most reasonable people simply don't look at professionals that way! The virtuoso, wide receiver, and traffic reporter can make or break a performance. They're difference makers, but they don't produce in a vacuum! While differences in skills exist, differences as professionals don't!

Professionals are recognized as worthy individuals, not worthy professions. The reason they're recognized as such is because they not only know what they're doing, but they conduct themselves in a manner that engenders trust. It is no more complicated than that!

Degrees of Sophistication

I realize this premise may threaten or offend some people's sensibilities. After all, how can two people be considered professionals when one's training and education may have taken years of study and thousands of education dollars, while another's may have been a one-year vocational program?

First, realize that I am not advocating equal titles, equal pay, or academic recognition profession-wide. Doctors, lawyers, research scientists, CPAs, and others engage in work with a very high technical degree of sophistication. These individuals should be recognized and compensated based on the complexity of knowledge required in their field of expertise, mastery in application of that knowledge, and degree of judgment required. Under this definition, levels of sophistication can vary wildly, especially technically. But both a loan officer and a cardiologist can show up as professionals, the only difference between them being the greater degree of sophistication of their vocation or how they conduct themselves. The clients of the loan officer and the patients of the cardiologist can experience each as professionals, although the degrees of sophistication between the two can be significantly different. While each is different, each exhibits the appropriate level of judgment, discernment, and care required for their clients.

Second, it is not my intent to delegitimize those in professions who are already considered professionals. Nor am I trying to diminish the hard work that many dedicated individuals have done to achieve their professional goals. These bright, production-oriented individuals have sacrificed personally and in other ways while contributing to society, their professions, and their companies. They are world thought leaders, Nobel Prize winners, business icons, brilliant doctors, professors, etc. Their value is immeasurable.

Third, I am not advocating a dilution of the term *professional.* I am, in fact, advocating elevating it! Rather than create more situations of "less than", I am advocating for more situations of "more than". I am encouraging a broader context for the word *professional* in order to re-legitimize those deserving individuals who epitomize the best their trades and professions have to offer. It's about seeing past the hierarchy to the potential and the contributions of individuals, regardless of rank or education. One isn't less of a professional simply because:

- She takes direction from you.
- His education or pedigree isn't commensurate with yours.
- Her technical competency is less sophisticated than yours.
- His star power is less than yours.
- Her title isn't on a par with yours.
- His degree of impact is less than yours.
- Her age is substantially less (or greater) than yours.
- The color of his collar is blue instead of white. In fact, being a professional has little to do with the color of one's collar.

In an article in the March 2007 edition of *Good Housekeeping,* Merry Maids was named the nation's best house cleaning company. Founded in Omaha, Nebraska, in 1979, Merry Maids now touts 950 service territories that include franchises and corporate-owned branches. Their secret? An emphasis on being trusted professionals.

One doesn't normally associate *professional* (white collar) and *maid* (blue collar) in the same sentence. Yet, according to Joy Flora, former president of Merry Maids, being trusted professionals is a huge part of the success of the Merry Maids brand. Their people deliver thousands of times daily, building a powerful brand in the process. Arguably, house cleaning isn't a profession as such, but it hasn't stopped the staff at Merry Maids from being professionals. The Merry Maid's success story is told in greater detail in chapter 4.

Affirming another individual (even a maid) as a professional does not devalue your own standing as one. It heightens it!

This chapter has identified three primary causes that, unfortunately, inhibit individuals from viewing themselves as professionals. Beyond deserving nurses, paralegals, flight attendants, and real estate agents, there are literally millions of people who (1) demonstrate mastery in their work and (2) conduct themselves in a way that engenders trust. You've met them and so have I. They're trusty auto mechanics, conscientious grocery store managers, and invaluable executive assistants. Most of these people don't view themselves as professionals. This is unfortunate. If they thought of themselves as professionals, their performance and morale would jump up another notch. For those who don't quite yet measure up, the aspiration to become a professional becomes a springboard in raising their sights and performance.

Look around you. How do the people you associate with view themselves? In chapters 13 and 14, you'll see how professionalism within a company's culture raises standards, promotes ethics and efficiency, and influences interpersonal relationships. People who view themselves as professionals have higher morale, better job satisfaction, and more job longevity. This was stated in chapter 1, but it bears repeating: organizations whose members view themselves as professionals outperform, outsmart, and outlast organizations that don't. There's plenty of room for everyone if you're willing to put up a bigger tent.

SUMMARY

- Any individual desiring to hold the lofty mantle of professional can do so, regardless of circumstances or background.
- Traditional definitions of *professional* (which have been influenced through strong academic leanings) places prescribed limits on who qualifies to be one. This excludes an innumerable number of deserving people.
- When people think *professional,* they think worthy individuals not worthy professions. Being a professional has everything to do with who you are and a lot less with what you do.
- Overwhelmingly, people define consummate professionals by *how* individuals conducted themselves, not by *what* they did. In other words, technical competence does *not* define a professional in the eyes of others.
- You don't need to pursue a traditional profession in order to be a professional, let alone demonstrate professionalism.

CHAPTER **THREE**

The Psychology of Being a Professional

If we do what we do because we chose to, we're committed.
If we do what we do because we have to, we're compliant.
Real professionals aren't compliant;
real professionals are committed.
Real commitment comes from the inside—it's who you are.

—Marshall Goldsmith

B*eing* a professional, which is the essence of this chapter, is a powerfully motivating force that raises standards. *Viewing* oneself as a professional is a precursor to *being* one. The foundation of this chapter is no more complicated than that. If you agree with the premise, it's not absolutely necessary for you to read this chapter. If so, consider skipping ahead to chapter 4. However . . .

I have three cautions for those who are considering skipping this chapter: (1) psychology junkies will enjoy this chapter, (2) Albert Bandura (called the world's greatest living psychologist) and his cutting-edge work on self-efficacy is highlighted in this chapter, and (3) Marshall Goldsmith made significant contributions to this chapter—including sharing his now-famous dinner conversation with Bono.

A New Identity

I once worked with a group of men in a service organization. As time passed, I watched one of them go sideways, compared to the other men in our group. This young man had potential, but he never fulfilled it. You probably know someone like him. While his peers were graduating from high school and going off to college, trade school, or the military, he was still living in the moment. He didn't seem to have much of a future, and I wondered what might stimulate a turnaround, hoping that it would be sooner rather than later.

This young man got married and, lo and behold, after a year of marriage, his wife was pregnant. The young man was thrilled—he beamed as he told me. I was watching the turnaround happen right in front of me. He described his hopes for the future, his role as a father, and his future relationships with his wife and child.

This man's thoughts and ideas included his future career plans as well. What is important here is not what his plans were, but rather the vision with which he now saw himself. Responsibilities he was formerly unwilling or unable to take, he was suddenly embracing with enthusiasm.

What brought about the change?

Each of us has varying identities or self-images. Mine include son, husband, father, author, etc. These views can be very motivating. They are precursors to our future behavior. They are, using a psychological term, an *aspirational identity.* It's about our wanting to become something. With fatherhood looming before my young friend, he saw himself in a very different way. A big part of his identity suddenly became dad, something that transcended merely a title and became a mission.

This new self-view was obviously positive and a motivating force for good, but he did not actually possess all of the attributes associated with fatherhood. For example, he still had to learn about feeding and diapering a newborn, how to console, how to discipline, and how to balance his role as father with his other commitments.

Yet dad was how he saw himself. Whether he had proven himself or measured up to the requirements of being a dad is not the point. His view, or aspirational identity, of himself *is* the point. That aspirational identity raised his sights and modified his behavior in ways that other circumstances to that point had not.

My friend Ellen Fletcher, an accomplished accounting professional, did extensive research for this book. She has a different self-view than my young father-to-be friend, but it is one no less motivating. Ellen was raised in the South and very much lives up to the stereotypical image of the Southern belle. She is gracious and calm under pressure. Her appearance is as important as her demeanor, all of which relates to how she feels about herself and treats others.

As she grew up, Ellen adopted the views of various respected mentors and rejected examples of bad behavior by others. She said, "My aspirational identity is one that has been created from the qualities I admired in teachers, acquaintances, other mentors, and those great managers and co-workers who I have been lucky enough to have in my life and professional career. I also recognized the qualities of those bad managers, . . . and I have made it a point not to exhibit those qualities." Because Ellen sees herself as a lady, she is just that.

Suffice it to say, being a lady has become Ellen's north arrow in terms of how she conducts herself. This aspirational identity is something affirming, and it elevates her view of herself and therefore influences her actions. These types of self-views stretch us and ultimately lift us to greater heights. One can't have enough of them.

The View from the Mirror

Our views are a big deal, especially when it comes to people. In *The Big AHA!* I noted that "the view we hold of others—for better or worse—is the single greatest influence in establishing and sustaining our effectiveness with people." Figure 3.1 shows the dramatic effect our views hold on our interpersonal effectiveness.

The views I wrote about in *The Big AHA!* was of others; in this book we're focusing on the views we hold of ourselves. In *The Big AHA!* we were looking through a window; in this book we're looking in a mirror. **The views we hold of ourselves are as important, if not more so, than the views we hold of others.** Thus, it shouldn't come as a surprise

Figure 3.1— Components of Interpersonal Effectiveness

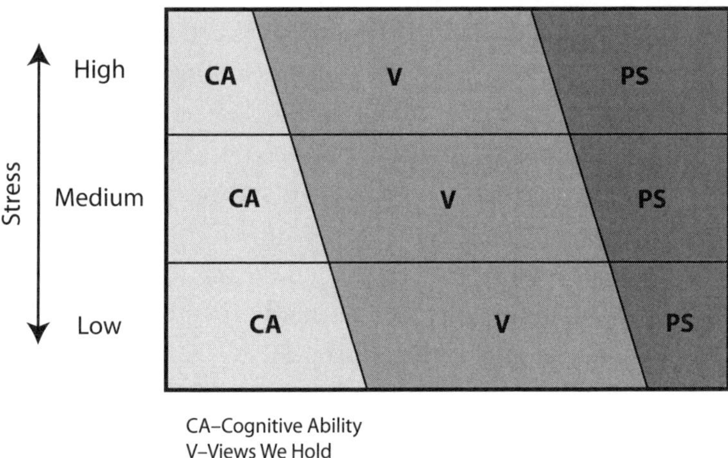

CA–Cognitive Ability
V–Views We Hold
PS–People Skills

that people who view themselves as professionals excel beyond those who don't.

The renowned psychologist Carl Rogers was a pioneer in his work on self-views. He actually referred to them as self-concepts.[1] Whether you call them self-concepts, perceptions, views or self-views, identities, or self-identities, it's really the same thing. I prefer the term *view* because it is particularly flexible, enabling descriptions not only of self but of others as well. These views really define who we believe we are, which is the substance of this chapter.

Jose Canseco was one of baseball's premier talents in the 1980s and 90s. Yet Canseco was known as much for his lackadaisical, almost showmanlike approach to the game than he was for his talent. When his manager reiterated the club's expectations and reminded him that he was first and foremost a baseball player, Canseco basically replied, "No, you're wrong. I am a performer." Canseco's view of himself as a performer certainly helped explain the way he conducted himself, namely, in a manner that drove the team brass crazy.

Our self-views are created by our life experiences. For instance, having a child who is incarcerated might lead one to develop a view that "I'm a bad parent." Other people, whether through gossip or meanspirited character assassination may indirectly contribute to or reinforce the same view. But we'll never really know whether anyone is, in fact, a bad parent or not, because these self-views are actually a history lesson, based on the past, about which we can do nothing to change.

While these self-views are instructional to a point, they describe what is; they do little to describe what's possible, which is something we're much more interested in. Thus the rest of this chapter is geared toward understanding a particular type of view—an aspirational identity—and why this is imperative to someone aspiring to be a professional.

Aspirational Identities

Renowned leadership expert John Maxwell noted, "It's how we perceive ourselves to be that determines who we are." That beautifully and succinctly sentence captures the fundamental concept behind this chapter, and while I'm tempted to leave it at that, there really is (as Paul Harvey would say) more to the story.

Earlier we looked at the concept of self-view (or self-identity) and why that is so powerful in helping you to see yourself as a professional. Now let's look at why that occurs and try to understand it in a little more depth. Before doing so, it's important to ask two critical questions: What is an aspirational identity? How does it differ from the popular (and arguably the most frequently discussed) type of self-perception, namely, self-esteem?

First, we have to define what we mean by the term *self-esteem*, because people understand this term in very different ways. Generally, self-esteem is a value judgment we make about our self-worth. It's the way we feel about ourselves, including the degree to which we possesses self-respect and self-acceptance. That seems straightforward enough.

The trouble is, as revolutionary educator Marva Collins notes, "Self-esteem is highly overrated." She adds, "There are criminals who rate highly and saints who score pretty low [in self-esteem assessments]." To date, there has been no correlation between high self-esteem and high levels of performance.[2] In fact, several researchers have argued that the opposite is true. Marva's observations, however, are consistent with a number of studies in education and other disciplines.

For myriad reasons, self-perceptions can simply be wrong. And even if they're right, those perceptions are defining what is, not what's possible.

For those with fairly accurate assessments of their self-esteem, it is significantly, although not exclusively, influenced by what you *do*—in other words, conduct. Each of us has certain standards of conduct—regardless of whether those standards originated from civil or ethical sources—that we understand to be appropriate. And our worthiness, if we're being honest, is measured against those standards. Cheating on an exam, for example, should lower your self-esteem if you understand that cheating is inappropriate.

Many will measure actual behavior versus desired conduct when assessing themselves. Because the results of these assessments are influenced by historical behaviors, it is not forward looking. It reflects what is. Current assessments are more like a report card or a snapshot; they do not reflect future possibilities.

An aspirational identity, however, is primarily about who you are or wish to be—as opposed to what you do. It's forward looking. It raises your sights. It suggests possibilities. Take the example of the young man mentioned at the beginning of this chapter who was about to become a father. His conduct, historically speaking, was not consistent with that of a successful father. But the once irresponsible young man suddenly became responsible, primarily as a result of his desire to measure up to his view of himself as a dad.

Many aspirational identities can be recognized by "I am" statements. "I am a dad" (our new dad). "I am a lady" (my friend Ellen). "I am a Smythe and proud of it." In business they might be, "I'm an IBMer," "I'm a surgeon," or "I'm a member of Local 240." Whether part of a company, profession, trade, or organization, each of these identifications connotes a positive image worth living up to.

Note these three important points:

1. Not all identities are necessarily aspirational. Joe introduces himself: "Hi, I'm Joe, and I'm an alcoholic." It's the standard greeting at an Alcoholics Anonymous (AA) meeting. AA has learned the power

of identity (or self-views) in helping their members to personalize and come to grips with their problems. While this identity is not necessarily aspirational, it is powerful nonetheless, constantly reminding people to be vigilant against the temptations to which they once succumbed.

2. A negative self-view can be just as empowering and motivating as a positive one. James Waldroop and Timothy Butler describe a negatively distorted self-image as one of the fundamental psychological issues that enables numerous undesirable behaviors (twelve in all) that hold businesspeople back at all levels.[3] A negatively distorted self-image is akin to an automobile accident at rush hour on a busy freeway, because it becomes the catalyst for a series of cascading problems everywhere we look!
3. Self-limiting beliefs are a first cousin to our self-view and also influence our behavior. A self-limiting belief (for example, "I'm lousy at math") differs from a self-view (for example, "I'm a professor") in that the first is a skill or attribute while the second has to do with an identity as a person. Self-limiting beliefs can be as debilitating as unhealthy self-views.

Aspirational Identities in Action

Imagine a new hire—let's call her Jane—on her first day on the job. She's full of enthusiasm and energy. But she has unknowingly joined a company that is lethargic and rewards mediocrity. What happens after six months? Is Jane still full of enthusiasm or has the unsupportive, uninspiring organization dragged her down? Most of us are all too familiar with the latter scenario. Still, there are exceptions. In Jane's case, despite the dysfunctional cultural issues of the company, she is still buzzing along with unhampered motivation and vision.

What was the difference? Simply put, when the company hired Jane, they hired a professional. From the moment she walked through the door, she viewed herself as a professional. Her aspirational identity as a professional transcended the culture of her organization. (I'll cover this extensively in chapter 9, Mind-Set 4: Professionals have personal standards that often transcend organizational ones).

In Jane's case, we have an example of someone *feeling* that they're a professional. They don't just hope to be one. They are not just interested in becoming one. They don't just think they are one. They feel it in their bones! It's a part of their being.

It's Not About Your Technical Competence

There aren't many like Jane who naturally show up the way she did, oozing professionalism.

I often ask groups, "How many of you consider yourself to be a professional?" There's a slight difference in the response between white-collar and blue-collar groups. In white-collar crowds, nearly all the hands go up. In blue-collar groups, about 85 percent of the hands go up. But despite these high percentages, I know that only a handful will show up as Jane did.

White-collar crowds respond the way they do, I've surmised, in part because of the perceived prestige attributed to being a professional and because they believe they're expected to think of themselves as professionals. This goes to the point in chapter 2: our society has defined professionals in white-collar terms. Blue-collar groups respond the way they do because of the pride they take in their work and because they want to be in the club with the impressive label.[4]

By far the biggest factor—the one that's shared by both groups—is that they base their professional identity on what they do, their technical competence. How they go about their work, especially in the blue-collar world, takes on less importance, at least when compared to what they do. While this seems natural (given the discussion in chapter 2), it misses the important point that our technical competence, as important as that is, is merely the greens fees that get us into the game.

For some, this is not an easy shift in thinking—that how you do your work is as important (if not more so) than what you do. To help make this insight stick, you have to engage in repetition and reinforcement. Figure 3.2 helps to visualize the concept.

Scissors require two blades in order to function properly. Over-dependence on only one blade (for example, technical competence) proves

Figure 3.2—A Professsional's Balanced Approach

to be ineffective. It's only when the second blade (how you go about your work) is added that the scissors become viable. Naturally, the sharper the blades, the better they function.

Both blades are essential. Most of us know from experience that when things go wrong, the root cause is frequently attributed to how the situation was handled. This is consistent with the comments of senior executives in chapter 1, namely that the antithesis of professionalism is not determined by technical competence. Instead, it's largely defined by conduct unbecoming of a professional. In other words, *how* a person goes about his or her work.

Being a Great Professional and Great Mom Too

Professionals are highly cognizant of the balance between their identities as professionals and their nonprofessional responsibilities. Many cried foul when Elizabeth Vargas announced in 2006 that she was stepping down as the anchor of *World News Tonight,* believing she had been pushed out by her bosses at ABC News. Not so!

Vargas, now a mother of two young children, said that she voluntarily left the anchor's chair to return to the network's newsmagazine show *20/20* because it demanded less time. Vargas said, "I was finding it more and more difficult to do the job the way I wanted to do it, which is 100 percent . . . and still be a great mother."[5] Despite the tremendous prestige and honor that came with the anchor's job, Vargas wanted a different role because her identity as a mom trumped everything else at that time.

Psychiatrist Nathaniel Branden, an expert on the subject of self-worth, said, "No factor is more decisive in people's psychological development and motivation than the value judgments they make of themselves."[6] In Branden's view, how we perceive ourselves to be, whether this is a healthy self-image or a negative one, determines who we are. Our self-image is the most significant key to our behavior.

Self-Efficacy Explained

Several years ago Albert Bandura, a professor of psychology at Stanford University and a preeminent psychologist, introduced the concept of self-efficacy—a term that is frequently confused with self-esteem. Many people refer to self-esteem when they mean self-efficacy. Self-efficacy is a self-impression or perception that you are capable of performing in a certain manner or capable of attaining certain goals.[7] Whereas self-efficacy relates to your perception of your ability to reach a goal, self-esteem relates to your self-worth—or how you feel about your individual value. The perception that you have about your self-esteem is often a building block that influences your efficacy. In other words, one influences the other.

For example, someone who has a high self-efficacy about being able to write a book is confident in his ability to do so. That perception may be well founded or completely misguided. Just as with self-esteem, self-perceptions involving self-efficacy can simply be wrong!

Suspending for a moment the inevitable tendencies to have an inaccurate and artificial self-perception that leads to an inflated sense of worth, the principles behind self-efficacy and aspirational identities are powerful. Both emphasize future-focused activities. Both speak to what is possible rather than simply what is. When accurately represented, self-efficacy and aspirational identities are powerful drivers.

Figure 3.3 illustrates the synergy between an aspirational identity and self-efficacy, or at least a self-efficacy that is based on an accurate self-perception. Figure 3.3 shows how you can progress from virtually

Figure 3.3—Aspirational Identity

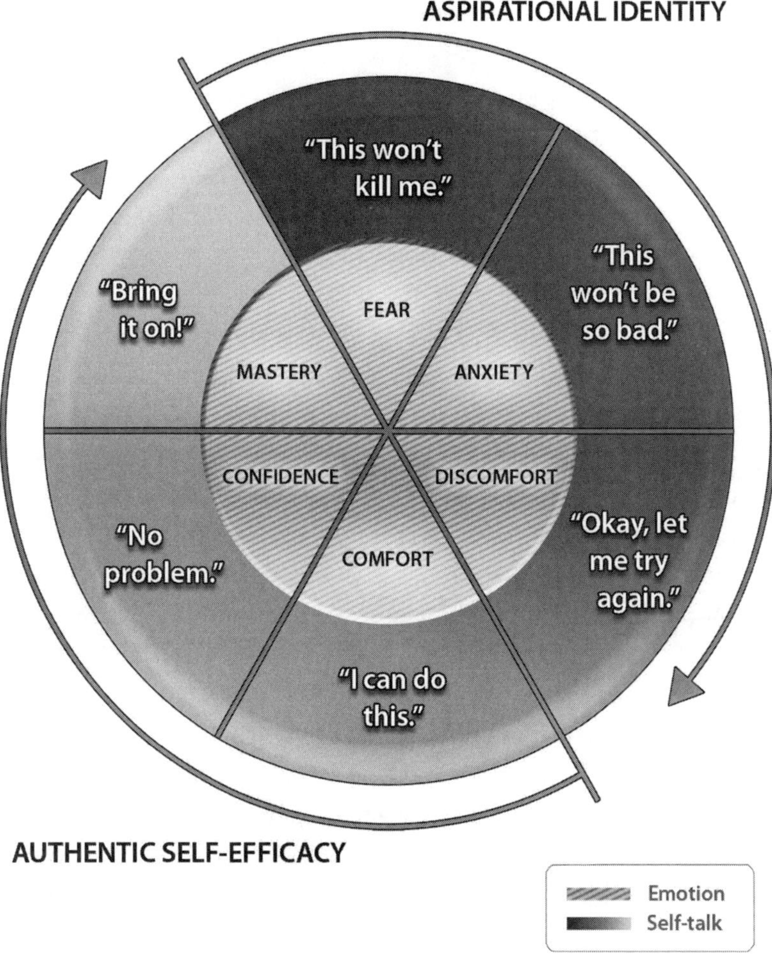

no skills and no confidence to virtual mastery and high confidence by leveraging your aspirational identity and your self-efficacy.

A new father attempting to calm a crying baby for the first time illustrates how this works. This new father knows little about babies, but he's a hearty soul, and despite his lack of experience, he takes his role as dad—his aspirational identity—seriously. Seeing himself as a dad gives him the fuel he needs to complete the task, despite the fear and trepidation he's initially feeling about calming his crying child. He tells himself, "This won't kill me," and it turns out that the experience doesn't. Initially his skills are woefully inadequate, but he realizes with each succeeding fatherhood experience that (1) it isn't nearly as bad as he's made it out to be and (2) with each experience this young father gains skills and confidence.

His view of himself as a dad sustains him through the initial and most difficult phase of this process, namely, getting him through the inevitable rough times and validating each small victory. He sticks it out despite the obstacles, frustration, and grief he experiences along the way. This process transcends mere visualization (which has a task orientation) and enables him to be something (a dad) that he sees as worthy and desirable.

Eventually this new father moves from feeling "This won't kill me" to "This won't be so bad." Thereafter he is only mildly discomforted by the thought of calming the baby. At this point his self-efficacy toward the goal of calming the baby has increased, and that confidence is well founded. Prior to that time, a high degree of self-efficacy is an illusion driven by bravado or worse. Ultimately, with the benefit of experience and reinforcement, he achieves a level of mastery. He has gone from nothing to something. Of course, the speed of his progress can be accelerated by encouragement from others, particularly his spouse and friends.

Notice how this man's aspirational identity of being a father and his self-efficacy of accomplishing the goal of being a father compliment each other. In this case, being something preceded accomplishing something. This is consistent with what we discussed in chapter 1, that leadership is a matter of how to be, not how to do. The young father exhibited personal leadership when his north arrow became his self-image of dad, with all its accompanying responsibilities.

This principle, as well as it works toward a good outcome, can also be used badly. Napoleon said, "A soldier will fight long and hard for a bit of colored ribbon."[8] The ribbon represented "how to be" for soldiers. Street gangs exploit this principle too, using the identity of the gang as a galvanizing force for new recruits and wavering members who are short on commitment. Members are coerced into doing something they wouldn't otherwise do. The approach proves to be quite effective, despite its manipulative nature and its dependency on fear as a motivator.

For instance, *Oakland Post* editor Chauncey Bailey was gunned down on August 2, 2007, in a brazen attack that shook an otherwise calm downtown Oakland neighborhood. Bailey had been preparing a scathing investigative report on a well-known community institution that had been marginalized through "fraud and forgery by a ruthless . . . criminally-minded family." As the *Contra Costa Times* noted following the killing: "When a journalist is ambushed and gunned down in broad daylight on a busy downtown street, our thoughts turn immediately to Russia, Latin America or some Third-World dictatorship."[9] Yet this happened right here in the good ole US of A. What possible explanation could possibly justify this despicable act? The suspect (a nineteen-year-old handyman) quickly confessed to the slaying, saying that "he considered himself a 'good soldier' when he shot and killed Bailey for writing negative stories about his beloved institution."

The handyman's family commented on how his values and demeanor had changed after he became associated with the institution and committed an act that he would have never committed otherwise. It was surmised that the institution's leadership programmed not only the handyman but many others like him into seeing themselves as good soldiers for the organization and ultimately participating in many hideous and unlawful acts. Regardless of how or why the handyman reached the point where he could murder Chauncey Bailey, self-efficacy became a powerful motivator for the handyman and became the source of much pain and misery for many others.

The Ultimate Aspirational Identity

A few organizations, although not many, have recognized the power of reinforcing their people's view of themselves as professionals. Both Peter Drucker and Jack Welch have stated that the world's best leadership development program resides within the U.S. Army. In her book *Be Know Do,* Frances Hesselbein stated, "The first line of the Creed of the Noncommissioned Officer states, 'No one is more professional than I.'" Notice how, right off the bat, the army emphasizes the importance of being a professional. (The organizational impacts of this principle will be discussed in chapter 13.)

Recall Steve's story from chapter 1, when he rose to the occasion in the aftermath of a plant explosion. He saw himself as a professional and acted accordingly. Steve later commented that the thing that meant the most to him throughout the whole ordeal was his business unit's vice president recognizing him as a consummate professional. In work there may be no higher compliment than to be considered a consummate professional.

Being a consummate professional means you're at the top of your game. You've earned the highest levels of respect and admiration from your peers. More important, you have built enormous levels of genuine self-esteem.

It's little wonder that people aspire to view themselves and be viewed by others as a professional. Despite the price involved, people willingly subscribe to it. This type of motivation (referred to by psychologists as autotelic[10]) is the highest form primarily because it is internally driven.

In the workplace, professional is arguably the ultimate aspirational identity. Recall, for example, how my self-view as an engineer (as well as my ego) got me into trouble when I turned down my boss's request to cover another desk. I had defined myself as an engineer (what I did) instead of a professional (who I was or aspired to be). Had I viewed myself as a professional, the outcome would have been drastically different—and I might add, for the better.

Notice how the aspirational identity of being a professional trumps:

1. a view based on I am my job (I am an accountant)
2. a nonaspirational view of one's role (I am just a clerk)
3. a negative self-view (I am second-rate)
4. a self-limiting belief (I am no good at managing people)

During your career you will have lots of jobs with lots of titles in lots of companies. The one thing that's common among all these is the importance of being a professional! In other words, you are a professional first. Your degrees, your job, and your title are simply appendages.

Be a professional who happens to hold an MBA or happens to hold the office of vice president—not the other way around! The way to master life's lessons in personal leadership (and in the process become a trusted professional) is to first aspire to be a leader.

Aspiring to Change

Molly, a business client, struggled with asserting her needs. She would often capitulate, consistently putting the needs of others ahead of her own needs. She avoided conflict, sometimes at the expense of an important deliverable.

Communications training is typically the perceived solution for someone like Molly. And while it's true that communications training does help with tactics and skill building, training of this type often does not address the root of the problem.

In Molly's case, the root of the problem lay in an unhealthy view of herself as second-rate. Regardless of how or why she held this view, it loomed like an eight-hundred-pound gorilla that influenced each of her relationships.

You can spend years and thousands of dollars in therapy to determine how and why negative views develop. But as Marshall Goldsmith has noted, "When you're over fifty, blaming mom and dad for your behavioral traits is weak."[11]

Knowing the why behind our behavior can lead to analysis paralysis, an intriguing intellectual exercise, but it often accomplishes little in terms of making meaningful corrections. In other instances, a desire to determine why becomes an avoidance technique that delays the necessary and inevitable action toward correction. While it is an all-too-human tendency to want to know why, it's a mistake to assume that knowledge of that type is a precursor to correction. Knowing why may give you a greater understanding, but it often does little toward developing new, more positive behaviors.

Recall that John Maxwell said, "It's how we perceive ourselves to be that determines who we are." In Molly's case, perceiving herself as a professional enabled her to subjugate the undesired view of herself as second-rate with one that held greater appeal and promise. Molly's desire to be a professional, despite her discomfort, enabled her to initiate discussions with people, even those who promised to be contentious. However, most of Molly's encounters resulted in successful outcomes.

Molly changed. She grew. Others noticed and responded by reinforcing her newfound confidence. Dave Ulrich noted, "Transformation will not likely endure until people assimilate a new identity."[12] In Molly's case, her change was sustained because she had assimilated a profound new identity.

Molly's self-view and internal changes were accomplished without the aid of formal communications training. Like the new father attempting an uncomfortable task, Molly achieved a greater sense of herself as a professional and increased her self-efficacy in order to handle unpleasant situations in the future.

A Challenged Self-View

Negative self-views have the opposite effect of positive self-views. A diminished view of yourself as a professional is unsettling, if not paralyzing.

My friend Jay, a consultant, missed an important deliverable for a client because of a misunderstanding and some questionable judgment. This was quite uncharacteristic of Jay. The impacts were significant to the organization and to the new player in his client's organization. After the dust settled, a debriefing was held to find out where things went wrong. The debriefing went poorly because it focused on assigning blame rather than determining root causes. The final straw was when the client told Jay that he was unprofessional.

Jay was devastated! He believed he had contributed to the problem, although he also believed he had acted conscientiously and in good faith. Jay had always prided himself on showing up as a professional. This was a bitter pill, one that shook him to the core!

As a result, over the next few months, I watched a normally confident and congenial guy become tentative and withdrawn. Eventually, Jay came out of it, but it took a great deal of time and an enormous amount of effort for him to shake off the feelings associated with being labeled as unprofessional.

Did he deserve the unprofessional label the client gave him? That's not for me to say and really isn't the point. The accusatory title went beyond mere hand slapping; it challenged Jay's personal self-view as a professional. In the end, Jay didn't merely feel guilt; he felt shame.

Waldroop and Butler point out, "Shame is personal . . . it's a feeling about who you *are*."[13] Certainly Jay was at fault for the mess-up—which by itself would warrant feelings of guilt—but his feelings were deeper, more persistent, and more personal—all of which were consistent with the shame he later felt.

Being considered unprofessional was paralyzing for Jay and would be devastating for most conscientious people. Being told you're unprofessional is an uncomplimentary slight of the worst type. It's really painful. It's something that most people would rather do anything to avoid, because it threatens a cherished view of themselves that is inseparably linked to their being.

A Study in Identity Change

Many of us think of our identity as fixed, but it need not be that way. Think of our new father example or Molly in the workplace. Both of their identities evolved with time and experience. Now consider Marshall Goldsmith's experience with Bono.[14]

At a charity dinner in 2007, Marshall Goldsmith was seated next to Bono. The older Goldsmith was not familiar with Bono's music, but the two found that they had much to talk about, and Bono fascinated his dinner companion with stories of his life's adventures. Afterward, Goldsmith described the evening in an article for *Businessweek*, and he told his readers, "After listening to Bono share his personal story, I realized that he is a wonderful example of a person who has not only changed his behavior but also his identity, or definition of who he is—while remaining authentic and not becoming a phony."

This metamorphosis dazzled Goldsmith, because he coaches high-level executives to "achieve positive change in their leadership behavior."

Part of his approach is to help others to take a long look at how they view themselves. What he saw in Bono was someone without pretense or facade. He saw the singer and musician as a "regular guy" and grasped that this was Bono's self-identity as well. He saw that Bono admired other singers and musicians, recognized the influence of his peers on his own work, and appreciated their many achievements in addition to his own. At no time, however, did Bono make a point of what his music had accomplished in terms of sales or status for him. Instead, Bono focused on what they had produced in the name of their art, their craft.

Still, there was no doubt that Bono enjoyed his rock-star status and the fame that accompanied it, because in addition to adoring fans, he had access to influential people, and this opened the door for his latest role as a humanitarian. As Bono recounted a tour of Africa during the famine years of the 1980s, Goldsmith couldn't help but recall his own time spent in Africa as a Red Cross volunteer. "He talked about his desire to help those who needed the help the most and to alleviate human suffering," Goldsmith said. "It was clear that a large part of the rest of his life would be devoted to doing whatever he could to make our world a better place."

Bono's greatest impression on Goldsmith came during his after-dinner speech. Despite an atmosphere that encouraged Bono to pillory public policy decision makers and governments around the world or anyone else whom he might want to criticize, Bono maintained focus on why he was at the dinner. "He was clearly there to raise money and help people in need—not to prove how smart or clever he was," Goldsmith said. "He was sincere in expressing gratitude to anyone who was helping out in any way. His need to help others far exceeded his need to be right. He is a man with a mission. He isn't pretending to be a humanitarian—he is a humanitarian." He added, "After having dinner with Bono, I reflected upon how he had changed. He did not let his definition of who he was limit his potential for who he could become."

As he looked back at his "dinner with Bono," Goldsmith saw that the musician-singer-rock star-humanitarian wore many hats simultaneously. But he was not a chameleon who changed to fit whatever role he was playing at the moment; he was the same person in each role. Goldsmith concluded, "In the same way that Bono changed not just his behavior but his definition of who he is, you can change your definition of who you are and change your role in the world."

Indeed! What great promise that holds! As we've seen in this chapter, our self-views (in whatever form they take) are powerful motivators. And as Bono demonstrates, changing one's view changes everything! I am not saying that our self-view is our only motivating source. There are numerous other motivating factors, such as performing meaningful work and dynamic leadership. But when it comes to self-motivation, our self-view is a huge motivational driver, and this element is too frequently ignored when we study this process.

Why This Resonates with People

If what you've read so far resonates with you, I suspect you've got plenty of company. Whenever I speak on this topic or use the material in a consulting process, people really soak it up, and it doesn't much matter whether I'm dealing with a senior team or frontline individual contributors. Here are a few reasons why.

It has intuitive appeal because of who they are and who they want to be. It is, for many, what they have always believed but never seen validated—until now. Surprisingly few in the workplace really view themselves as professionals. This is unfortunate because it promises a free and previously untapped source of motivation that proves beneficial to both employees as well as their organizations.[15]

Being a professional appeals to our better natures because it is a force for good. By understanding what's required of professionals, people have a much better defined target to shoot for. In this era of declining standards, it is a target that is desperately needed.

Since being a professional does not require a stereotypical professional profession, applicability is universal. It gets to the root of a very big problem, regardless of the type of work you do. Professionalism is compatible with any set of values, an individual's or an organization's, as you'll see in chapter 13, where the emphasis will be on how organizations can achieve a competitive advantage by encouraging these views in its people.

SUMMARY

- Because self-perceptions determine who we are, wanting to be something is powerfully motivating.
- Wanting to be a professional recalibrates your own expectations and raises your standards. Viewing yourself as a professional is a precursor to being one.
- Viewing yourself as a professional is likened to having an aspirational identity. It's about becoming something, in this case something honorable, namely, a professional.
- Seeing yourself as a professional is one of the highest forms of motivation because it's intrinsic, internally driven.
- In the workplace, professional is arguably the ultimate aspirational identity, transcending your title, vocation, or educational pedigree.
- Having an aspirational identity as a professional gets you through the initial and most difficult phase of personal change (learning new skills, learning to cope with distasteful situations, etc.).
- For many, being considered unprofessional can be traumatic, largely because people typically associate unprofessional with character flaws.
- People who view themselves as professionals tend to excel beyond those who don't, because they expect more of themselves.

CHAPTER **FOUR**

Trust: The One Thing You Have to Get Right

The competitive advantage of trust has never been more important or more valuable.

—Ken Chenault

Because of distrust, nations go to war, economies fail, and cynicism breeds. In many ways, human history has been charted by the impacts of distrust. It's a game changer. With trust, people tend to be more confident, proactive, and hopeful. Without trust, people tend to be more skeptical, withdrawn, and pessimistic. Trust is to mental health what clean air and clean water are to physical health. George MacDonald observed, "To be trusted is a greater compliment than to be loved."

This chapter is all about trust. It's covered in a way that, I hope, will broaden your perspectives on a topic that seemingly needs none.

As of this writing in the summer of 2010, trust is at an all-time low in both government and business.[1] Not surprisingly, the economy is running on fumes. Frances Hesselbein noted that in her lifetime she's "never seen higher levels of cynicism and lower levels of trust." She knows all too well how critical this is because "a democracy becomes unsustainable under low levels of trust."[2] The same principle holds for organizational health as well.

The seven mind-sets are thoroughly illustrated in part 2, and since trust and trustworthiness are central to the premises underlying the mind-sets, it's important to understand how these terms are defined. That may seem odd because the word *trust* is used so commonly and seemingly understood by most. But trust is multifaceted and conjures up an array of complex emotions based on one's experience.

Trust is personal. With few exceptions, the connotation of the word is positive and affirming. However, "trusting Rebecca" and "trusting the sun to rise" are two different experiences. For the purposes of this book, we are focused on trust as it relates to people. At a very fundamental level, it's really quite simple: do I trust so-and-so? The answer to that question is often based on a confidence that others have a genuine concern for our welfare rather than a desire to inflict harm.[3] And when we say we trust someone, we're usually referring to his or her character. As we'll see in this chapter, there is more to it than that.

"John, I trust you. You do what you say you will do. You exercise good judgment and you're good at what you do." As a manager, Judy couldn't ask for more. She wished she had ten more employees like John. Because of the trust that John had built over time, he received many desirable assignments, had a great working relationship with Judy, and had become a serious player in the greater organization.

The German word *trost*—which suggests comfort—is the linguistic root for the word *trust.* Judy and John trust each other and enjoy the comfort that comes with that trust as the foundation of their working relationship. That's vitally important because of the interdependence of their work.

Yet the word *trust* can be used when attempting to prove a negative. "Trust Patty? I don't think so!" Note the cynicism, sarcasm, and disappointment in this comment. The speaker has definite negative and dubious feelings for Patty's work. Because trust is assumed to be affirming (a good thing), the speaker makes clear that her use of the word here is sarcastic so as not to confuse the listener.

Sometime ago my family redid our backyard, which included dealing with maddening inclement weather. And that meant mud—lots of it. After the umpteenth time our beloved dog Nikki tracked mud into the house (she has a doggie door), I was exasperated and looked her in the eye, pointed my disapproving finger, and said, "You cannot be trusted!" This conclusion came after spending an endless amount of time vacuuming and negotiating with my wife over the cleaning of muddy paws.

Nikki could not be trusted to stay clean, but I *could* count on her to always find the biggest mud hole in the yard. In her case, I could depend on her all right—to do the wrong thing! But because it was the wrong thing, my statement to her ("You can't be trusted") was not affirming. Just because we can count on someone's consistent behavior does not mean that we trust them. For example:

- I can trust Judy to be on time, and I can count on Alex to be fifteen to twenty minutes late.
- I can trust Mike to do the right thing for the organization, and I can count on Daniel to always look out for Daniel.
- I can trust Robin's work to be very thorough, and I can count on Mika's work to have one or two troubling flaws.

Because trust tends to have an affirming and positive connotation, we hear statements in the workplace like: "From the perspective of the controllers office, 'Danny' and 'trust' don't belong in the same sentence. Please provide us with a new representative from your department ASAP!" For our purposes, I will emphasize the positive, affirming connotation of the word *trust.*

Trust Is Personal, Very Personal

Because the nature of trust is so personal and so intuitive, it's difficult to capture in words a definition that does justice to such a unique emotional experience. Yet it's important that we try to define it because trust impacts the important, tangible, and practical aspects of our lives.

My experience with Nikki illustrates why trust is so personal. Trust represents something more than just an impersonal, interpersonal insurance policy. When someone says (or thinks) that so-and-so can't be trusted, there is usually more to it than that. What he really means is that so-and-so can't be trusted with things that are important to *him.* Thus the most predictable and powerful way to demonstrate concern for the welfare of others is to prove one's trustworthiness with the things that are of greatest importance to them.

With all due respect to the dozens of other definitions of trust we're familiar with (which are largely clinical in nature), this is my working definition: **Trust is the emotional glue that supports one's priorities, protects one's self-interests, and ensures respect for one's values.**[4] When someone is found to be untrustworthy, almost without fail, it is because of a violation of one of these three concerns. Taken collectively, what trust does for individuals also applies to organizations. I believe this definition frames the discussion—both in nuance and in substance—surrounding trust.

Supporting Priorities

Our priorities are reflected in how we invest our time, energy, and resources. In the workplace, it's all about producing and getting the right things done—starting with the items of greatest importance. Those who deliver inconsistently on their commitments—whether through haphazard effort, questionable quality, organizational drama, unimaginative solutions, or lukewarm organizational support—will all register pretty low on the trustworthiness scale. Likewise, bosses who provide ragtag resources, less-than-forthright information, weak political support, confusing priorities, suspect promises, emotionally distant encouragement, and self-serving pronouncements will give their employees very little reason to consider them trustworthy in light of the priorities for which they have responsibilities.

Other groups that bear noting are those who are high maintenance. These people tend to be either technically incompetent, emotionally dependent, or organizational contrarians (hell-raisers). Each has his own story and pathology, although it's not our purpose to address these here. What is noteworthy is that these people tend to sap precious time and valuable energy away from important priorities.

In her own way, my Nikki was a little hell-raiser because she siphoned off a great deal of my time and energy to clean up after her. Given other important priorities at the time, cleaning up after her was something I would have preferred not to do.

Protecting Self-Interests

Protecting our self-interests is about ensuring our well-being, whether it is financial, emotional, psychological, social, or physical. Those who trash talk (harm another's reputation), demean (attack another's self-esteem), take credit from another's work (steal another's credibility), or take shortcuts with safety (put the well-being of others at risk) are unlikely to be viewed as trustworthy.

Yet it's heartening to observe colleagues in high-trust environments giving credit where credit is due, defending others' reputations in their absence, or taking a bullet for a peer. In addition to protecting the self-interests of others, trust is also built by advancing another person's self-interest. We've all observed employees who would walk through walls for certain managers. This is because those managers extend trust by offering a challenging assignment, opening up their networks, or personally mentoring employees. Simply put: they cared about their employees.

Having one's self-interest championed by a third-party can be a defining experience, particularly when it involves a high-stakes issue or when you are unable to represent your own affairs. David Maister shares the following experience from his book *The Trusted Advisor.*

Regina M. Pisa, chairman and managing partner of Goodwin Procter LLP, one of Boston's largest and most prominent law firms, describes an unusual and special trusted adviser relationship.

"I had a CEO client call me," she said. "He was leaving an appointment at Massachusetts General Hospital and wanted to come over right away. He walked in with his wife and said that they had just been told he was terminally ill, with not much time left. He said, 'I'm fearful for my wife. She doesn't have someone like you in her life who she can call on for anything, and I want you to do for her what you did for me. We're putting ourselves in your hands to help us through all this.'

"Getting the estate planning in order was the easy part. What they were asking for was for me to help them deal with the whole thing, before and after death. There's no greater definition of a trusted adviser, no greater reward than when you develop bonds with clients that run so deep."[5]

Ensuring Respect of Values

Values reflect the essence of who we are by providing meaning for our life and purpose for our work. Values help us make sense of our world because they are inseparably connected to our core beliefs. They tell us what's important and what isn't, what's right and what isn't, what's worth pursuing and what isn't. **In the workplace one's personal values are the fuel that advances personal growth and job satisfaction.**

For instance, someone who values freedom and has their freedom artificially throttled by a command-and-control manager will likely view management as untrustworthy. Alternatively, managers who create special assignments for stymied employees (such as those who value creativity) in order to use their creative talent will be fondly remembered as being especially trustworthy. Likewise, managers who are especially innovative in developing work-life balance alternatives will be viewed as trustworthy by employees who value quality time with their families.

Interdependence Between Values and Self-Interests

I'm not suggesting that our self-interests should come at the expense of everyone or everything around us. Quite the contrary! Borrowing from the wisdom of actor and humanitarian Paul Newman, I'm not advocating that people should be deified. I am suggesting that people are entitled to fundamental self-interests that should be protected and nurtured in the workplace.

Just as a mechanical governor moderates the output of an engine, values moderate one's self-interests. Our values help us determine the difference between being ambitious and being greedy, between being assertive and being aggressive, between being a steward and being a tyrant. It's knowing when to let a confrontational peer win an inconsequential argument, when to place the spotlight on a colleague instead of yourself, when to take one for the team. For instance, recall Steve's experience in chapter 1 wherein his sense of responsibility in dealing with the plant disaster temporarily preempted a well-deserved promotion. This is an example of putting values into action—in Steve's case putting the greater good ahead of his personal interests.

David Foster, one of the world's greatest songwriters and producers, was honored at a tribute concert held on May 23, 2008, in Las Vegas by Andrea Bocelli, Michael Bublé, Celine Dion, Barbra Streisand, Josh Groban, and many others. When asked how he attracted so many incredibly busy, in-demand, high-profile entertainers for a rare, one-night event, Foster simply said, "I'm the glue."

How true! Foster had played a significant role in the early development of the careers of most of the performers at his tribute concert. Described as the man behind the world's greatest singers, Foster indeed provided the emotional glue for these top performers based on his years as a trusted mentor and confidant. As this example illustrates, trust unifies people in unique ways and jump-starts those things that are most important to us.

As mentioned earlier, Judy and John shared a high-trust relationship; they had an emotional glue. Rules were few, freedoms were abundant, candor was normal, and information flowed freely between them. Authenticity was expected, and one-upsmanship was nonexistent. This enabled focus and speedy execution of the things that mattered most, which created a freedom for them to jettison clutter. You know the clutter all too well: debilitating office politics, misplaced priorities, rumor mongering, and suspicious motives.

For Judy, John's character is an important piece of the trust puzzle but not an exclusive one. Judgment and competence are other important pieces too. It is important to Judy to know that whenever a new situation comes up, John has the judgment to do the right thing. Likewise, as the department's top performer, John generously shares his knowledge with others, which is invaluable to Judy. This illustrates an essential truth: our trustworthiness is not only a natural consequence of the perceived qualities in our character but also of our judgment and competence as well. For Judy, John measured up well on the three legs of the trustworthiness stool illustrated in Figure 4.1.

Figure 4.1—Trustworthiness

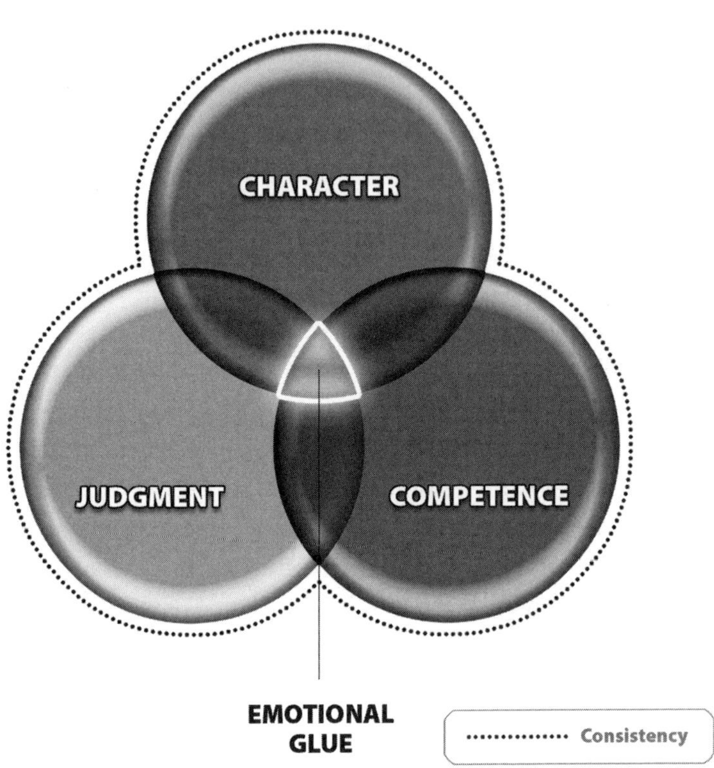

As Noel Tichy and Warren Bennis point out, "With good judgment, little else matters. Without it, nothing else matters."[6] Judgment assures others that you're doing the right thing. Competence assures them that you're doing the thing right. But competence, while imperative, doesn't protect you from doing the wrong thing in the first place. Theodore Levitt, a renowned management professor at Harvard, captured this point beautifully when he observed, "Nothing is more wasteful than doing with great efficiency that which should not be done at all." John Gardner, in a conversation with a new CEO, asked his opinion of the second-in-command he had inherited. The CEO said, "He's a superb crisis manager, which is fortunate because his lack of judgment leads to a lot of crises."

At a purely practical level, it's pretty hard to trust someone who lacks good judgment. Think squandered effort, incessant wheel spinning, and needless frustration. Judgment is about critical discernment and wisdom; competence is about smarts and skills.

Character—that oh-so-personal component of the three-legged trustworthiness stool—is our personal credibility passport. Most people feel that the deepest level of trust surrounds issues involving character.

Together, these three qualities—judgment, competence, and character—determine our worthiness as to whether others will trust us with things that are important to them. And we must never forget, **we're the ones taking the trustworthiness exam, others do the grading.**

It's important to note that other people may have great confidence (trust) in our competence but little confidence in our judgment. Likewise, our character may be a source of great trust, but our competence is lacking. The point is that people trust us in different ways and on different levels. Not trusting someone to return phone calls is very different from someone who betrays a trust by joining the competition. Rest assured that those things that are of greatest importance to us, almost without fail, are graded the harshest when a violation of trust occurs.

A quarterback who values the low-risk swing pass to a running back coming out of the backfield, but who can't throw a touch pass to save his soul will be trusted for his good judgment, but he won't be trusted for his ability to execute. Good judgment with questionable competence doesn't cut it. Likewise, poor judgment accompanied by good character *or* solid competence accompanied by questionable character will produce the same result: you'll be on the bench. All three elements are needed—character, competence, and judgment—in order to build trust.

So aside from character, competence, and judgment, is anything else expected of someone to be considered trustworthy? Yes! In a word, *consistency.* There's an inseparable correlation between trust and consistency, especially when it comes to behavior. **You can have consistency without trust, but you cannot have trust without consistency.**

Years ago, as a sales director, I had an account executive who was exceptional in keeping me informed about what was happening with our major accounts. Not only was the information helpful, but I could always count on him to provide me with two or three critical updates each week—without fail. I was never caught flat-footed by not knowing what was going on. Not once! This was invaluable—good news or bad. When it came to emotional glue, he and I had it in buckets. The consistency in his communication played just as important a role as the information itself.

Without consistency, you don't know who or what you can count on. And it's that uncertainty that can become an insurmountable barrier in developing trust. **Aspiring professionals must commit to consistently show up as a professional should, not merely when it suits their needs.** There's nothing like a mixed message, a double standard, or creative rationalizations to undermine one's credibility.

No Mixed Messages

Do his or her words translate into deeds? When they don't match, people's antennae go up and they naturally become suspicious. "There is something wrong with a party that preaches capitalism to single mothers while practicing socialism toward corporations," said Joe Scarborough, host of MSNBC's *Morning Joe* and a former Republican congressman, on the importance of consistency for the Republican Party to reestablish the political moral high ground.

Consider the following:

- After declaring a company-wide fiscal policy of constraint, the leader who called for the constraint engages in lavish spending.
- After publicly declaring her support for the company's important new initiative, the department head decides to wait it out and only go through the motions.
- After committing to fulfill important assignments on a task force, a team member then fails to do his part.

Whether it's a leader issuing an organizational edict, someone declaring her intention, or an employee making a personal commitment, if one's words and deeds don't match up, they simply won't be credible. Ultimately, these people won't be found to be trustworthy.

A colleague friend recently turned down a lucrative last-minute assignment with a generous client after having previously committed to another client for the same dates. Her actions were consistent with her original commitment. To her credit, she didn't put off her original client simply because a new (and presumably better) situation arose that suited her needs.

No Double Standards

This is the age-old test of consistently defending important organizational values. Professionals don't play favorites, don't promote situational ethics, and don't use their position or knowledge to take advantage of, punish, or intimidate others—especially those who may not agree with them. Professionals know that doing so suggests bias, hidden agendas, or worse. In addition to reflecting poorly on them personally, it also poisons the organization's environment.

Consider:

- Two people publicly disagree with the boss over an impending decision impacting operational strategy. Nothing happens to one; the other is bad-mouthed by the boss to senior management.
- Two equally competent people double their annual sales quota. One is invited to lunch with the division president. The other is ignored.
- Two equally competent people have serious ethical violations of a similar nature. One is fired; the other (who happens to be favored by the leadership) receives a slap on the wrist.

These examples of inconsistencies are illustrative of an environment that would surely produce distrust.

A client of mine, a plant manager, made a commitment to his people that he would never compromise the needs of the plant. True to his word, he fired an employee for cause because he believed the employee's action jeopardized the well-being of the plant. The employee happened to be his good friend. It would have been easy enough to justify any other action short of termination (while suiting the manager's needs), but the manager took the action that he felt was appropriate for the circumstance, regardless of how unpleasant or personally difficult. As a professional, he did what he felt was right.

No Creative Rationalizations

Renowned psychologist Seymour Epstein warned "never underestimate the ability of the human mind to rationalize." Succumbing to the temptation of justification is a latter-day way of rationalizing doing something you know you shouldn't. Professionals are expected to maintain high ideals despite difficult or trying circumstances. That means, among other things, being objective, compartmentalizing personal feelings, and being authentic. In short, that means getting the right result the right way. Anything less isn't measuring up.

Consider:

- A retailer charges a premium for a plus-size (the premium being justified by the extra fabric required) but does not provide a discount for petite sizes. Given the lack of a discount for petite sizes, the extra-fabric argument is intellectually dishonest.
- A senior leader cherry-picks a few useful facts that support the argument for relocating the company headquarters to a new location (which happens to be within seven miles of the leader's home). An objective comparison shows that the cons for such a move clearly outweigh the pros. Just because the senior leader can approve the decision, it doesn't mean he should.
- A politician who adamantly opposes policy X when the opposition party is in power suddenly becomes an outspoken supporter of the policy when his own party returns to power. Being a reed instead of an oak when the wind blows simply reveals a lack of principle as well as weak character.
- An athletic coach condones taunting by his players—behavior that more often than not leads to heightened hostility during competition and altercations afterward. Defending the indefensible not only makes you look foolish, but it is one of the fastest ways to lose your personal credibility.

Each of these examples demonstrates some form of creative rationalization that people use when it suits them. Most of us view such people as unprincipled, undisciplined, and opportunists. This all leads to inconsistent behavior and distrust by people who are expected to hold themselves to a higher standard rather than merely look out for themselves.

Consistency Alone Is Not the Answer

Recall that consistency alone doesn't guarantee trustworthiness. My dog Nikki was consistent in finding mud holes in the backyard, but that didn't translate into mutual trust because so much of my time and energy involved cleaning her up. When it came to the backyard, we had no emotional glue.

Likewise, someone in the workplace who consistently fails to pull his own weight, who consistently exhibits poor judgment, who isn't up to the technical demands of the job isn't someone you're likely to have warm and fuzzy feelings about. How could you? She is unable (perhaps unwilling) to support your priorities and perhaps those of your organization.

Consistent behavior combined with incompatible values also produces distrust. For example, as a fiscal conservative, I don't trust politicians who are consistently fast and loose with the public purse. Taken in excess, I believe this practice ultimately leads to excessive debt and the unconscionable burden of financial bondage for our children and grandchildren. As someone who holds fiscal responsibility as a core value, I'm unable to generate any emotional glue for politicians (regardless of their political party) who act contrary to that core value. These same loose-spending politicians may be acting consistently, according to their values, but I still don't trust them.

Simply put: no emotional glue = no trust, regardless of another's consistent behavior. Trust is possible only when both the emotional glue and consistency in behavior are present.

Seems like a tall order, this trustworthiness business! To a perfectionist, it may seem like a challenge; for the rest of us it may just seem overwhelming. The good news is that one need not be perfect to be considered trustworthy. Psychologists have concluded that for people to be found trustworthy, their behavior needs to meet a 70 percent threshold of consistency. In other words, perfection isn't required.

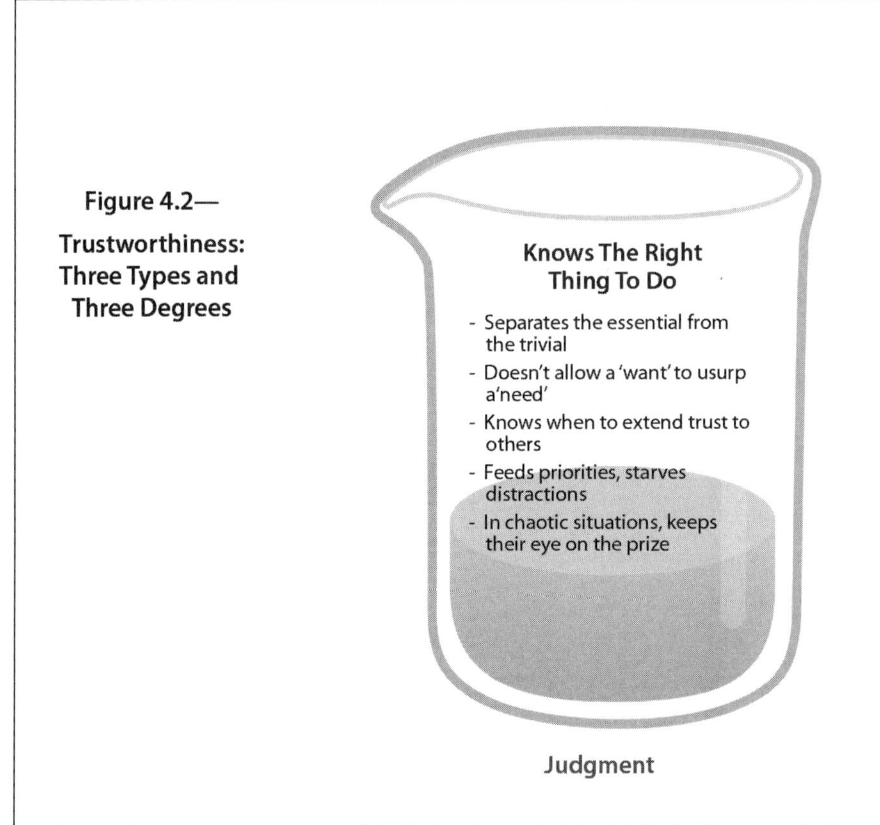

Figure 4.2—
Trustworthiness: Three Types and Three Degrees

Figure 4.2 shows how the core elements of trustworthiness (character, judgment, and competence) support the things of greatest importance to others (values, priorities, self-interests, etc.).

As Figure 4.2 suggests, there are varying types and degrees of trust. Some have a greater impact than others, especially those related to character. The nature of the trust generated by someone who consistently demonstrates superb judgment is very different from that which we experience when someone comes to our defense against an unwarranted political attack or proactively works to promote our career interests. As

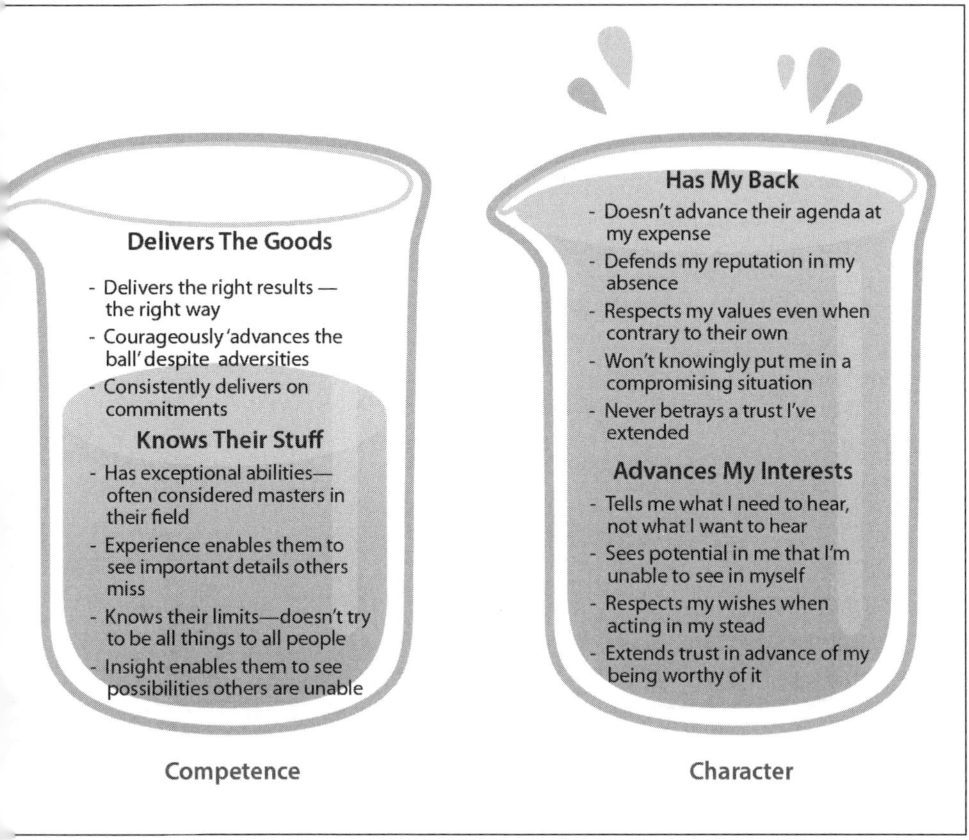

Delivers The Goods

- Delivers the right results — the right way
- Courageously 'advances the ball' despite adversities
- Consistently delivers on commitments

Knows Their Stuff

- Has exceptional abilities—often considered masters in their field
- Experience enables them to see important details others miss
- Knows their limits—doesn't try to be all things to all people
- Insight enables them to see possibilities others are unable

Competence

Has My Back

- Doesn't advance their agenda at my expense
- Defends my reputation in my absence
- Respects my values even when contrary to their own
- Won't knowingly put me in a compromising situation
- Never betrays a trust I've extended

Advances My Interests

- Tells me what I need to hear, not what I want to hear
- Sees potential in me that I'm unable to see in myself
- Respects my wishes when acting in my stead
- Extends trust in advance of my being worthy of it

Character

we move from left to right in Figure 4.2, the depth of trust increases—it's stickier, it carries greater significance. After all, trust is personal.

I noted earlier that answering the question "do I trust so-and-so" is pretty straightforward. Despite involving many complex emotions, most of us have little trouble confidently answering that question. It's straightforward because the answer is usually pretty intuitive. Figure 4.2 helps us to understand why. Individuals exhibiting the traits shown in Figure 4.2 (and many more like them) will be seen as trustworthy; those who don't, won't. Part 2 brings to light many more examples.

SUMMARY

- Human history has been charted by the impacts of distrust.
- The absence of trust in organizational affairs (especially business) portends that things will end badly.
- Trust is uniquely personal. With few exceptions, the connotation of the word is positive and affirming.
- Character, competence, and judgment (when they are consistently applied) are all determinants as to whether we trust someone or not.
- Someone's consistent behavior does not necessarily mean that we trust them.
- Trust is the emotional glue that supports one's priorities, protects one's self-interests, and ensures respect for one's values.
- We're the ones taking the trustworthiness exam, others do the grading.
- The types and degrees of trust are different. A character-blunder, for instance, carries with it a higher degree of severity than one of judgment.

CHAPTER **FIVE**

The Big Picture

These guys are professionals. They're the best.

—Woody, *Toy Story*

This chapter focuses on why we need to correct the current trust deficit, not only for business, but for the nation as well. Here I want to advance the premise that the mind-sets held by the Founding Fathers (the same mind-sets to be examined in part 2) animated our country's freedoms and prosperity from the beginning. In the end, I contend that professionalism is a must-have, not a nice-to-have, in order to reestablish trust in our political institutions, our free markets, and our leaders.

Living in an Era of Declining Standards

With the advent of legislation like Sarbanes-Oxley, it might appear that standards are improving rather than declining. It's true that compliance, ethics, and a myriad of other regulations have never been so much in the forefront than in today's business climate. The reason? An overall decline in standards. Just as civil laws emerge in response to increasing levels of unacceptable behavior, corporate compliance and regulatory schemes do likewise.

Illegal behavior (fraud, embezzlement, conspiracy, insider trading, etc.) in corporations has certainly grabbed its share of headlines in recent decades. So pervasive were the problems with corporate malfeasance that Andy Grove, a former chairman of Intel, admitted, "I find myself embarrassed and ashamed to be a businessman." John Bogle, the founder and former chairman of one of the world's largest investment management companies, the Vanguard Group, noted, "We must address the remarkable erosion in the conduct and values of our business leaders."

Unprofessional—although not necessarily illegal—behavior has also been on the rise, but it has received less attention. Marshall Goldsmith said, "Far too many have fallen away from the lost art of being a professional. The twenty behaviors outlined in my book *What Got You Here Won't Get You There* are all demonstrations of how not to be a professional." How often do we hear about the tyrannical leader who intimidates and demeans, the top-producing salesperson who disdains others, or the brilliant scientist who is too full of himself? Regretfully, this type of behavior is widespread.

Ralph Keyes, author of *The Post-Truth Era: Dishonesty and Deception in Contemporary Life,* notes, "The obvious cause of dishonesty's rise is ethical decline. From this perspective, moral[1] compasses have broken down. Our sense of right and wrong has gone into remission. Conscience is considered old-fashioned. Conviction has been replaced by cynicism."

Consider when former San Francisco mayor Willie Brown observed, "I don't know anyone who doesn't lie on a résumé." This wasn't a wink and a nod from a big-city mayor but a public pronouncement. Brown's statement is emblematic of the types of behavior (yes, unprofessional) that were unthinkable just twenty years ago. It's unprofessional conduct that slowly but surely erodes our environment and poisons our culture. Standards decline, behavior slips. Then standards decline again, worse than before, and behavior slips even more. It's a vicious downward cycle that so many simply ignore. The causes are debatable, but the fact remains that behavioral norms can no longer be taken for granted. Consequently, trust is on the decline in an era in which it has never been more needed.

Sinking Confidence in the All-Important Financial Services Sector

James Madison wisely observed, "The circulation of confidence is better than the circulation of money." Public confidence is especially important in the financial services sector because it's the lifeblood of the nation's economy. But the decline in trust today has impacted every area of the business world, and it has been particularly prevalent in the financial services industry. According to the 2009 Center for Public Leadership study of confidence in leadership, Wall Street received the lowest confidence ratings of all—even lower than the media. In light of the 2008 economic downturn, that shouldn't be terribly surprising, but this lack of confidence is indeed troubling.

While reading several articles about the credibility meltdown in the financial services sector, I found that most of the authors described numerous levels of financial chicanery that seemed to one-up a different tragedy within the same industry the week before and the week before that and the week before that. Despite the degrees of wrongdoing, it seemed as if the culprits had forgotten how to blush.

I was astounded as all the business writers generously referred to the guilty institutions as professional. Did they really mean to say that? Perhaps they used the word *professional* out of habit. After all, the financial services crowd is a white-collar bunch. Or perhaps it was a bequeathing of the much-envied professional label to some people generally considered to be experts. In this case, experts in financial engineering. Recall from the discussions in chapters 2 and 3 that trusted professionals transcend mere technical competence. As I use the word in this book, professionalism comprises both the *what* and the *how* of getting things done.

Why Professionalism Matters Most

As you'll see in chapter 8, professionals should create more value than they extract. There are some who argue that the sophisticated financial engineering now prevalent in the financial services sector too often creates little or no mainstream economic value. Rather, this type of financial engineering mostly transfers wealth from one part of the economy to another. Many of the resulting financial instruments are highly leveraged, and with natural connections to Monte Carlo–type probability scenarios, they are more akin to high-stakes gambling than investing. Of course there are those people (often with interests to protect) who dismiss this concern out of hand.

John Bogle, considered by many to be the conscience of the financial services industry, railed against what he saw as the dangers of financial engineering. As we watched the meltdown on Wall Street, we saw just how much financial engineering was behind the complicated financial instruments known as credit default swaps (CDS) and collateralized debt obligations (CDO) that were being popularized by so many financial services companies. Bogle, however, warned, "The innovation of derivatives has enriched the financial sector (and the ratings agencies) with their enormous fees, even as the overrated, as it were CDO's have wrecked havoc on the balance sheets of those who purchased them and are now left holding the bag, surprisingly including the banks and brokers that created and sold them. Since virtually all the main mutual fund managers also run pension money, their broad embrace of CDO's has in addition eroded the retirement plans of tens of millions of citizens."[2]

Warren Buffet has dubbed derivates "financial weapons of mass destruction." These were the same types of instruments that shook AIG, Wachovia, Lehman Brothers, Bear Stearns, Morgan Stanley, and others to their foundations. Collectively, they nearly pushed the economy over the edge.

This doesn't lend itself to confidence, nor does it portray the players as professionals who are interested in creating mainstream economic value—in spite of the impressive and sophisticated financial engineering behind these instruments. These tools were created by the best and the brightest minds on Wall Street. But the adage, "Just because you can doesn't mean you should" certainly applies here.

Time magazine business writer Stephen Gandel[3] suggests there has been a sea change in Wall Street's culture, with traders now holding the preponderance of power once held by investment bankers. This means that they are making money in a very different way than they did before. He suggests that this has translated into greater risks, a short-term focus, and a devil-be-damned attitude toward the consequences of the traders' actions.

Gandel writes, "The term IBG, YBG became popular on the Street. It stands for 'I'll be gone, you'll be gone'; [that is,] someone else will have to pick up the mess." He quotes trader Phillip Meyer: "If running the economy off the cliff makes you money, you will do it, and you will do it every day of the week." Even in today's era of declining values, that statement is troubling beyond words.

Some in the industry repudiated these sentiments. "That's not representative of my firm." "We're not like that!" "I've never worked with a group that had greater integrity." "They're giving everyone else a black-eye!" Truly innocent and upstanding employees at the vilified firms were quick to point out that their division did nothing wrong, that it was the flyboys down the hall who messed it up for everyone. After all, each division has its own subculture, which is related in form but not necessarily in substance to the greater corporate culture. And it's true that many groups practicing exotic trading functions gave a black eye to their firm's mainstream meat-and-potatoes divisions. It's the timeless story of the few undermining the many.

At the same time, some argue that the media tends to vilify Wall Street. Writers such as Gandel, they say, cherry-pick their facts to suit their purposes. While that may be true in some instances, there is no question that over the past decade Wall Street took brazen risks with unproven financial instruments without truly knowing what the consequences might be. Some argue that CDOs and CDSs are appropriate financial instruments. But you have to wonder if these people could hold these positions if the taxpayers weren't backing up the risk. Pursuing self-interests must be done responsibly—at least that's how trusted professionals go about it.

Of course, the goal in business is to make money. But as you'll see in Mind-Set 2, how you go about making money determines whether people see you as trustworthy or not. Someone once observed that a professional is someone who has the freedom to act like a scoundrel but chooses not to.[4]

Fair or not, the public (at least at this moment) does not have a great deal of confidence in Wall Street. For those working Wall Street's mainstream functions—loaning money for homes, cars, education, and small business—that's unfortunate. In his description of America in the early nineteenth century, Alexis de Tocqueville noted, "I know of no country, indeed, where the love of money has taken stronger hold on the affections of men." That observation still holds as much weight today as it did more than 180 years ago. De Tocqueville specifically mentioned the *love* of money, echoing the New Testament.[5] The biblical teaching advances the premise that money itself is not evil, but the *love* of money is.

When we measure our self-worth and all that goes with it in terms of financial wealth—as is so often the case today—we often do things we wouldn't otherwise do. Dee Hock, former CEO at Visa, rightly observed, "Money motivates neither the best people, nor the best in people."

Perhaps the most damaging consequence of the recent excesses—which was driven largely by the love of money—has been the loss of trust. John Bogle reminds us, "The modern world of business was built on a system of trusting and being trusted."[6] And as I discussed in chapter 1, violations of trust are synonymous with being unprofessional.

Today, the difference isn't in substance but in scale. Two hundred years ago it was about snookering someone out of forty acres of land. Today, it is a billion-dollar windfall emanating from a clever but less-than-transparent deal.

Lest you believe this is just about Wall Street, it isn't. Certainly Wall Street is the latest poster child for today's excesses and the caviler me-first attitude, largely because of the draconian impacts that have been felt on Main Street, but the problem transcends Wall Street. In varying degrees, it impacts every industry. John Bogle observed:

> When managers are seduced by the siren song of unfathomable riches, largely unfettered by the notion of serving the interests of the corporation's long-term owners, they are easily tempted to focus on driving the stock price higher. When earnings growth goals are unrealistically high and the investment community brooks no interruptions in a regular progression of growth, the temptation to run the business around becomes overwhelming.

> To meet "the numbers," important long-term initiatives may be the first cost to be cut, with down-sizing (artfully renamed right-sizing) next in line; then financial standards are pushed to the limit; finally, earnings become so illusionary and subjective that credibility is lost.[7]

And lest you believe the downward spiral in trustworthiness is merely limited to business, you may want to revisit those deplorable statistics cited in the preface. The lack of trustworthiness, it seems, is an equal opportunity offender. This does not bode well for the republic, as every aspect of a democracy—commerce, political, legal—is dependent on trust, currently something we are sorely lacking.

This era of declining values has resulted in cynicism being at an all-time high and trust being at an all-time low. It's unfortunate but true. Absent trust, a republic can collapse. Centuries ago, Augustine of Hippo suggested that self-love led to the fall of the Roman Empire.[8] Thus we must be ever watchful about becoming too complacent, too arrogant, and too ungrateful for the freedoms and opportunities we enjoy. This certainly feels odd for a country accustomed to being a world-beater—the eight-hundred-pound gorilla in world affairs.

It's no wonder that we hear a lot today about the need to return to homespun values, getting back to the basics, and remembering what made us great as a country. It's about acting responsibly, being self-reliant, demonstrating loyalty, being industrious, exercising discipline and restraint, taking pride in one's work, and having a reputation of being trustworthy. Consider the following perspectives on the change in mind-sets within the greater business community:

- John Bogle warns that "no nation can take its greatness for granted" and cites his disgust of the "remarkable erosion in the conduct and of values . . . of our business leaders."[9]
- Jeffrey Immelt speaks passionately about renewing American leadership and how "we've forgotten the fundamentals [that brought us] a successful modern economy."[10]
- Paul Orfalea speaks with conviction of how the nation has "lost our immigrant mind-set." Immigrants, he reminds us, built this country.

What is the embodiment of homespun values? In a word, professionalism. Of course, that means *being* a professional. That's what this book is about—*being* something. *Being* honorable—something that characterizes professionals to a tee. Everything that goes with them is harmed when the dark side of a few egotistical, high-flying capitalists gets the better of them.

As you saw in chapter 1, we need better professionals—and more of them—to be the great antidote for what ails business today.[11] Trustworthiness provides an unshakeable foundation for success, both individually and organizationally. But in order to leverage the power associated with professional ideals, people must understand them with some level of specificity and appreciate why it matters to them. Considering what we've discussed in the preceding chapters, we've all got a ways to go.

Recall:

- The term *professional* is ubiquitous and, with greater use and widespread application, has lost a great deal of its essential meaning.
- Senior officers—who naturally self-identify as professionals—could not adequately explain what it meant to be one.
- Far too many hold the outdated notion that they don't qualify to be considered a professional due to their inferior vocation or because they lack a certain degree or preferred pedigree.
- Far too many fail to view themselves as professionals, something that could define a critical aspect of their identity positively.
- Few organizations (even white-collar groups and professional service organizations) explicitly reinforce the notion of their people as professionals.

At some level, this shouldn't be terribly surprising, as people have largely had an implicit understanding of what it meant to be a professional. Yet when I Googled the question, "Has U.S. business lost its way?" nearly *159 million* hits were generated.[12] Even optimists should take that number as a sobering reality check.

Almost two centuries ago, Alexis de Tocqueville toured this country and wrote, "The greatness of America lies not in being more enlightened than any other nation, but rather in her ability to repair her faults." A return to professionalism and professional ideals is the key to addressing our underlying ills.

The good news is that people are anxious to learn more about professionalism and are motivated to live up to the ideals represented by the seven mind-sets. As you'll see in part 2, this holds great potential for us as well as our country.

My favorite line from the film *Toy Story* is uttered by Woody: "These guys are professionals. They're the best." This echoes what many of us have always believed: professionals make all the difference. There are no games. No sleight of hand. Just providing value. Isn't that what most people expect professionals to do?

The remainder of this book is centered on the application of professional ideals as a means toward enhancing business performance. Simply put, it's about leveraging business opportunities. But let's put this in perspective. Opportunity in America is what water is to a fish. It's all around him, he doesn't think about it. He takes it for granted. And he doesn't know how it got there. For him, it just works. The fish, like those who are afforded opportunities to pursue business interests in this country, is fortunate—very fortunate. But the fish doesn't know he is fortunate. Let's not be like the fish!

Freedom, like opportunity, should never be taken for granted. In light of the disturbing times in which we live, I feel it both appropriate and necessary to briefly address how we came to have this opportunity in the first place and how the mind-sets described in part 2 played a role in that opportunity.

Free markets[13] are, of course, an integral part of this system in that they seek to provide products and services people need, want, and desire. To do so, the market fosters innovation and inventiveness. To remain relevant, the market continually reinvents itself. Thus free markets create the greatest level of prosperity and opportunity for the most diverse groups of people than any other comparable economic system. The remarkable success worldwide of microcredit[14] in creating entrepreneurial opportunities in nontraditional environments shows just how transformative free markets can be.

For the United States, what helps make our free markets work especially well is what compliments them, namely, individual freedoms, an ingenious monetary system, a broad-minded educational system, religious liberty, an impartial judicial system, and personal property rights. This has been proven to be a powerful formula.

Many have postulated that no country on earth provides its people with as great an opportunity for wealth creation as does the United States. That's because of the previously noted intangibles that surround U.S. free markets. Some argue, for instance, that the type of megacommercial successes such as Facebook (founder Mark Zuckerberg started in a Harvard dorm room) and Google (cofounder Sergey Brin is a Moscow-born entrepreneur who started his enterprise in a Menlo Park garage) could have originated only from within the United States. That said, there are tens of thousands of more modest but successful commercial enterprises founded by citizens and immigrants each year. But wealth, whether mega or modest, isn't the point here. The point is that our economy is replete with opportunity for a better life for everyone, and this is only limited by an individual's self-determination, which is enabled by the unfettered freedoms we all experience.

The great American experiment described by historian Catherine Drinker Bowen[15]—chronicler of the convention that produced the Constitution—has borne fruit. And it has borne lots of fruit.

The foundation for this success is directly attributable to the Founders. With all due respect to Tom Brokaw,[16] the Founders embody the nation's greatest generation. And imitation, as the saying goes, is the greatest form of flattery. As you will see in chapter 6, the handiwork of the Founders—this democracy—has, in some form, been copied or modeled in the founding documents of more than 120 countries!

So what, you ask? It's critical because the existence and the evolution of the United States are modern-day miracles. In less than two hundred years—a blink of an eye in terms of world history—an idealistic, ragtag rabble of revolutionary colonies has been transformed into the world's most powerful nation. The United States is one of mankind's greatest success stories. I believe the Founders possessed the very same mind-sets that I will chronicle in this book. Said another way, at some level the mind-sets played a significant role in the nation's founding and subsequent success.

These mind-sets, when acted on, proved to be like bedrock in demonstrating trustworthiness to every person who ever tread on this soil. For the Founders, they proved to be instrumental in earning independence by winning a grueling war against all odds, the incomparable genius contained within the much-debated Constitution, and the wisdom and foresight reflected in the country's fledgling institutions that propped up the young democracy (namely, the legal and monetary systems).

Warts and all, the Founders were found to be trustworthy because of their values and their mind-sets. I don't expect you to blindly agree with me about the role the mind-sets played in the nation's founding and subsequent success. This is simply my point of view, which I have based on what history teaches us about the values these men held and the way the nation has sustained its success—its fruits,[17] so to speak. Each chapter in part 2 carries a story about the Founders that illustrates this point.

The opportunities we enjoy today are special, and the mind-sets in part 2 enhance those opportunities. How ironic that these same mind-sets have been shown to have an inseparable connection to the nation's success, namely, providing abundant opportunities for each of us! Lacking the mind-sets of the Founders, the freedoms and opportunities we enjoy today would be a mere mirage.

If there is a scintilla's amount of truth to this premise, then at some level we are the latter-day benefactors of the Founders' mind-sets. They've provided us with a priceless gift: freedom and a superior system of commerce that provides opportunities for individuals, while sustaining the well-being of the country at large. Yet none of this should be surprising, because trust always proves to be a foundational component of success.

As you move on to part 2, I hope that you will appreciate this case for the importance of professionalism, whether it be for the nation or an organization or an individual. When you're creating something special, something enduring, something of substance, something that shouts success, professionalism is not just nice to have—it's a must-have!

SUMMARY

- Despite the adoption of enhanced ethical standards by corporations and the advent of regulation like Sarbanes-Oxley, undesired (unprofessional) behavior remains a serious problem.
- Far too many have fallen away from the lost art of being a professional—or perhaps they never knew what it meant in the first place.
- The lack of professionalism can not only give an industry like financial services a black eye but has the potential to run the greater economy off a cliff.
- No other country on the face of the earth provides so many opportunities for wealth creation than does the United States. The Founders' mind-sets are in the roots of this extraordinary success story.
- Given the era of declining values in which we live, professionalism is not just nice to have—it's a must-have!

PART II

The Seven Mind-Sets

The Seven Mind-Sets of Trusted Professionals

1. **Professionals Have a Bias for Results.**
   - The quality of their work speaks for itself.
   - They exercise superb judgment.
   - Accountability means advancing the ball, often in spite of adversity.

2. **Professionals Realize (and Act Like) They're Part of Something Bigger than Themselves.**
   - They commit to the success of their firm, organization, or client.
   - They realize that success transcends their own parochial interests.
   - They collaborate as an effective team member.

3. **Professionals Know *Things* Get Better When *They* Get Better.**
   - They are emotionally invested; it's more than just a job.
   - They are always learning, ever vigilant, and thoroughly prepared.
   - They are willing to advance a point of view and work toward what's possible.

4. **Professionals Have Personal Standards That Often Transcend Organizational Ones.**

   - They have personalized a set of core values.
   - They do what's right over what's expedient by taking the long view.
   - They avoid pointless drama. They rise above the fray. They stay focused.

5. **Professionals Know Personal Integrity Is All They Have.**

   - Authenticity and honesty are paramount.
   - They consistently deliver on their commitments, both explicit and implicit.
   - They refuse to violate the trust others have extended.

6. **Professionals Aspire to Be Masters of Their Emotions, Not Enslaved by Them.**

   - They are respecting even when it's difficult to be respectful.
   - They maintain their objectivity and keep their wits about them.
   - They manage their ego and resist the urge for immediate gratification.

7. **Professionals Aspire to Reveal Value in Others.**

   - They readily extend trust to those who need it.
   - They recognize the value other professionals bring to the table.
   - They aspire to lift others through their demeanor and actions.

CHAPTER **SIX**

MIND-SET 1

Professionals Have a Bias for Results

There is a difference between interest and commitment.
When you're interested in something,
you do it only when it's convenient.
When you're committed to something,
you accept no excuses, only results.

—Ken Blanchard

Good intentions are admirable. Hard work is a virtue. Being proactive is to be applauded. But if these traits don't produce sustained results, they are superfluous. There's no substitute for sustained results. Consider:

- A vice president of operations who increases productivity 10 percent annually for three consecutive years while making his department a great place to work, as was noted in 86 percent of departmental surveys.
- A creative team that wins a three-year advertising contract with a major new client.
- An attorney who successfully lobbies policy makers to include his company's next-generation technology in industry-wide product standards.

Deliver results and you'll get noticed. People will know they can count on you. Simply put: they'll trust you. Equally important, you'll trust yourself.

Professionals feel a tremendous sense of responsibility to deliver sustained, meaningful results—results that both they and their organizations can be proud of. This is what I mean by a bias for results. Thus it should not be surprising that a bias for results is the first mind-set of the trusted professional. In many ways, it's first among equals. As you'll see, the six other mind-sets emanate from it.

Recognize, though, this mind-set is not a bias for action. Nor is it a bias for execution or a bias for success. It is a bias for *results.* It's the bottom line. But the results must be the *right* results. Suffice it to say, results based on illegal activities or unethical behavior are, even in the best light, unacceptable imitations of the real thing. Likewise, results based on convoluted business models, while legal, later prove to be not only unsustainable but foolhardy. For instance, the 2008–2009 financial crisis that was caused in part by intricate and sophisticated financial engineering schemes is a striking example of delivering the wrong results.

There has never been more pressure to deliver real sustainable results at all levels of an organization. In an era of great distrust, it's pretty simple: producing results demonstrates trustworthiness. Recall that we're the ones taking the trustworthiness exams; others do the grading. So regardless of whether the deliverables are self-imposed or dictated from above . . . regardless of whether there are extenuating circumstances beyond your control . . . regardless of whether the results are easily quantifiable or maddeningly subjective . . . regardless of whether you think the process is fair or not . . . it's important to deliver valid results, at least if you want to be found trustworthy.

Having the bank call you on the carpet during your first week as chief executive officer of the Covey Leadership Center isn't something Stephen M. R. Covey relished. Despite his company's amazing growth, great intellectual property, and a wonderful staff, the firm had had eleven consecutive years of negative cash flow. Eleven years of losing money and digging a bigger and bigger financial hole. The bank, in effect, gave the company a no-confidence vote by asking the principals to renege on personal guarantees. The bankers did not trust that the company could show a profit, and so they were ready to pull the plug.

Fortunately, the company received a reprieve. Under Covey's leadership, the balance sheet quickly turned from red to black, and the value of the company exploded to $160 million (an increase of 6,500 percent) within two and a half years of his taking the helm. Crisis averted—as the achieved results satisfied all impacted parties.[1]

In the for-profit world it's wonderful to have great products, a virtuous staff, and loyal customers, but in the end, you'll soon be out of business if you're not making money. The same fundamental principle holds for nonprofits, nongovernmental organizations, etc. Delivering results demonstrates trustworthiness. Without it, you'll ultimately be forced out of the game regardless of how high-minded your people are or how noble your cause.

Just as important is the need to deliver the right results in the right way—ensuring that the outcomes are sustainable and not just a flash in the pan. Anyone can hit the bull's-eye once, but it takes professionals to do it time after time!

The individual contributor who leaves dead bodies in his wake after achieving an important goal doesn't cut it. Likewise, a manager who mortgages an organization's future by foolishly slashing and burning important organizational resources in order to look good is irresponsible. The naysayer who hits her numbers while undermining the organization's cultural norms is poison. Sustainable results are dependent on going about your business in the right way.

Don't Start Out in the Penalty Box

Allow me to let you in on a little secret: getting results is much easier when you're passionate about what you're doing. When your work is stimulating, aligned with your values, and complements your skill sets, you have a natural nexus for generating the right results. Seems obvious, doesn't it? You see it so infrequently in practice.

But just being passionate about your work is not enough to produce results. It is true that doing what you love does not make it feel so much like work—arguably, a good thing—but being fervent is not a panacea. Passion does not guarantee the right outcome. Ask any author in the midst of a book project how he feels when he's on his fifth rewrite. Ask any researcher during the development of a new drug how she feels when she's on her seventh clinical trial. Ask any attorney how he feels when he's months into prepping for a monumental trial. If any of them are honest, they will likely tell you they are sick of it. What gets them to the starting line is their passion for positive results. What gets them to the finish line—especially when things are tough—is their professional will.

For professionals, having a bias for results naturally reveals:

- their choice to be personally accountable: a willingness to advance the ball
- that the quality of their work speaks for itself
- their habit of exercising superb judgment

Accountability Means Advancing the Ball

The truth is we constantly run across more skunks than doves in our attempt to fulfill our professional responsibilities. Thus we need to constantly overcome adversity in order to achieve our objectives. The pros make it happen without buck passing, whining, or finger-pointing. Professionals are focused and accountable.

Accountable people are, by their nature, trustworthy. Trust is an emotion. And emotion, by definition, means "to move." When trust exists, things happen—mostly good things.

Dave Ulrich is a partner and cofounder of the RBL Group, a business professor at the University of Michigan, and is considered to be the world's preeminent human resources consultant. He notes, "Recessions are difficult for all industries, but some industries struggle more than others. In a recent downturn, revenues across one particular industry fell 40 percent in less than six months. Leaders in some firms were slow to respond and lost share and momentum."

To illustrate his point about how critical leadership is in such situations, Dave shared with me his experience with Roger (not his real name) and his leadership team, who were fast to recognize the downturn. "They looked at their backlog and saw it falling," he said. "They reviewed previous economic downturns to anticipate what might happen next. They saw customer sentiment changing with less demand. Rather than hide or hoard this data, they quickly shared it with their management team and with a broad section of employees via town hall meetings. They shared with employees the anticipated course of the downturn and potential implications. They enlisted employees in coming up with ways to reduce costs, maintain customer service, and gain market share. When they had to make difficult decisions (such as closing facilities), they listened to employee questions and concerns and still were able to act. Roger's leadership team reduced their base salary by a larger percent than the hourly employees. They spent time with customers in order to build relationships for future business, and they invested time with employees in order to describe situations and listen to suggestions. The results of their actions were favorable. Attitude surveys showed that employees had increased confidence and trust in their leadership. Productivity, even during the downturn, stayed high. Cash flow and gross margins remained among the highest in the industry. The company gained market share by winning new contracts and by using its cash for consolidation."

Roger and his team chose to be accountable. They realized that because they had earned the trust of their employees, they were able to move quicker than their competitors. Dave pointed out, "The speed of trust also helped them to anticipate and respond to changing industry conditions and build customer share. They were well positioned when a recovery came."[2]

Trust is a universal key to achieving these types of results—especially under such challenging conditions. Creating it needn't be limited to senior executives. Think you need gray hair and a world-class résumé to produce game-changing results? Think again.

Excellence Personified: A Shining Light for the FBI

George Piro, at the age of thirty-six, helped mastermind one of the most significant accomplishments in the history of the FBI: the interrogation of Iraqi dictator Saddam Hussein. Piro's results after seven months yielded some of the most provocative and insightful intelligence ever extracted from the Middle East—intelligence that for years had eluded every major international intelligence agency.

Piro is well known in law enforcement circles, but he deftly deflects any credit by suggesting that the success belongs to the FBI. You can tell he believes it. It's not hype. The evening I'm with him he's addressing an invitation-only packed-house on the interrogation of Saddam. George has them spellbound one moment and in stitches the next, and ninety minutes flies by. George is in his element—he's having fun.

Piro clearly embraces the "service above self" motto he was taught years earlier in the air force. His smile is infectious, and he is surprisingly playful for a hardworking, button-down guy. He's serious about his work, but he doesn't take himself too seriously. He's the kind of man you hope your daughter will marry. Still, his public service career is anything but predictable. As far as his interrogating Saddam, well, no one saw that coming.

George Piro's family is Lebanese. Prior to his thirteenth birthday the family moved from civil-war-torn Beirut to California. The teenager could not speak English then, yet now he is fluent in three languages. After a stint in the air force, he became a police detective and earned two college degrees in his off-hours. In 1999 he joined the FBI. Five years later FBI agent Piro was summoned to Baghdad.

Shortly after Saddam Hussein was captured in December 2003, the CIA turned to the FBI to conduct his interrogation because the results would need to be delivered to an Iraqi court to facilitate prosecution. Although he had only been with the FBI for five years, Arab-speaking Special Agent Piro was dispatched to head a team of CIA and FBI analysts, specialists, and behaviorists to obtain the answers to many questions from the deposed dictator and other key leaders of Saddam's regime.

Interestingly, no one expected much to come of the interrogations. In fact, any revelations would have been celebrated. When he told me about the experience, Piro said, "The initial expectations were that Saddam would not talk to us. Saddam had no motivation to talk to us . . . no incentive to talk to us . . . so the common belief [among our people] was that Saddam was not going to provide any information." That's understandable when you consider that (1) Saddam knew what the U.S.

government hoped to gain from his interrogation and (2) Saddam knew war crimes charges were pending against him. Speaking up would mean self-incrimination. If that was not enough to frustrate any questioning, Saddam also knew that he was categorized as a prisoner of war—which meant Geneva Convention protections. So, at any time and for any reason, Saddam could terminate the process or even refuse to be interviewed. Piro's interrogation team faced long odds indeed!

The questioning of Saddam produced especially remarkable results. How did that happen? Look no further than George Piro for the reason why. He told me, "I personally expected to have success. I would not have been satisfied—nor would anyone on my team have been satisfied—with anything except success." He certainly achieved it.

Piro learned that Saddam believed Iran, not the United States, was the most significant threat to his rule in Iraq, which is why he claimed to have weapons of mass destruction. He wanted the Iranian government to believe he was as lethal as he had been at the height of the Iran-Iraq War of the 1980s. "He told me that if he would have allowed [United Nations] inspectors in, they would have revealed his secret," Piro said. "Instead, he misled the entire world." And in doing so he all but signed his own death warrant. Though Saddam didn't have such weapons in his arsenal at the time, he had every intention of rebuilding his weapons program as soon as the threat of UN inspections passed. He admitted to Piro that Iraq possessed the technology and the will to reinstitute the program. All he had to do was wait for the UN sanctions to be lifted.

Saddam also told Piro that he believed Osama bin Laden was "a fanatic" and a threat who couldn't be trusted.

Of his own situation, he confessed that he had horribly miscalculated the intentions of the Bush administration. At most, he expected the U.S. military would conduct no more than a brief air campaign as a kind of saber rattling that would allow him to buy time by making concessions, probably by allowing more inspections. He seemed to have no idea how much the world had changed as a result of the terror attacks of 9/11.

Regarding the widespread belief that Saddam used look-alikes or body doubles, the former Iraqi dictator explained that there were none.

Demonstrating his huge ego, he said that no one could play the part well enough to convince him, much less his enemies. Reports of his whereabouts during the invasion of Iraq were mostly correct, including two instances when the information led to high-powered attacks on specific bunkers. In truth, Saddam had been at both places and had only just departed when the bombs fell.

Of the first Gulf War, Hussein stated that his decision to invade Kuwait in 1990 was staged on the basis of an insulting comment by a Kuwaiti emir.

The information is both fascinating and instructional. Fascinating, as it showed (for whatever reasons) how ineffective the world's collective intelligence efforts had been in understanding the psyche and tactics of this ruthless dictator who all too often had dominated the global political stage. Instructional, in that Piro's interrogation demonstrates how professionals go about their business with an eye toward producing nothing less than game-changing results.

Just how did Piro acquire this information—information that had previously eluded "the best and the brightest" within the world's intelligence community? He did it as only a professional would: by committing himself to achieving the best possible result and by paying the necessary price to attain that outcome. Piro began his work with rigorous preparation, largely through a meticulous study of his subject in order to develop powerful insights into the man so he could discern if Saddam was being honest with him.

Positive results came almost immediately in their first meeting when Piro demonstrated a familiarity with the four novels Saddam had written, as well as an extensive knowledge of Iraqi history. So effective was this all-important initial session that, at its conclusion, Saddam asked to meet again with Piro.

Deft decisions by Piro made Saddam totally dependent on the agent for all his needs. Chief among these was that Piro became the prisoner's only human contact. Piro knew that Saddam would have no regard or respect for a field agent, so he perpetrated an elaborate ruse. By seeming to bully the guards around Saddam, Piro manipulated the prisoner into believing that his newfound friend was a high-ranking official dispatched by and in daily contact with the U.S. president.

Piro played the role of appreciative audience when Saddam would recite his own poetry. At the same time, because Saddam was kept in a windowless cell, Piro had power over day and night. No clock was allowed in the cell, and all guards relinquished their watches. Piro, however, wore the largest wristwatch he could find. Saddam had to ask him the time, thus the interrogator also controlled this aspect of existence. But more than control Saddam, Piro would also provoke him occasionally.

Saddam was an egoist, anxious about his legacy, not so much now, but in the distant future. Piro knew this and annoyed him by showing him videos of U.S. military successes in Iraq interspersed among images of the destruction of statues of Saddam by Iraqi civilians.

"I wanted him to get angry. I wanted him to see those videos and to get angry," Piro told me.

One night a medical necessity required Piro to fly Saddam to a hospital by helicopter. The aerial view of Baghdad glistening in the night emboldened the agent to comment that the city and the people and the nation were moving on without him.

In a subtle way Piro's mother assisted in his breaking through the dictator's last defenses. Heretofore, Saddam's birthday, April 28, had been observed as a national holiday. But in 2004 the only people who marked the occasion were the former dictator's interrogator and guards. How did they celebrate the day? Cookies. But not just any cookies. Piro asked his mother in the States to bake a batch of Lebanese cookies and send them to him overnight. He knew that Saddam had great regard for the Lebanese people, and the prisoner reveled in the birthday cookies. After she later learned that her cookies were meant for Saddam, George's mother playfully smacked the back of her son's head.

Notice the creativity, the turn-on-a-dime flexibility Piro employed. In Hebrew there's a word that describes what Piro did: *tushiyta.* It means pushing the limits, inventing as you go, improvising when curves are thrown your way. For our purposes, it means to be resourceful and to exert your professional will to accomplish the mission.[3]

In George Piro's case, Saddam's revelations made the seven-month grind especially fruitful. Virtually no one anticipated such remarkable results when the process began. Piro's work speaks for itself. John G. Perren, Special Agent in Charge of Counterterrorism for the Washington

Field Office, commented, "George Piro exemplifies what is best in our agents—integrity, professionalism, and dedication to the mission."[4]

Day in and day out, professionals of all stripes go about their business in much the same way. The marketing consultant, the customer service representative, and the principal electrical engineer are all renowned for the quality of their work. These are people who become the standard-bearers for their organization of what it means to perform exceptional work. Their reputation is renowned. Everyone seems to know them—or claims to!

Professionals, it seems, have far more to do with purpose and attitude (*tushiyta,* if you will) than with either age or time spent on the job. Neither George Piro nor his superiors knew precisely what successful results would look like in the interrogation of Saddam Hussein—after all, they were on a fishing exhibition. In Piro's case the quality of his results was subjective. That's not usually the case. Rather, most well-run organizations establish clear performance objectives for their people. They establish—in advance—what successful results should look like. This practice proves largely effective for both management and employees alike in terms of generating results.

Some well-intended managers, however, sometimes shoot themselves in the foot by establishing performance objectives that fail to motivate their employees or produce unintended consequences that harm the organization's greater good. Note: sometimes the de-motivating part for employees isn't the performance objective itself but rather the person who issued it.

Washington: First in War, First in Peace, First in Judgment[5]

In 1775 the American colonies were hardly a unified, cohesive group when the war for independence from Britain erupted. Declaring independence is one thing; winning it is quite another. Eighteenth-century oddsmakers would have made the upstart colonials a very long shot in the conflict. After all, these revolutionary soldiers were largely a bunch of ragtag farm boys up against the world's finest professional army. This was not just the few against the many; it was the destitute and poor against the well schooled, rookies against seasoned veterans. There also was the question of who should lead them into battle. The Continental Congress tagged George Washington with the task despite the fact that he had never commanded an army in battle before. He accepted the assignment much as the other Founding Fathers who risked everything to pursue independence from the British Crown. As commander in chief of the Colonial army, should the war be lost, Washington would be one of the first to be hanged.

Things did not go well for the Colonial army. Washington lost major battles on Long Island and on Manhattan, thus leaving the city of New York to be occupied by the British army. Much to his chagrin, Washington immediately found himself on the run. As historian David McCullough observed, Washington "made dreadful mistakes, particularly in the year 1776. They were almost inexcusable, inexplicable mistakes." Certainly some of this is understandably attributed to the general's steep learning curve, but the war was almost lost right out of the starting gate. Many historians believe that if the British commanders had made a bigger push early against the Continental army, they would have squelched the uprising and possibly ended the war without having to advance much beyond New York City.

Yet Washington never lost his focus on what mattered most: victory. And this was not just because his own hide was on the line but because of the conviction Washington held for the glorious cause of America. As Washington commenced a long retreat into New Jersey, his men were demoralized, their ranks were decimated, and their supplies were almost nonexistent. In December 1776, with the future of the Continental army hanging in the balance, Washington—against all odds—rallied his men in famous fighting that resulted in major victories at both Trenton and Princeton. These unexpected triumphs changed everything—psychologically speaking—and provided a dramatic boost to the revolutionary morale.

As important as these New Jersey victories were, Washington was not lulled into thinking that these were prescient events that held the key to winning the war. Rather it was Washington's judgment that victory was not to be won on any single battlefield but rather dependent on outlasting the British in the field. On paper, the British army was superior in every way.

Most desktop generals believe that ultimate victory comes with winning more battles than the enemy. Not Washington. He knew he had a home-field advantage, and if he could sustain the morale of his troops and maintain his political support, eventually the will of the British would collapse. He was right. It took seven years—until 1783—before Washington's judgment was validated. But in the end, his opponents capitulated.

Victory for the colonists meant independence from the British, and it meant all Americans would determine their own destiny. Despite the high price of victory (twenty-five thousand Americans were killed—1 percent of the population), it was cause for celebration as the great American experiment in democracy began in earnest. Washington, along with his unsuspecting cast of heroes, had delivered the right results!

The colonies quickly learned that as significant as winning independence was, it was like having the soda without the fizz. After some fitful years the fizz came in 1787 with the ratification of the Constitution—dubbed the "Miracle at Philadelphia" that former Chief Justice Warren Burger commented was "as great an impact on humanity as the splitting of the atom." One (independence) enabled the other (the Constitution). No independence, no Constitution!

One shudders to think what would have happened had the colonists had lost. Imagine America unable to shine as a beacon of democracy and freedom to the world. Approximately 120 democracies exist worldwide today. They all started in 1787 when the first modern democracy came into existence—the United States of America. Our lives as we know them would be radically different had the colonists failed. George Washington's leadership changed history—transcending generations and billions of people.

Washington was an unlikely victor who had to overcome astronomical odds. What ultimately enabled him to prevail? In a word—judgment. While he was chosen to lead the Continental army because of his character and integrity, his lack of command experience in the field was at first like a boat anchor. He was not a great military leader—having served the Crown and Virginia in uniform less than ten years before returning to farming and overseeing the rise of one of the richest fortunes in the colonies. Fortunately he was a fast learner, a wonderful judge of talent, and most important, a natural leader. He was a leader others would follow. These things kept him in the game against multiple British commanders until he himself became a master of the game.

Washington never took his eye off the prize of victory. Results mattered to him. Everything else was secondary. Washington was what management guru Jim Collins calls a Level 5 leader: "fanatically driven, infected with the incurable need to produce sustained results." This kind of fanaticism is driven from a desire to make something great, in Washington's case, a fledgling nation.

Victory—Washington believed—could be won by staying in the field against all odds. Outlasting the enemy became his strategy, and he did not deviate from it. It wasn't fancy. It wasn't sophisticated. It wasn't cutting-edge. But it worked! This tenaciousness proved to be a simple and highly effective plan. And it was good enough to defeat the world's finest army. The rest of the story is history.

Judgment also is essential in achieving results, regardless of whether you're the leader of a modern democracy, a pharmaceutical sales representative, or a construction manager for a snazzy new sixteen-story uptown high-rise. You've got to have an overall strategy (judgment with a capital *J*) and good tactics (judgment with a small *j*). These tactical judgments involve:

- *people* (being an exceptional judge of talent and character, knowing who to trust and who you shouldn't, knowing which battles are worth fighting and which aren't, assembling a top-notch team, etc.)
- *resources* (making the best use of time, being prudent with limited capital, understanding the important difference between needs and wants, feeding priorities, starving distractions, etc.)
- *self-awareness* (leveraging your technical strengths, knowing what you don't know, being committed to have others help you with your blind spots, compensating for technical weaknesses, recognizing and compensating for your biases, complementing your viewpoint and personal temperament with their own unique perspectives.

Washington was intelligent, but he had not been schooled formally in military tactics. But he quickly realized that winning would require leveraging the collective skills, ingenuity, and wisdom of every soldier in the Continental army. He asked lots of questions, sought advice, discovered people's strengths and weaknesses, and gave capable individuals important responsibilities. In many ways, these are lessons right out of Management 101. These tactical judgments—when subordinated to a core strategy—ultimately proved to be the winning formula.

The essential point here is that Washington's judgment compensated for his inexperience. Said another way, his keen judgment compensated for his questionable competence. And so it is (or can be) for each of us. We get a new job, a special assignment, a change in scope in our current job. There's so much we don't know. Right off the bat, our technical competence isn't where it needs to be. It's a scary (and often humbling) experience. Fortunately, good judgment compensates for questionable competence. Good judgment buys time—allowing us to make wise choices about resources and people—while we learn from our mistakes, thus enabling our competence to catch up to us as we attain our goals. All of this takes work, patience, and discipline, but in the end we will achieve the results we seek.

One last thought on Washington: he received the ultimate compliment through the process that resulted in his presidency. By a nearly unanimous consensus his compatriots knew that Washington would be the country's first chief executive. Initially, the role of the chief executive had been contentious at the Constitutional Convention. The delegates were obsessively suspicious about centralizing power in any single office. After all, the colonies had just endured a painful eight-year war with the mother country to escape that kind of unquestioned control. After much debate, the delegates reluctantly agreed that the office of the presidency was a necessary evil.

As the work of the Constitutional Convention concluded, compared to the legislative and judicial branches of government, the executive branch was left less defined, less prescriptive. The delegates left the office of the presidency slightly ambiguous with George Washington in mind, allowing him to define the office as crises confronted him. In effect, the delegates said to him, "The sun is rising on this budding, yet fragile, nation. You represent the best among us. Show us the way. Be our exemplar, not only for today, but for all of our tomorrows."

This was an ultimate demonstration of trust. These delegates, stalwart leaders in their own right, submitted themselves to Washington's leadership. The thirteen independent sovereignties demonstrated their confidence in his skill as a unifier, all while defining the all-important—yet mysterious—office of the presidency for future generations.

Washington completed two terms but refused to run for a third. In the end, "Washington became the supreme example of the leader who could be trusted with power because he was so ready to give it up." Exemplar indeed![6]

So where does a bias for results come from? Is it innate or learned? The answer is it's both. For some, this kind of judgment comes naturally, as part of their value system; for example, an achievement-oriented individual. For others, though, such judgment has to be acquired, developed along the way, learned in the crucible of experience. Regardless of how one comes to possess a bias for results, the experience of producing great results is reinforcing in its own right. Since people find you trustworthy, they gravitate toward you. In the workplace you're seen as the go-to guy. Your bosses and your co-workers want more of you.

On this latter point, self-trust and the confidence that goes with it are important, because confidence is a key element in ensuring that you will continue to achieve the right results. This involves keeping promises to yourself, not believing your own lies and exaggerations, and being able to achieve challenging goals.

Two months short of her tenth birthday, my daughter Natalie hiked to the top of Half Dome in Yosemite National Park. Considering it's a seventeen-mile round trip, almost five thousand feet of vertical elevation, and a harrowing four-hundred-foot final ascent so slick and steep (50+ degrees) that it requires cables for assistance to ascend to the summit, the hike is a remarkable accomplishment for an adult, let alone a child. Natalie to this day draws on this achievement whenever she faces a challenge. She remembers how daunting that ascension was and how she overcame it. Simply stated, her past success (results) enables her current success (results) largely because of the confidence (self-trust) she has in herself as a result of her achievement. Equally important for Natalie: that experience—despite the difficulties encountered—reinforced her desire (a bias, so to speak) for more experiences like it.

A final footnote on George Piro: since his return from Baghdad, he's received several impressive awards and two promotions. Just as my Natalie has a quiet confidence about herself, George possesses that same inner strength as well. He looks forward to meaningful work and big challenges. Just as he did with Saddam, he expects to have success—which means delivering results. His latest job responsibility? Protecting the nation's capital from possible al Qaeda attack. It's comforting to know he's on the job.

Dave Ulrich puts this chapter into perspective: "The stories in this chapter clearly show that a bias for results drives success. Ironically, when we ask seminar participants to fill in the sentence, 'To be effective, a leader must . . . ,' what we often get are attributes: have a vision, communicate, have integrity, be authentic, have emotional intelligence, treat others well, and so forth. We seldom get responses about delivering results. Without results, leaders may be well liked, but they will not be respected and admired. We like to begin our leadership coaching sessions with the question, 'What are the results you need to focus on in the next time period?' These results may be about financial performance, employee productivity, customer commitment and share, investor confidence, or community reputation. Without being clear about what we want, leaders may demonstrate noble actions but lack lasting impact. A bias for results means clarity about desired outcomes. A bias for results requires thinking about multidimensional results (for employees, customers, investors, and communities). A bias for results means being accountable to oneself and holding others accountable. A bias for results looks to the future and what can be more than the past and what has been. A bias for results is fundamental to being a professional."[7]

SUMMARY

- Mind-Set 1 is the first among equals because all other mind-sets emanate from it. This mind-set was integral in the founding of the United States, as evidenced by George Washington's success in the Revolutionary War.
- Professionals feel a tremendous responsibility to deliver sustained and meaningful results. The quality of their work is obvious; thus, they're seen as trustworthy.
- Producing results often means overcoming adversity in various forms. And despite inevitable obstacles, they remain accountable, invoking their professional will to get them to the finish line.
- Despite any gaps in competence, judgment can compensate sufficiently to make up for this deficiency and enable one to achieve the desired result.
- Through success, professionals develop the right amount of confidence (self-trust) and reinforcing experiences to enable them to deliver desired results again and again. Plus, producing great results is often sustaining, as people often want more.

CHAPTER **SEVEN**

MIND-SET 2

Professionals Realize (and Act Like) They're Part of Something Bigger than Themselves

I'm not sure if we remember how to give something up for the long-term general good.

—PETER G. PETERSON,
Former Senior Chairman, Blackstone Group

The price of three hours of sleep just kicked in. Unable to effectively concentrate any longer, he calls an end to our meeting. It's 9 p.m.—five hours past our original end time. He's still got another hour of work ahead of him.

This is par for the course. But no one should feel sorry for him. He is a self-made man of means and status and has a long and distinguished executive career. People respect him.

The irony is that he doesn't need the job, let alone the headaches. The board recently asked him to serve as CEO after his predecessor flamed out. He immediately fell in love with this well-known S&P company. Performance has been spectacular, and the future is brighter yet. He sees the potential and expects the company to realize it on his watch. He believes all of this in spite of the fact that his wife would be ecstatic if he retired.

That's what makes it so frustrating.

"We seem to be succeeding despite ourselves. We're fortunate to be in the sweet spot of our market niche because our executive team is largely dysfunctional. Trust, respect . . . you name it, we're rock bottom. Our customers trust us, but we don't trust each other. Go figure!

"Issues that should take five minutes, take forty-five. Some of our people have messiah complexes. Others are conspiracy theorists. Long chains of accusatory, CYA e-mails are everyday occurrences. People keep book on their colleagues and never forget the times when they feel they were wronged by someone. Agreements are short-lived. Even when people reach an agreement, somehow they feel tainted by the experience and want to take a shower afterward.

"It's wasted energy. Worse yet, it brings everybody down. We need to be investing our best energies into our market, not fighting arcane battles with people who are supposedly on the same team. That's just not how I want to be spending my time. It's gonna stop."

It did.

This mind-set arguably warrants a book of its own. I have more interview notes, more anecdotal stories, and more reference materials embedded with tape flags on this mind-set than perhaps any other. More important, through my consulting experience I've seen how the lack of this mind-set contributes so much to the angst and ineffectiveness of so many teams, especially executive teams. And it's the lack of this mind-set that also proves so impactful in subverting meaningful organizational change.

Marshall Goldsmith, an extraordinarily generous man, considers this mind-set to be an acid test for professionals, especially today. In speaking of professionals, he noted, "I want to know that I can trust you to do something other than just look out for yourself." As you'll see in this chapter, it's next to impossible to be perceived by others as a professional (and trustworthy) without being able to some degree to get beyond yourself.

Think about the above CEO's situation. He has leaders in his organization, although not necessarily professional ones. Their energy was principally spent playing gotcha games and making themselves look good in the process. Several factors are in play (think: big egos), but the gist of the problem is that his team lacks the discipline to be a part of something bigger than themselves. They have a chance to own an extremely desirable and highly profitable market niche if they will just apply themselves. Instead, they are stuck in the weeds. Even worse, they are stuck in interpersonal weeds—the worst kind.

For those who don't yet hold this mind-set, it's more about what they get rather than what they give. It's about careerism, not professionalism. It's more about status and less about substance. It's more about scoring points than team play. Gen. Richard Myers notes, "One of the worst things you can do in the military is to do things for the wrong reason—especially if that reason is to get ahead. Self-aggrandizement is a really bad trait—as bad as a lack of integrity. It's usually recognized early, and once it is, you're toast!"

The motives behind these behaviors are varied, but the behaviors themselves can be especially prevalent in executive teams. It's not our purpose here to diagnose why they show up, but to simply acknowledge that they do.

There are a myriad of ways of dealing with these undesired behaviors, ways of lessening their impact. For instance, General Electric (during the Jack Welch CEO succession) and Ameritech (during the Bill Weiss CEO succession) both told their succession candidates that if they were caught undercutting another succession colleague (or anything like that) they would be out of the running for the top job.[1] And to affirm their values and desired behaviors, both companies reinforced the carrot of collaboration to all their succession candidates as an important decision-making criterion in selecting the next CEO.

Teams—those that outsiders would describe as professional—have subjugated themselves to something bigger (and arguably more important) than their own pocket book, ego, status, or power. They're building something that transcends self. In organizational terms, it's building something that outlasts you, something that becomes bigger and better with time. Some like to think of it as an organizational legacy.

What these teams quickly come to realize is that there are important implications that stem from this mind-set, namely, that it means collaborating with people who may not be among your favorites. It's learning (sometimes painfully) that fighting over turf is a fool's errand. It means not always getting your way. It means resisting the urge to pull rank. It means learning to sacrifice. It means not trying to prove how smart you are. It means putting the company's overall business performance ahead of your own business unit's performance. It means that any number of your assumptions about people and things may be wrong. In a nutshell: it's about keeping your eye on the prize, demanding excellence from yourself and your colleagues, and holding your nose when you have to in order to do things you don't like.

This chapter will focus on how this mind-set (or the lack of it) impacts primarily business organizations. But rest assured it also impacts virtually every other facet of U.S. culture as well.

To be clear, I believe this mind-set is a big deal. In fact, one can argue that it was primarily this mind-set that enabled the colonists to win their independence from the British monarchy (but more on that later). I further believe that it's the lack of this mind-set that is at the core of much of our nation's ills. That said, when it comes to this mind-set, there's an elephant in the room—one that's important to examine from a business context.

Marshall Goldsmith tells of the CEO of a multibillion dollar company who communicated in a company-wide memo that he wanted to create a culture where everyone contributes to the best of their ability and contributes to their colleagues across the company based on need. Seems hard to argue with, right? Trouble is, Karl Marx advocated precisely the same thing. Marx, for example, espoused "from each according to his ability, to each according to his need."

How could a free-market capitalist CEO and a communist icon be of one mind on such a fundamental issue? Perhaps they weren't. Or perhaps the CEO misspoke. Perhaps there's another explanation. Nevertheless, the story gives rise to an important observation.

How is it that someone living in a capitalist society (one that promotes self-interests) is supposed to suddenly become a communist when you work for a corporation? That may sound shocking until you realize that most corporations ask individuals to suspend individual benefits (think: self-interest) and to sacrifice for the larger corporation (that is, the greater good). For an individual employee, the core dichotomy becomes "What's in it for me?" and "What's in it for the corporation?" With the demise of job security, ever-increasing globalization, fewer promotional opportunities, etc., Marshall believes "it's increasingly difficult to expect that people will sacrifice (willingly, at least) for the larger corporation to the degree they have in the past." Granted, they may do so unwillingly in an attempt to keep their jobs during a bad economic cycle.

An individual employee asks to what degree does she look out for her own self-interests and to what degree does she invest in being a corporate team player? Of course, the answers are specific to the circumstances and values impacting each individual.

I mention these dichotomies for the benefit of senior leaders, because the dynamics facing employees have changed significantly in recent years. In fact, the clarion call for sacrifice (for example, telling employees not to focus on self-interest) from senior leaders who are receiving lucrative compensation rings hollow. Marshall captures the point well: "So I'm supposed to knock myself out for the larger corporation while the CEO is knocking down $50 million a year!" Admittedly, there are few executives whose compensation is that high, but the disparity in executive compensation (whether real or perceived) is a trigger for such disdain.

Marshall continues: "So absent the security commitment on the part of the corporation, you basically have people on their own, looking out for themselves. Everyone pretends to have no self-interest, but they really do have self-interests. And make no mistake, one way or another, those self-interests get played out."[2]

So let's put this chapter in perspective. I'm not advocating that anyone be a doormat for an organization. Nor do I espouse the idea that an employee must do anything at any time and at any place the organization demands just to be perceived as being a corporate team player. People are not wind-up, mindless automatons. Being invested is great; being taken advantage of isn't. In other words, I'm not advocating you allow yourself to be exploited.

I am, however, advocating that each of us, as professionals, has an inherent obligation to the organization (or client) we are a part of to put its interests ahead of our own. Consider the alternative: an organization full of people holding a me-first mind-set. It won't be long before the organization is out of business. And, of course, organizations don't lose, people do. In this instance, owners and employees alike.

Of course, putting the organization's or client's interests ahead of our own—in the extreme—can be self-defeating. You cannot be married to your work, and yet there isn't always a black-and-white distinction. There's plenty of gray in these matters. So you've got to be prudent. You've got to be smart. But one thing is for sure, the individual who consistently looks out only for himself will quickly be shunned by conscientious colleagues and disdained by managers because he has proven himself to be untrustworthy. Those employees who do prove themselves to be trustworthy do so because they have allowed their successes to be a by-product of their organization's or client's success. As a professional they:

- Commit to the success of their firm or organization or client.
- Realize success transcends their own parochial interests.
- Collaborate as an effective team member.

Let's look at these distinctions individually.

Commits to the Success of Their Firm or Organization

We've all heard the joke about the bacon-and-egg breakfast: the chicken is involved, but it's the pig that demonstrates real commitment. There's obviously a big difference between the two. Sometimes in our professional life we unknowingly confuse the two. Or, looking through a more cynical lens, some have perfected the art of making involvement look like commitment. When I think about commitment—the type that's worthy of emulation—I think of the Founders, especially those who signed the Declaration of Independence.

The Declaration of Independence is viewed today as one of the two most important documents in the history of the United States. During the summer of 1776 its adoption marked a turning point in the conflict that became the American Revolution, namely, after this, there was no going back. Thus the last sentence pointedly states that the fifty-six delegates "mutually pledge to each other our Lives, our Fortunes and our sacred Honor" for the support of the Declaration. John Hancock, president of the congress, supposedly warned his colleagues, "We must be unanimous; there must be no pulling different ways; we must all hang together." In response, Pennsylvania delegate Benjamin Franklin added, "Yes, we must, indeed, all hang together, or most assuredly we shall all hang separately."[3]

If there had been any question prior to their affirming the Declaration with their signatures, the fifty-six delegates were now avowed rebels, traitors to the British Crown, and liable to the punishments involved with such an act. These delegates now put everything on the line; the representatives from Massachusetts had as much to lose as the delegates from South Carolina, Virginia was as liable as Rhode Island, New York as Georgia. Everyone's head was in the noose!

But there was much more to declaring independence than the crafting of 1,337 words on paper. While there were no fireworks to mark the occasion, there was cannon fire. And while cannons thundered between armies in the field, the delegates attacked the arduous task of crafting a government for the fledgling nation. Funds needed to be secured from reluctant European sources. Alliances needed to be brokered. The war effort needed to be sustained. A government had to be framed in which the autonomy of each former colony—now deemed a sovereign state—was protected. The tough nut was devising a weak centralized government that could successfully wage a war of independence. It was no small feat that they succeeded.

The delegates fully invested themselves in these tasks. Their devotion to their work, however, included the neglect of their personal affairs and lengthy separations from their family. With the fortunes of war, the Congress twice had to flee from Philadelphia and set up shop again in Baltimore, Lancaster (very briefly), and York.

Their wives and families also shared in these hardships. When the Continental army went into winter quarters in Massachusetts in 1775, George Washington asked his wife, Martha, to be with him. Her 475-mile journey from Mount Vernon to Boston was not an easy trek, especially with the onset of winter. The roads were little more than dirt paths, and each river crossing was a formidable challenge surmounted only by fords and ferries. Accidental drownings were not uncommon.

Add to this difficult feat the scarcity that characterized the winter camps of the Continentals—sparse rations, shoddy housing, bitter cold, and inadequate sanitation—and the picture is not a pleasant one, especially for a woman. Without complaining, Martha left the comfort of Mount Vernon for the frozen hell of the army's winter quarters. There, she acted as far more than a hostess in the hovel in which Washington lived; she went out of her way to offer hospitality and encouragement to the soldiers in the miserable camp. Like her husband, she was an exemplar to the solders, and they universally extolled her thoughtfulness to them. What man would complain when she did not?

Martha did this every year for *eight* years when the army withdrew into winter quarters, including the notorious winters at Valley Forge, Pennsylvania, and Morristown, New Jersey. She once commented that she had heard the last shots of every campaign and the first shots of the next one. She wasn't exaggerating.[4]

Other Founders' families endured similar trials. John and Abigail Adams scarcely saw each other for ten years, beginning in 1774. During the war years, Abigail alone tended to their four children as well as to all the needs of the family farm in Quincy, Massachusetts. She also lost a daughter in childbirth in 1777 while John was hammering out the new government in Philadelphia. Thomas Jefferson constantly worried about the health of his wife, Martha. She was extremely frail, and this weighed heavily on his mind—especially when he was asked to pen the first draft of the Declaration. Benjamin Franklin's heart broke when he could not convince his son William—then the royal governor of New Jersey—to join in the struggle for independence. Despite that disappointment, the elderly Franklin accepted the ambassadorship to France with the mission of winning financial and military assistance for the cause of freedom in America.[5]

In our generation, few truly understand the level of commitment demonstrated by the Founders. They put it all on the line—and their families did too. It's true that the Founders were fighting for a better life (their own self-interests, if you will), but the cause they embraced—freedom along with a democratic form of government—clearly was bigger than themselves. Without the type of real commitment demonstrated by the Founders, it's difficult to build something extraordinary.

Many have argued that America has gone soft, lost its way, become inattentive to that which made the country great. That's understandable—especially when the latest pop icon garners more media attention than the nation's gruesome national debt.

Emboldened traders on Wall Street, Stephen Gandel argues, have been the ones responsible for much of the high-risk financial engineering schemes that have led to the country's current financial mess. Making money for their firms, regardless of the consequences, was apparently all that mattered. As former trader Phillip Meyer, has noted, "If running the economy off the cliff makes you money, you will do it, and you will do it every day of the week."[6] This is self-interest run amok!

Consider the warning issued by Founder George Mason: "America is a republic. A republic is based on the people and dedicated to the common good. If the people put the common good before their own interests, the republic flourishes. If they pursue only private gain, the republic dies."[7]

The degree to which the country has lost its way is debatable, but what's not debatable is the degree to which we've culturally "deified the individual" (as Paul Newman described it). That typically means maximizing self-interests at the expense of more important things.

Rakesh Khurana, a professor at the Harvard Business School, defined the conduct of a true professional as "create[ing] value for society, rather than extract[ing] it."[8] Of course, the principle Khurana is teaching can also be applied to organizations and individual clients. Khurana's definition is spot-on and captures the spirit of being a part of something bigger than yourself. It also puts a much-needed emphasis on professionalism in an era when careerism is so prevalent.

Being part of something bigger than yourself is impossible when you're already the center of the universe. Using the principle taught by Professor Khurana, true professionals create more value for their organizations or clients than they extract from it. True professionals are always looking out for the common good (that is, health) of the organization of which they are a part.

In the workplace, it's disconcerting to see how ready some are to take more than they give, how prevalent irresponsibility can be, how discipline seems to be a virtue from a bygone era. One needs look no further than the sports world for outrageous, illustrative examples.

If ignorance is bliss, then Gilbert Arenas must be in nirvana. In January 2010, Gilbert, a guard at the time with the NBA's Washington Wizards (who ironically had a reputation as a gunner), was suspended for the remainder of the 2009–10 season after he brandished an unlicensed firearm in the club's locker room. Arenas, the Wizard's franchise player, was the team's only hope of going anywhere during the season. As it turned out, Arenas's suspension sealed a season of mediocrity for the Wizards.

What a knucklehead! The incident left the team in disarray, his teammates mystified, team management feeling betrayed, and Wizards fans up in arms. Yet Gilbert demonstrated commitment all right—to himself![9] Self-centered people are hard to warm up to and even harder to trust.

Arenas has plenty of company. Professional sports has many excesses and certainly provides a target-rich environment of such self-centered examples. As entertaining as the individuals involved might be, I'll spare you from highlighting any more.

Granted, the all-too-prevalent me-first attitude we see in professional sports is generally less common when contrasted against a normal work environment. But make no mistake, the me-first attitude, while comparatively muted, is plenty prevalent in the mainstream workplace. That's why people who demonstrate this mind-set really stand out. They're responsible. They're committed. They do their best even with the challenging aspects of their responsibilities or when the business climate gets tough.

Lest you think me naive, I realize that battles and commitment in the workplace are not analogous to the battles and commitment that led to our nation's independence. But the difference is in scale, not in substance.

Note: there will be inevitable conflicts between one's personal values and philosophies and those espoused by an organization. Whether the conflicts are consequential or not, it shouldn't provide justification for doing less than you're capable or (at worse) actively undermining the organization's objectives. In the case of a serious clash in core values, individuals would be well served to seek an organization that is more aligned with their values, rather than create a lose-lose scenario for everyone.

A recent Gallup poll asked Americans, Who do you admire? The military finished first, with a 77 percent approval rating.[10] Certainly there is a level of empathy and appreciation for the job these soldiers are doing. This appreciation and admiration continues after soldiers have exchanged their uniforms for business attire. Savvy private-sector firms respect military veterans as an important source of leadership for their companies. For instance, both General Electric and Home Depot consider veterans to be an integral source for their talent pool.[11]

Gen. Richard Myers observed: "We've seen some of America's most admired companies actively pursue veterans as part of their staffing strategy. For instance, GE has over eleven thousand veterans working for it. The private sector knows a thing or two about talent. After all, they're dependent on top-notch talent to give them an edge, so the interest in vets shouldn't be terribly surprising. These are people who have lots of 'leadership molecules.'

"Their stint in active duty," he added, "often involved decisions that carried life-and-death consequences, so they truly understand what 'service before self' means. Plus, consider that 10 percent of an officer's time in the first twenty years is spent on education. That means taking them out of their job and developing them as individuals. That's not learning how to drive a tank, not learning how to fly a plane. It's not merely technical training. It's honest-to-goodness education, developing the whole person. But the best part comes when we set them loose to apply that education in meaningful, real-life situations by giving them tremendous responsibility early and often in their careers."[12]

Jeffrey Immelt, chairman and CEO of GE, speaking on December 9, 2009, to the cadets at West Point in a speech entitled "Renewing American Leadership," commented, "We actively recruit from the military because we have learned that the values you bring to our company are essential to our success. . . . We want people who see a purpose bigger than themselves."

Success Transcends Their Own Parochial Interests

Superintendent Gary Peters had just completed another successful year—at least on paper. Peters (whose employer is a well-known Fortune 200 company) is one of several geographically based superintendents with the responsibility of keeping critical oil pumping stations humming—standard fare for an operating company of this type.

Peters and his colleagues rely heavily on maintenance budgets in the tens of millions of dollars to achieve annual operating objectives. Peters is an up-and-comer, and so he is a hard charger. He seems oblivious to the good fortune he's been dealt: his division has comparatively newer equipment with better technology and is less impacted by the inclement weather patterns that his colleagues endure. Per common practice, Peters aggressively expended his entire annual maintenance budget, which happened to be generous, given the division's circumstances. From Peter's point of view, he wanted everything to look great, including himself.

Four months into the next budget year, an especially critical pumping station operated by another superintendent failed. The impacts were bad—really bad. Markets were adversely impacted, media coverage was unrelenting, and company management started hunting heads. Everybody lost something.

The station failure was attributed to inadequate maintenance—a failure that clearly could have been prevented. While Peters wasn't consciously hoarding his maintenance dollars, he certainly hadn't been forthcoming with his colleagues about his overly generous maintenance budget. The problem wasn't that Peters ensured that all his maintenance was done promptly and correctly (a great deal of it was discretionary), it's the fact that equipment maintenance overseen by the other superintendents (who had far greater importance to the company) wasn't done. It's the age-old story of doing with great precision that which should have never been done in the first place.[13]

The catastrophic failure not only dramatically impacted the business unit's bottom line but tainted the reputation of everyone involved—including Peters, much to his chagrin. Had Peters offered to redirect some of his maintenance budget to the other superintendents, the failure likely would have been averted.

This kind of thing happens far too often. Managers become insular. They look exclusively at their own world and little else. While it's admirable to act responsibly with those things for which we are directly accountable, professionals must be able to see the bigger picture and always act in the best interests of the business. In Peter's case, he won the battle and lost the war.

Peters hadn't yet developed the something-bigger mind-set. As a result, he had great difficulty in realizing that his long-term success was dependent on factors beyond his short-term parochial interests. Peters has plenty of company.

There may be a myriad of reasons why someone doesn't hold this mind-set. Some may be inherent to the organization's culture. Some may be inherent to the individual—wanting to perhaps make themselves look good (or someone else look bad). Perhaps they just want to get a leg up on the competition. Perhaps Peters subscribed to the dog-eat-dog theory of career management.

Peters needed to become interdependent with his fellow superintendents so that their results *collectively* met the overall business objectives of the operating company. That meant interacting with his colleagues in a completely different way, a way that had each of them owning not only their individual objectives but their collective ones as well.

Consider how this mind-set plays out in practical terms:

- One division develops an exceptional number of high-potential employees, all of which ultimately go on to higher levels of responsibility at corporate headquarters. The division didn't hoard the talent it developed. Rather, the division did everything it could to have the corporation make the best use of that talent, which happened to be at headquarters. The division, in affect, acted as a farm club for corporate.
- Steve (from chapter 1) passed on his well-deserved promotion and addressed the consequences of the unfortunate plant explosion. The more important issue for the company, at least in Steve's mind, was

heading up the company's internal investigation, which is exactly where he put his priority.

- A senior executive rescues a fellow panel member at an industry conference (someone who is enormously knowledgeable but terribly introverted and handicapped by underdeveloped communication skills). The seasoned, articulate senior executive could have stolen the spotlight at the expense of a vastly inferior panel discussion. Instead, she chose to draw out her colleague, which made for a rich panel discussion—which is exactly what was intended by the conference organizers.

When Your Industry Sneezes, You're Bound to Get Sick Too!

It's easy to forget that our success is dependent on the health and vitality of our industry. All it takes is a single unfortunate accident, a bad-news incident that turns into a media frenzy, or someone cutting corners three thousand miles away to adversely impact your business or your industry. Consider:

- The 1979 accident at the Three Mile Island nuclear power plant that prompted the cessation of new plant construction throughout a once-vibrant industry for nearly thirty years.
- The 2008 salmonella scare that brutally impacted farmers after tomatoes were pulled from bins and menus nationwide.[14]
- The unprecedented scandals in financial services (for example, Bernie Madoff and Allen Stanford) that rocked the confidence of the investor community and the credibility of the industry that served them.

Professionals know that it doesn't take much to turn an entire industry upside down. And when an industry experiences a downturn, it takes a lot of people with it. Responsible professionals are ever-vigilant to avoid such outcomes. They realize they aren't on an island but rather a part of an industry (something bigger), not the other way around. So naturally their success is contingent on their industry's success.

Change Headed Straight at You

The lack of this mind-set is perhaps the greatest impediment to creating vital, sustainable organizational change. It goes without saying that change is hard. Naturally, most people are inept at change. Change elicits feelings of fear ("I'm going to lose my job.") or just plain antipathy ("Things are fine . . . leave me alone"). Plus, change suggests new ways of doing things, the need for learning new skills, all of which takes people out of their comfort zone.

Yet an essential part of being a professional is an ability to deal effectively with change. It has been aptly stated that today "the only constant is change." That's true. Organizationally speaking, a company that isn't constantly questioning, evaluating, and ultimately changing is on its way to the scrap heap. But I'm not defending any leader's boneheaded decisions for the sake of change that proved to be unwise or imprudent. Certainly, all of us can point to plenty of examples of change-motivated errors in judgment. Fortunately, there are many more well-thought-out efforts to affect change that have made sound business sense.

If a professional's success is largely the by-product of her organization's or client's success, then it's imperative for all professionals to get behind their organization's change efforts. Professionals, as hard as it sometimes is, do what is in the best interest of their organizations or clients. With that as a context, it's much easier to invest one's energies in constructive activities (like making the business better) as opposed to wallowing in self-pity and railing against management. Plus, from a career point of view, it's been my experience that those who embrace organizational change fare far better than those who fight it.

I have a special word to anyone who might be in a situation to initiate change. You may be at the zenith of your career. You may be making more money than you've ever made. People may be responding to your beck and call. They may be laughing at *all* your jokes. This is likely the best job you've ever had. With such a sweetheart deal, there's a tendency not to rock the boat. After all, why mess up a good thing by introducing an unpopular change initiative? This is true even if the change is imperative for the continued betterment of the organization.

Professionals—even with such creature comforts—still act in the best interests of their organizations. And if change is warranted, then so be it. Leaders willing to make tough calls such as these become role models for the organization's next generation of leaders. They are remembered as the consummate professionals they truly are.

Collaborating as an Effective Team Member Is the Norm

Procter & Gamble's (P&G) renowned former chairman A. G. Lafley observed, "We're perfect for Derek Jeter, but A-Rod would not work out here," alluding to P&G's collaborative, distinctively loyal, midwestern, and hierarchical culture.[15] A-Rod's "stats-first" attitude and tendency to undermine good team karma[16] certainly wouldn't cut it at P&G.

Every organization has its own unique cultural norms, expectations about how to conduct business, aspirations that reinforce the organization's values, ideas of what's acceptable and what isn't, and behaviors that are rewarded as well as activities that are not. All the elements of this corporate culture comprise the norms that materially aid the organization in achieving its objectives. Today, you'd be hard-pressed to find an organization that doesn't include collaboration as an important expectation. And "collaboration" is often synonymous with "trust."

Richard Kovacevich, the retired chairman of the board of directors and former CEO of Wells Fargo, noted that he's been at his best when he applies what he learned on the basketball court to his financial services responsibilities. Kovacevich, an avid athlete, notes, "You learn very quickly playing sports that it's all about team. It's the *best five* players that win the basketball game, not the *five best* players."[17] Collections of individuals rarely outperform teams working in a concerted manner.

Imagine the five overachieving commanders who comprise the Joint Chiefs of Staff. Each branch of the service—army, navy, air force, and marines—has a chief (typically homegrown in the respective branch) who is charged with advising the top leadership of the civilian government. The chairman is the nation's highest-ranking military officer. Gen. Richard Myers acted in that capacity from 2001 to 2005.

General Myers's responsibility was to transform the five best players into the best five players. He said, "There had been times in the past when the Joint Chiefs would meet and things would become contentious. . . . The chiefs sometimes had difficulty getting beyond the parochial interests of the branch they represented. While that's admirable, at the end of the day it's ineffective. Our charge was to provide, in a unified way, the best advice we could to the president, the secretary of defense, and the Congress. To accomplish this, we ultimately agreed that, before our deliberations, we'd remove our 'branch hat' and put on our 'chief hat.' The change of hats, of course, was symbolic but really helpful. It served as a powerful reminder to look at something bigger than one's own branch. As a result, we dramatically increased our level of collaboration. The law says that I, as chairman, must state another branch's view even if it differs from my own. But I never had to do that because of our ability to achieve consensus."[18]

The general made giant strides in developing his team and putting the best five players on the floor. He was successful in focusing the Joint Chiefs on the bigger picture, something beyond the parochial interests of their service branch, their personal curiosities, and their personal ambitions.

Unfortunately, too frequently, we hear about instances such as:

- A department's unwillingness to provide constructive feedback on operating issues to its director—after the director viewed earlier feedback as dissent (think: bad news) and disloyalty to him.
- An especially talented research and development department that ignores critical input from the marketing department about user preferences—thus ultimately developing a much-hyped and technologically superior product that was unfortunately and embarrassingly trashed in the marketplace, because it proved to be innovation for innovation's sake.
- An operations superintendent who obfuscated and contrived safety concerns in an attempt to undermine an important department initiative that involved a first-class external contractor the company had chosen to partner with.

Each of these entities didn't fully appreciate how they were a part of something bigger. Instead, they allowed their fears (manager), curiosity (R&D department), and resentment (superintendent) to interfere with the greater good their organizations were trying to achieve.

When you hold a something-bigger mind-set, it profoundly changes how you think. General Myers commented to me that *real* transformation isn't really about advances in technology; real transformation occurs "between the ears" and profoundly changes how people think. As a result, you see things differently, which naturally leads to higher levels of collaboration.

Often the first thing you see differently is yourself, which is vitally important. The something-bigger mind-set helps to recalibrate one's self-view as a professional (recall the transformative power of one's self-view discussed in chapter 3). While still holding a healthy ego, professionals know that what they do is not about them. Rather, what they do is always about the all-important "something bigger" that they are trying to bring to pass. And, as a professional, that means collaborating with other professionals to get it done.

Professionals, in effect, become advocates for something bigger, whether that something bigger is meeting a critical project milestone, an organization attempting to achieve marketplace preeminence, or a nonprofit exceeding an important fund-raising milestone. Recall also, in the discussion of Mind-Set 1, for professionals, there's an inherent responsibility to advance the ball in achieving the desired result.

In addition, because people are typically more comfortable representing third-party causes (as opposed to their own), they naturally become emboldened and driven to act in ways they might not otherwise. Consider:

- The team that learned how to effectively challenge one another, hold one another accountable, and provide one another timely, constructive feedback. They accomplished this after years of being too conflict adverse, too apt to reward loyalty instead of performance, and too dependent on the team's leader for critical feedback. This change enabled the team to, among other things, become team-centric instead of leader-centric.

- The organization that learned to readily share critical operating information across departmental boundaries. Previously the departments had been isolated, insulated in their own world, and focused on only their own issues. Because information is power, there had been a long-standing reluctance to share such information. This change broke down these ancient barriers and enabled greater collaboration.
- The organization that institutionalized candor as a cultural norm after years of hiding bad news until the problem ultimately festered and metastasized. This change especially enabled the executive team to confront brutal facts more quickly and with greater effectiveness. No topic or person was off-limits.

When you're trying to create something bigger than yourself, seeing yourself as a professional engages an extra gear in driving it home. Notice how collaboration played an integral role in the following examples. The first thing you will notice is that you will see problems differently, and your approach to these problems will be different from how you might have previously approached them, because:

- You're considering a bigger picture, one in which you may have only general knowledge. As a result, you are forced to listen, gather more information, and be a bit more introspective. It forces you to see other points of view. This requires more interdependence with others. This was true of what happened with the Joint Chiefs of Staff in the earlier example.
- All of a sudden, the issue isn't just about you. It's about something bigger than yourself, which usually brings greater responsibility, involves more people, and requires more oversight. The consequences naturally become bigger.
- You see yourself as a professional, with all the inherent expectations. You no longer act instinctively and interpersonally when under pressure, when the heat's on, when emotions are running high, when in conflict. You begin to handle matters with greater decorum, with more tact, with more collaboration—just as a professional would.

A professional holding the "something bigger" mind-set thinks differently than those who don't. The difference is profound.

Pursuing a Higher Purpose

Twenty-five yards separated Philadelphia Eagles running back Brian Westbrook from scoring a late fourth-quarter touchdown against archrival Dallas on the Cowboys' home turf in the closing weeks of the 2007 regular season. After Westbrook broke loose, it was clear that no one was going to stop him. The end zone was as good as gift-wrapped for him. Instead, the All-Pro running back surprisingly stopped just short of the goal line, at the one-yard line. His maneuver shocked everyone in the stadium as well as the national viewing audience.

It was a smart move. Dallas was out of time-outs, and with Philadelphia's newly minted first down, all quarterback Donovan McNabb had to do was take a knee three times to run out the clock. The Cowboys never got the ball back, and Philadelphia won the game by four points. The only thing missing was legendary Cowboys quarterback and broadcaster Don Meredith singing "Turn out the lights, the party's over."

"It was brilliant," commented Eagles coach Andy Reid on Westbrook's tactic. The running back passed up an easy touchdown and all the personal glory and individual accolades that go with it in order to ensure the Eagles' win. Westbrook knew that the game wasn't about him; it was about advancing his team in the divisional standings. Philadelphia kept alive its play-off hopes and lived to fight another day![19]

Brian Westbrook had a higher purpose than just making his stats look good or inflating his ego. His higher purpose was the success of his team.

What Westbrook did in the "look what I've done" NFL is really unusual. Mike Ditka, a Hall of Fame tight end and NFL coach, commented on how unusual it is in professional sports today to see honest-to-goodness teamwork. Ditka contrasted that against his playing days—an era when "team-first" thinking was the rule rather than the exception.[20]

Not surprisingly, the NFL teams that have enjoyed the greatest degree of success in the last decade were those that have worked hard to throttle back the me-first attitude and had their players subjugate themselves to the team. Consider the New England Patriots—winners of three Super Bowls in 2001, 2003, and 2004. In the 2003 Super Bowl, the Patriots played the Carolina Panthers—a game New England won 32–29. From the introductions to the final whistle, the Patriots embodied professionalism.

During pregame introductions, the Panthers introduced their starting offense by name, and then the rest of the team ran on to the field. When the Patriots were to be introduced, the announcer said, "New England has chosen to be introduced as a team." Without any individual identification or collective fanfare, the Patriots ran on to the field, went about their business, and won the game.

The Patriots viewed themselves first and foremost as professionals. It's part of their mind-set. They envision "team" as one of their most important values. Coach Bill Belichick insists on it. When it comes to personal-foul penalties, the Patriots historically have been among the least penalized teams in the league. Individual outbursts are strongly discouraged. When a player acts out inappropriately on the field, a posse of teammates escorts the offender to the sideline. For the Patriots, it's not only what they do but how they do it.

The degree to which the lack of this mind-set negatively impacts executive teams and their organizations cannot be overstated. The same trend that Mike Ditka observed among professional athletes is often just as prevalent on the ball field as it is in the boardroom. The manifestations are different, but the impacts are the same.

I have been a member of two organizations that were especially high performing. Most of those who were a part of those organizations held the something-bigger mind-set, although we didn't call it that at the time. Both were amazing experiences. We worked hard, yes. But we had fun. We cut through our issues fast, with little gamesmanship. Results were spectacular. Camaraderie was off the charts. Trust was the rule, not the exception. Not surprisingly, those who strongly held the something-greater mind-set converted those who were initially undecided or cynical to ultimately see the power inherent in teamwork.

That kind of experience shows you what's possible, organizationally speaking. And once you understand what's possible, you never want to go back. No one misses the wasted energy, the head games, the political positioning. The absence of this mind-set (organizationally speaking) is like having a number of small pebbles in your hiking shoes while trekking over a steep, rugged trail. The pebbles ruin the hiking experience. You wonder how something so small, so unassuming could wreak so much havoc, cause so much pain. The really maddening part, though, is that the pebbles are uninvited, unwanted guests.

It's not until you remove the pebbles that you can truly enjoy the experience. Yes, your elevated heart rate and exaggerated breathing remind you of how hard you're working, but you expect that. After you get rid of the pebbles, you're not really bothered by the exertion—the pristine wilderness is reward enough. Finally—with the pebbles gone—you can focus on your journey without the unnecessary aggravation or needless annoyance.

It was those same metaphorical pebbles that were giving our CEO fits in this chapter's opening story. The staff's histrionics, the pointless drama, the subversive vendettas were all uninvited, unwanted guests. As the CEO knew, his company's journey to own its market niche was hard enough. Making it harder by tolerating such unprofessional behavior just didn't cut it. Finally, the CEO issued an ultimatum: get behind our initiatives or get off my team! His people got behind the initiative.

Of course, anyone choosing to put an organization's interests ahead of his or her own must be prudent about that decision. It requires great judgment to evaluate the integrity of both the organization and the people leading it. Consider the employees at Enron and the people who worked with Bernie Madoff.

When you see that you're part of something bigger than yourself, you grasp a defining experience for your career. When I ask groups (typically experienced folks in their forties and fifties) to share their most satisfying, fulfilling, and meaningful professional experiences, they speak of being part of a high-performing team, developing a wildly successful cutting-edge product, and the success their colleagues achieved. Leaders speak with pride about the wonderful jobs they helped to create, the economic benefit they helped to generate, and the great leaders they helped to develop. Noticeably absent is any mention of bonuses, promotions, awards, or the egotistical status symbols like a corner office or other enviable perks to which so many aspire.

Notice how all these satisfying, fulfilling, and meaningful achievements were not about individual rewards. The origins of their greatest sources of satisfaction, their greatest sources of pride, was a "we" thing, not an "I" thing. It was about things bigger than themselves.

Many have postulated that people are at their best when they are engaged in something bigger than themselves. That's certainly been my observation. After all, countries, communities, and families don't become great by putting a self first. The same is true for organizations. I have found that people who are doing work that they are proud of are likely to have embraced this mind-set in a very significant way.

Being part of something bigger than yourself also has the added benefit of contributing to your own well-being. Leadership expert John Maxwell noted, "To live a worthwhile, meaningful life, a person must be a part of something greater than himself." Being part of something greater than yourself, it seems, not only builds trust with others, but it builds esteem in yourself, especially when the something greater is aligned with your values. Such achievement provides immeasurable satisfaction and meaning.

SUMMARY

- The underdevelopment of this mind-set contributes to more dysfunction in organizations than perhaps any other. It is especially problematic with senior teams.
- The lack of this mind-set is, arguably, one of, if not *the* biggest barriers in implementing organizational change.
- Taken to an extreme, this mind-set can lead to people being taken advantage of by their organization. Great judgment is required not to fall into this trap.
- In the end, professionals should "create value for society, rather than extract it." Thus, to be found trustworthy, it's imperative for professionals to do something other than just look out for themselves.
- This mind-set often proves to be greatest opportunity to shift people's thinking away from *me* and ahead to *we.*
- For many, having worked with a team that held this mind-set often proves to be a defining experience in one's career.[21]

CHAPTER **EIGHT**

MIND-SET 3

Professionals Know *Things* Get Better When *They* Get Better

It seems that organizations and individuals that focus more on their responsibilities and less on their rights tend to outperform.

—Seth Godin

If, collectively, the mind-sets were a premium soda, this mind-set would be the fizz. It brings life to the soda and gives it an edge.

At first blush we might think that this mind-set is simply about what many today call personal growth. It isn't, at least not in the conventional sense. Today, personal growth is largely akin to so many other "self" movements in the greater culture, such as self-actualization, self-gratification, self-improvement, self-awareness, self-esteem, and self-fulfillment. And too often personal growth is just a euphemism for getting rich.

Personal growth, while having many admirable intentions, is more like a mirror than a window: it's *self*-centered. Its primary objective and benefits are directed largely toward self. It's inward looking.

Mind-Set 3—which builds off and is dependent on Mind-Set 2 (Something Bigger)—has as its aim the need to satisfy something bigger than oneself. It's outward looking. Its aims are to advance the interests of someone (or something) other than self (which is consistent with

Mind-Set 2). This mind-set enables things to get better, but make no mistake, in the course of achieving something bigger, personal growth (and perhaps personal wealth) occurs. But that wasn't the principle objective or the professional's motivation. Growth happens as a natural and powerful by-product of practicing Mind-Set 3.

For instance, talk to anyone who has worked in a disaster relief effort (Hurricane Katrina–that devastated New Orleans, the 2010 earthquakes in Haiti and Chili and China, the islands recovering from the 2004 Indian Ocean tsunami). Every aid worker comes back changed for the better, but that change wasn't their original intention, aspiration, or motive. Nevertheless, a profound change occurred as a by-product of their selfless efforts.

This phenomenon is not limited to individuals in the midst of such altruistic deeds. Similar changes occur in the lives of people in the for-profit world. You see this metamorphosis in the members of an especially high-performing team involved in bringing an important product to the market (such as Medtronic), people who are transforming an industry (such as Apple), and especially in such transformative times as recessions and economic recovery in the men and women devoted to revitalizing a brand (such as Ford). A professional's devotion to the task at hand requires your best thinking, a willingness to be personally invested in the outcome, an effort to go beyond yourself and even sacrifice for a greater good. In the process of doing this, you cannot help but find your best self along the way. The process stretches you in ways you never knew were possible. These experiences often mark some of the most dramatic professional growth of a person's career, but this isn't growth for the sake of growth. Growth comes as a by-product of serving a higher purpose.

In speaking about leaders, Jim Collins attributes these aforementioned characteristics (among others) as being central to people who have earned his much-envied Level 5 distinction: leaders who helped to build truly great companies. Collins notes that they did what they did for the sake of what they could build, not for what they could get (money, prestige, power, etc.). In other words, their motives were pure, their "ambitions [were] first and foremost for the company."[1]

Note, though, that high-minded ambitions are not always limited to our organization or company. They may also be directed toward our vocation (for example, education, public health, etc.) or to sources of personal services (teachers, physicians, etc.).

Marshall Goldsmith knows all too well how misplaced motives can undermine genuine, sustainable personal growth. Marshall, the world's preeminent executive coach, will not work with clients who he believes engage his services merely to get promoted. Marshall limits his consultations to those who are trying to *be* better (having the improvement become a part of who they are, thus having a greater likelihood that it becomes sustainable).

Being Your Best Self

When our ambitions are primarily directed into a purpose other than ourselves, our willingness to make emotional investments in being part of the solution rather than being a part of the problem rises dramatically. This often means upgrading our skill development, dealing with our own demons, giving others the benefit of the doubt, developing better coping skills in dealing with emotionally maddening situations, upgrading our knowledge base, appropriately extending trust to others, forging nontraditional partnerships, and committing to see things more objectively. All else being equal, these are things that most people would normally prefer not doing. But they do it anyway. Simply put, it's about being better. This isn't merely attitude; it's attitude with a purpose.

In organizational settings this includes situations such as:

- implementing painful but necessary change
- dealing with situations productively and constructively when things go wrong
- getting an edge back after complacency starts to rear its ugly head

Things become better because professionals don't act like victims. They're responsible. They're mature. They're seeking an upside to an otherwise negative situation. They don't bring everybody down around them. And they don't publicly support and privately subvert. For individuals it includes situations such as:

- taking action when you finding yourself unmotivated at work (namely, doing something about it)
- realizing that old approaches won't work in a new environment (for example, developing new skills and approaches)
- asking "what's possible?" when everyone else is focused on what's not working (that is, changing the tone)

Things become better because professionals maintain high standards (see Mind-Set 4) and don't settle for mediocrity. They are willing to bite the bullet on things that matter. They are willing to make future-focused investments. And they avoid the tyranny of the urgent.

Each of the forgoing examples is principally attributed to an internal desire to get better. External factors certainly exist too. But when people are motivated by external factors, their aims are not always about being better; their motivations can become more superficial or survivalist. For instance:

- fear (If I don't get better, I'll be fired.)
- ego (If I don't get better, I'll look bad.)
- pride[2] (If I don't get better, others will pass me up.)

Granted, fear can be a great motivator. Or, more accurately, it is a great *short-term* motivator. Long term, it's unsustainable. Likewise, ego and pride are poor substitutes for positive, affirming motivations. After all, who really trusts anyone who is motivated solely by ego and pride?

This trait of getting better isn't terribly common in our me-first culture. But when it's evident, it's obvious. Take, for example, Simone's situation. In a workshop the instructor makes a learning point about how people unknowingly alienate others. Most of the attendees immediately think of how others had done that very thing to them. In other words, the first thing they do is put on their victim hat.

Such, however, was not Simone's initial reaction. She immediately applied the learning to *herself*. She did not obsess as a victim would, but instead she tried to integrate the learning so *she* can avoid alienating others. In short, she's concerned about getting better and wanting things to get better.

Still, Simone is no pushover. She can assert herself when that's appropriate. She is also very skilled at providing constructive feedback to others without criticizing the individual. What is essentially impressive is her ability to learn from experience, which relates to her lack of defensiveness. She has confidence in her abilities but also realizes she's an unfinished product.[3]

Thinking of ourselves as an unfinished product helps us to remain humble in our quest to realize our potential. Humility (which is covered in greater detail in Mind-Set 6) is an especially important trait in realizing the potential of all seven mind-sets. But it is particularly so in this one.

Some have postulated that Jack Welch chose Jeffrey Immelt to succeed him as CEO at GE because Welch believed Immelt was "a leader with an insatiable thirst for *being* better."[4] The willingness to get better, the willingness to look in the mirror, the willingness to be a lifelong learner, and the willingness to take the high road is compelling. It naturally demonstrates trustworthiness and, as I said earlier, getting better. It's the fizz that brings the soda to life.

Three areas warrant particular mention as to how professionals get better:

- Professionals are emotionally invested, which is evident in their preparation and anticipation of key issues.
- Professionals are persistent, always learning, ever vigilant.
- Professionals are willing to advance a point of view; embrace a "what's possible" sense of optimism.

Professionals Are Emotionally Invested, Which Is Evident in Their Preparation and Anticipation of Key Issues

As I was writing this chapter, my daughter Heidi was contemplating a job change. She called for advice. Her job had become routine, and she wasn't learning anything new. She was a player in her firm, but the only challenging aspect of her position was her trying to do more work in less time—something that had limited appeal. Unfortunately, growth-oriented opportunities within her firm were few.

She had just interviewed with a new and bigger firm. The company, she felt, was top-notch. The position would broaden her industry experience although her degree of impact would be less than she'd been accustomed to. She was also concerned that she'd master the position too quickly and face again the distinct possibility of getting bored at some point. Those concerns led to the following discussion.

HEIDI: "You know, it might be great not having as much responsibility. Just mentally checking out at five o'clock."

ME: "Yeah, perhaps."

HEIDI: "It might be cool, you know, to just go along for a while. After all, it's just a job."

ME: *(sarcastically)* "Sure. When pigs fly!"

HEIDI: "Why do you say that?"

ME: "I've never seen you *not* be emotionally invested in your work. And besides, when you're bored, it saps your investment. Remember when . . . "

After some reflection, Heidi realized she was kidding herself. She just wasn't a go-along type of person. She was responsible and conscientious. It was as if she was incapable of *not* seeing how things could be better. She had a willingness to improve things and, when appropriate, to bring about meaningful change. While she initially didn't always know how to do it, she was always willing to learn.

For professionals, their work isn't just a job where you put in your time and collect a check. That doesn't mean, however, that their work takes over their lives. But emotionally, work definitely plays a meaningful role in their lives.

Getting the Basics Right

Much has been written about the importance of having passion for what you do, including earlier in chapter 6, Mind-Set 1. Passion is especially important today. Competition is fierce. There's always someone willing to work harder than you and for longer periods of time, so in order to excel at what you do, desiring to be deserving of success, it's important to do something you love. Your work has to hold meaning for you. It needs to reinforce your values. It needs to be something you believe in. This passion will help you to get through the inevitable tough times ahead, times that require extra grit, extra stamina, and extra resolve.

That's why it's important to be emotionally invested in what you do. Professionals bring that emotional investment to their work as well as to their relationships. It's a compelling and natural source of motivation. Fear, ego, and pride are insufficient motivations and become unsustainable at some point. Without being emotionally invested, we're likely just doing a job, just going through the motions. And under such circumstances, you can't do your best work. Ultimately others will lose confidence and trust in you, and you'll lose confidence and trust in yourself.

But passion alone will not absolutely ensure our achieving results. Conviction and professional will are sweeteners that compliment passion in this quest. Still, getting the basics right is essential.

Professionals take great pains to ensure that they've got the right fit in their work. They're doing the right job for the right employer. For some, that means starting their own enterprise, one that reflects their values and interests. In either case, the right fit provides professionals with an environment that best enables their emotional investment in their work. This is foundational for the professional.[5]

Showing Up Prepared

In today's business environment our knowledge and skills have a definite shelf life. The pace of change is breathtaking, even punishing, for those who are unwilling or unable to keep up.

Gen. Richard Myers observed, "In an era of transformation, the inability or unwillingness to develop certain skill sets has proven career-ending for some. For instance, consider the possible promotion of a three-star general to a four star. The three-star may be brilliant, have a great pedigree, and be performing well. But it's problematic promoting the three-star to four when the type of command he would hold requires getting things done effectively with and through others—something that has proven to be his Achilles heel. The need to get things done through others frankly transcends his own personal brilliance. So we passed on him simply because of our lack of confidence that he could take the organization to the next level."

The general's illustration isn't about what it takes to get promoted; it is about having the right stuff (knowledge and skills) to be successful in whatever professional situation we may find ourselves. And because change is inevitable, the frequency of jobs and professional situations will likely be greater than we have ever imagined. Professionals realize that old approaches won't always work in new environments, whether it be in a new job or a changing market condition. So personal change is inevitable for professionals, and being emotionally invested is even more important in making that change.

Not Everything Always Goes as Planned

Timothy Clark and Conrad Gottfredson[6] point out that each of us (leaders especially) may face periods of "temporary incompetence," when the demands of today's reality outpaces our ability to deliver. Thus, our credibility becomes just as dependent on our ability to learn and adapt as it is on our being expert. Just as important is the willingness to acknowledge (both publicly and privately) that we don't know something, which may be unsettling for a professional.

This is especially important for leaders, but it presents a paradox. On the one hand, acknowledging our inadequacies. And on the other, engendering confidence in the future.

Being able to adapt, and quickly, is important. For professionals, the process of learning is nearly as important as the learning itself. Essentially, successful professionals have learned how to learn.

Anticipating Problems, Spotting Future Trends, Mitigating the Impacts of Risk

Having an emotional connection to your work suggests that you care about what you do. It suggests that you're concerned about the impacts of risk to the enterprise. That's important, because the world is getting smaller and flatter, and competition is constantly increasing.

Andy Grove, former CEO of Intel, wrote about being vigilant against the impacts of risk (specifically, crisis points) in his book *Only the Paranoid Survive.* He notes, "Business success contains the seeds of its own destruction. The more successful you are, the more people want a chunk of your business and then another chunk and then another until there is nothing left. I believe that the prime responsibility of a manager is to guard constantly against other people's attacks and to inculcate this guardian attitude in the people under his or her management."[7]

Being emotionally invested suggests being vigilant against external competitive threats and anticipating internal problems that can threaten the viability of an operation. It means knowing what's going on in your industry, what's going on with your competitors, what's going on with regulatory requirements, and taking appropriate action. It means anticipating operating problems before they occur. In other words, professionals are dubious of the viability of the status quo. They know how untenable the present can be. This usually requires effort that's above and beyond what's normally required in the employee handbook. It's evidence of someone who is invested, someone who cares. That's why being emotionally invested is so important.

Sometimes the importance of something becomes even more evident by its absence rather than by its presence. Being emotionally invested is one of those things. When we're not emotionally invested, we:

- Likely won't have the curiosity to proactively seek better solutions.
- Likely won't have the motivation to thwart off organizational complacency.
- Likely won't have the staying power to take the long view.
- Likely won't care much when the organization comes under political attack.
- Likely won't have a sense of urgency when things go wrong.
- Likely won't have the courage to fight off cultural conformity.
- Likely won't have the patience to work through bureaucratic obstacles.
- Likely won't have the energy to be at the top of our game.
- Likely won't have the enthusiasm that will attract others to want to work with us.

The impacts of not being emotionally invested quickly become all too evident. It's the difference between merely surviving and flourishing. For professionals, being emotionally invested in their work is a given. It's something they expect, something they relish.

Professionals Are Persistent, Always Learning, Ever Vigilant

In the early twentieth century, Herbert Hoover was largely considered to be one of the most gifted men in public service at the exact time when his extraordinary skills were needed. By training, he was a mining engineer, and he traveled worldwide as a mining expert and efficiency consultant. He lectured on mining at Columbia and Stanford and wrote the standard textbook on mining. When the First World War erupted, Hoover was enlisted to organize the return of Americans from Europe and to meet their food, clothing, and travel needs. He also managed wartime relief efforts in Belgium. When the United States entered the conflict, Hoover was tabbed to head the Food Administration. After the war, he directed relief efforts in Central Europe, including Germany and the new Soviet Union. As a result, both national parties courted him to be their next presidential candidate. In 1921, Warren Harding drafted him as secretary of commerce, but Hoover's personal energy and innovative programs led some to dub him the "undersecretary of everything else." Very quickly he was seen to be the best secretary of commerce in the country's history. Through it all, Hoover proved to be indefatigable in everything he did.[8]

Consider Hoover's oft-quoted "grind it out" formula for success: "Nothing in the world can take the place of persistence. Talent will not; nothing is more common than unsuccessful men with talent. Genius will not; unrewarded genius is almost a proverb. Education will not; the world is full of educated derelicts. Persistence and determination alone are omnipotent. The slogan 'Press On' has solved and always will solve the problems of the human race."

The world certainly throws us lots of curves, some from our outside world, some from our inside world. That we'll face challenges and adversity is a given. That we'll succeed in overcoming those challenges without being persistent is doubtful. While seeming overly simplistic, this essential trait (persistence) is required of us as a prerequisite to the success we seek—in spite of any other natural and God-given advantages we may have.

Note the observation of Dee Hock, founder and former CEO of Visa International: "You learn nothing from your successes except to think too much of yourself. It is from failure that all growth comes, provided you can recognize it, admit it, learn from it, rise above it, and then try again."[9] In other words: dogged determination wins the day. Consider:

- Conrad Hall at Trader Publications started his classified advertising business by purchasing just one small publication (*Auto Trader*) as an experiment and worked out his recipe for success there. He then launched an exact replica in another market, learned from that experience, and ramped up to the national scale in just two years.[10]
- Educator Geoffrey Canada's pioneering efforts at the Harlem Children's Zone (a charter school) produced remarkable results—bridging longstanding performance gaps between minority and white students—that were thought unattainable. Through dogged persistence and experimentation, Canada's program now serves children in ninety-seven square blocks—up from twenty-four square blocks when the program began.

Persistence Personified

The eleven-year-old trudged uphill with newspapers bursting from overpacked sacks. It was New Year's Day, and the newspapers were heavier than usual, due to the post-holiday sales advertising. What a day to start a new paper route! Was this a case of biting off more than one could chew? The skinny kid, now out of breath and somewhat frustrated, suddenly wondered what kind of a mess this was going to be.

When a customer glimpsed the out-of-sorts carrier, he said, "What are *you* doing here? You don't have any business doing this. It is a boy's job. You'll never last!"[11]

The paper carrier? John Ireland's middle daughter, Kathleen. You probably know her as Kathy.

Kathy Ireland knows a thing or two about persistence. She not only lasted in this job, but she was named district carrier of the year for three consecutive years. Her entrepreneurial spirit was lit in her youth. Long before her paper route, four-year-old Kathy sold painted rocks out of her wagon. In the years since then, she overcame long odds, gender bias, and even a few self-doubts. In 1993 she founded kathy ireland WorldWide (kiWW), a design and marketing enterprise, which today is a billion-dollar empire. She did this after being one of the world's most successful supermodels.

Ireland, a natural beauty with piercing green eyes, was discovered at age seventeen and went on to appear in *Sports Illustrated*'s swimsuit issue for thirteen consecutive years. And she was the cover model of three of those issues. She also has appeared on the covers of such prestigious fashion magazines as *Glamour, Cosmopolitan, Mademoiselle, Seventeen,* and *Shape.* Who would have predicted such success from a self-described skinny, socially awkward teenager from Santa Barbara with no celebrity connections?

Despite her natural gifts, Ireland was never enamored with modeling. Rather, she saw herself as a businessperson who happened to be a model. Kathy wanted to be behind the camera, not in front of it. Today, Kathy is CEO and chief designer at kiWW, a woman's lifestyle brand. She employs thirty-seven and holds a majority stake in the Los Angeles–based company. The firm has forty-five thousand individual products in tens of thousands of stores in seventy countries and generates an estimated $1.5 billion in annual sales. *Forbes* magazine dubbed Kathy a supermodel turned supermogul. Today, she is one of America's most accomplished entrepreneurial CEOs.

Her post-modeling business success wasn't immediately evident, as there were several inevitable speed bumps to contend with. First, Kathy invested about two years in learning to brew beer, becoming involved with a microbrewery. She sold her interest in the business after she realized she didn't have a passion for beer. Kathy said, "I investigated other businesses, but I didn't have the right partners, and they failed." Ireland attributes the inadequate vetting of partners as a major factor in many of those failures. "But those failures have been learning experiences for me," Kathy added. "I failed so many times in business before starting our [kiWW] brand in '93. I look at failure as education, and in that respect, I'm very well educated."[12]

But adversity didn't build Kathy's character; it revealed it. She persevered and then persevered some more. Although she describes herself as headstrong and sometimes unintentionally controlling, her mind always turns toward meeting exceptionally high standards.[13] Like so many dynamic entrepreneurial leaders, Kathy has a strong sense of self-determination. This is why people often see her as having an independent streak. It's also why she really likes being self-employed and running her own company. True to form for someone with an entrepreneurial mentality, Kathy loves the business adventure and the freedom to create, but she also acknowledges that she's learned a lot of things the hard way.

Kathy knew intuitively what she wanted for kiWW, namely, to build a powerful brand. "I wanted a brand that had longevity, and I wanted to be involved every step of the way,"[14] she said.

When asked about her transition from modeling to branding professional, she answered, "It was a blessing that [at the end of my modeling career] I didn't have that celebrity and that fame as a model. No one was offering me endorsements. . . . That rejection served me very well in business, because when I hit the streets here in New York, and people slammed doors in my face, . . . it really didn't faze me. And that perseverance caused me to work with a team. . . . When others were buying fancy cars and designer clothes, . . . I invested in an art director, building a team."[15]

Kathy was first approached by John and Marilyn Moretz from designer sock company Moretz Sports to model their socks. At the time, Kathy had a small business and an undersized branding team in place.

Kathy's response? "I did not want to do an endorsement," she said. "I wanted to start a real brand from the ground up. People said we were absolutely crazy, but we thought this could be a really great beginning. What better place to start a brand from the ground up than with socks?"[16]

So she started on the ground level—literally. "With very little resources, no ad budget, but good people, good products, and hard work, my business partner, Jon Carrasco, and I loaded up our backpacks and traveled around the country presenting our socks to retailers."[17] They slept in airports to save money. Turns out, socks were the ticket. More than one hundred million pairs have been sold since Kathy received the fortuitous offer from Moretz.

What Kathy does comes from her entrepreneurial spirit, and how she conducts herself as an entrepreneur is inspired by her faith. Her Christian ideals are integral to everything she does, from family priorities to how she expects her business family to conduct kiWW's affairs. An admiring Bill Cosby once noted that Kathy's character is beyond reproach.

Kathy has received a number of impressive awards and honors because of her business success. Yet many are unaware of her efforts as a world-class humanitarian, supporting causes ranging from poverty to the Special Olympics, and doing everything with a quiet, low-key dignity. Laura Morton, Kathy's coauthor of *Powerful Inspirations,* commented, "Rarely, if ever, have I met someone who inspires me to *be* more, *do* more, *expect* more, and *give* more of myself to others."[18] Kathy has that sort of impact on people.

When Kathy launched kiWW, many simply saw her as a pretty face pursuing an admirable but foolish dream. So much for those who underestimated the once-pampered twenty-something supermodel who possesses business acumen by the bucketload and the perseverance to back it up. As of 2008, kiWW ranked twenty-third of all companies in licensing revenue at $1.4 billion. By contrast, Mattel was sixteenth at $2 billion, and Ralph Lauren was seventy-ninth at $154 million![19]

Over thirty years later, Kathy Ireland is still the girl with the paper route—only now, the sacks are a little fuller.

Professionals Are Willing to Advance a Point of View, Embrace a "What's Possible" Sense of Optimism

You're in a staff meeting. The boss asks for feedback on the presentation just made by Melinda on a new procedure proposed for project reconciliation. Before finalizing the proposal, getting a reality check with the staff is imperative.

Initially there's silence. Then there's mindless chatter. After two minutes no one has said anything worthwhile. When someone finally says something coherent, it's merely to placate the boss. In many organizations this gets played out regularly day after day.

The topic doesn't much matter. Instead of project reconciliation, the topic could have just as easily have been a department consolidation or new safety standards. People just aren't forthcoming. The boss doesn't know what the staff is thinking or why they might be thinking it.

It's true that some organizations are traumatized by their leadership.[20] When that happens it stifles feedback and breeds cynicism. But absent that problem, all too frequently people who have important points of view don't speak up. I've been around the barn a few times, and I realize political dynamics sometimes get in the way of speaking up. It's unfortunate but true.

People who consider themselves to be professionals should be sharing their point of view. Withholding our thoughts does not build trust, but rather raises suspicions about our intentions, motives, and support. Consultant Sandra Walston observed, "Silence is really conformity in disguise."[21] In organizations, mindless conformity rarely enables things to get better.

In such cases, others may ask if silence means that we are hiding out, hoping to remain anonymous, or perhaps wishing to remain disengaged? Are we lacking the courage to speak up on something we believe is wrong? Are we waiting it out to see how the political wind will blow? Are we withholding support while hoping the initiative will die of its own weight? Are we privately working against the initiative in the hope of punishing the boss?

Perhaps our silence means none of these things. The trouble is, when we don't speak up, people don't know where we stand.

It's important for professionals to advance their point of view in the spirit of helping things to get better. Roger Enrico, former head of Pepsico, advanced the notion that "having a point of view is worth 50 IQ points."[22] Here's why that's so important, not only for the individual, but for the organization:

1. For individuals, it creates a positive, new habit. It counteracts complacency, prevents us from just going along or hanging out in the weeds.
2. By thinking more like an owner, our actions increase our ownership in the issue. It broadens our thinking, whether exploring a new market opportunity, solving a problem, or revising a policy.
3. It provides a catalyst for new approaches and new possibilities. It challenges traditional thinking—this book is a prime example.
4. Organizationally speaking, it allows others to participate in refining new ideas by enabling others to challenge underlying assumptions, test the fundamental hypothesis, and add complimentary viewpoints. This process helps jump-start innovation.
5. It helps to avoid misunderstandings. Declaring our expectations (albeit a personal point of view) about how a project should be run, about how successful performance should be assessed, about what roles are appropriate all help to clarify our perspectives, which allows others to understand how we see the world.
6. It enhances our level of professionalism in the eyes of others. Sharing our point of view demonstrates transparency and shows intent.

When it matters, professionals should speak up. This is consistent with our commitment to advance the needs of their organization.

Embracing Optimism

There's a great line in a Billy Joel song: "Every time I've held a rose, it seems I've only felt the thorns."[23] Too often the naysayer in us squashes the upbeat optimist in us.

Seeing the possibilities, instead of just the problems, is an important trait for professionals. I'm not referring to blindly leading cheers for an organization's ill-conceived initiative or being Pollyannaishly naive about rectifying a product's critical design flaw. I am referring to maintaining an optimistic state of mind, one that seeks to be ever vigilant about getting better and revealing what's possible. It's being able to think more like an owner.

Let's consider this optimism through the lens of organizational change. First, self-initiated change, and second, change initiated by others.

Self-Initiated Change

It's been my observation that too many people sit on good ideas, especially in larger organizations. In other words, some of the organization's best thinking never gets utilized because people don't speak up. And speaking up is an important subset to being proactive, which is one of the most important habits effective professionals can cultivate.[24] At the same time, I have to acknowledge that some organizations' leadership may have created cultural norms that don't reinforce sharing our ideas.

However, too often, we simply fail to advance our ideas. We just don't speak up. This is inconsistent with the professional's aim to have things get better. An individual who withholds her ideas may have had a cultural upbringing or a personality type that acts as a barrier toward this aim, but it's important that our professional ideals trump these barriers.

Organizations that foster an environment that enables these ideas to bubble up are often richly rewarded. For instance, Brian Dunn, a forty-nine-year-old veteran and CEO of Best Buy, noted, "I don't believe that the model is any longer that there are a few really smart people at the top of the pyramid that make all the strategic decisions. It is much more about being all around the enterprise, and looking for people with great ideas and passionate points of view that are anchored to the business and connected to things our customers care about."[25]

Best Buy, like many organizations, has found ways to culturally reinforce the notion of having their people feel free to verbalize their best ideas. Without exception, this practice has overwhelmingly support among the employees.

But even professionals who find themselves in environments apathetic about such practices should be vigilant in looking for opportunities to espouse their ideas. Sometimes it takes nothing more than a big success from such an idea for management to catch the vision of what's possible.

Strategic Inflection Point for Procter & Gamble

Questions cannot only be powerful sources of insight, but they can be inspirational too, especially when we are asking about what's possible. The fruits of this question have brought pride to an entire nation (for example, the Apollo Moon landings), brought entire villages out of poverty (for example, microcredit), or generated amazing new products (for example, the iPhone).

This was precisely the question that A. J. Lafley asked himself in 2000 shortly after he unexpectedly took the reins as CEO at Procter and Gamble.[26] Innovation, which historically had been a competitive advantage at P&G, had waned. Growth had slowed, profits and the company's stock price were sliding, and P&G's biggest brands had lost significant market share.

Lafley's most critical strategic question was, "When it comes to having innovation jump-start P&G's performance, what's possible?" He found two fundamental options being advanced by his senior team. Both were based on conventional thinking. They could (1) continue to generously fund P&G's research and development department, as his predecessor had, or (2) redirect a portion of research and development's generous resources into marketing and brand development.

This strategic question was not only practical in nature, but it spoke to an even bigger question. What would P&G be as an entity? A research and development company or a marketing and branding enterprise?

Roger Martin, a former advisor to Lafley, notes that Lafley assumed the real problem "lay within himself."[27] Lafley said to himself, "I haven't yet found a creative resolution that meets my standards. That's not the world's fault. I just haven't thought hard enough yet."

His ultimate course of action? He needed to find sources of innovation *outside* of P&G and use P&G's huge resource advantage to develop and commercialize the innovation. Lafley set a target that 50 percent of all new innovation originate outside of P&G. It worked. P&G partnered with solo inventors and small companies that had developed breakthrough ideas. In doing so, he jump-started innovation as a P&G competitive advantage and enhanced the productivity of P&G's research and development function by two- to threefold.

Today, P&G remains known as one of the most admired companies in the world, due largely to their much-envied core competency of marketing and branding expertise. The company has regained its long-standing prominence in consumer goods marketing. Lafley's "What's possible?" question set those wheels in motion, rethinking the problem and yielding fruits that, while not initially obvious, proved to be prescient.

Change Initiated by Others

Change in organizations today is widespread and inevitable. Most, however, are recipients of change, not initiators of it. That makes it even harder.

In the first place, people generally dislike change. Initially they're likely to conjure up nightmare scenarios about the impacts of change, many of which are patently off base. Then, when the inevitably unpleasant aspects of change descend on them—Hey, I didn't sign up for this!—it often becomes even more distasteful.

Gen. Eric Shinseki observed, "If you don't like change, you're going to like irrelevance even less."[28] Fighting change often proves to be counterproductive. Finding ways to productively embrace change is not only the right thing to do, but it is consistent with how professionals perform. That's why being open to what's possible is important during times of change.

Interestingly, in speaking with those who have gone through some form of dramatic change in their professional life (for example, reorganization, merger and acquisition, job loss, etc.), the vast majority report that they are doing at least as well after the change as they were doing before the change.[29] Looking retrospectively, most would agree that they overdramatized the potential impacts of the change at the time it was initiated.

Sponsors or initiators of change have important viewpoints. Recall that when Gen. Richard Myers served as chairman of the Joint Chiefs, he served with Donald Rumsfeld, who was secretary of defense. Myers repeated to me Rumsfeld's well-known goal of getting the military ready for the twenty-first century.[30] *Transformation* was the watchword in all four branches of service.

During that time there was a lot of emphasis on who they were picking for certain jobs. All other qualifications being equal, Myers indicated that Secretary Rumsfeld always had two critical things he wanted to know about every candidate: (1) can I work with this person? and (2) does this person cling to the dogmas of the past?

Sponsors and implementers of change know how tough their task is. Getting the right people on their team is imperative. That means they need people who are supportive of the change effort, those who are open to exploring what's possible. That doesn't suggest that these people know precisely how they'll achieve their aims (they don't), and it doesn't suggest that they aren't full of questions and concerns (they are). It simply means that they are supportive of the change effort.

Donald Rumsfeld was like virtually any other leader in that he wants to work with people who are open to what's possible. In short, it means that if you're clinging to the dogmas of the past, you'll likely find yourself quickly becoming irrelevant, because leaders won't want you on their team.

The Prepared Political Monk

James Madison is widely considered to be the Father of the U.S. Constitution. While Madison himself disavowed the title,[31] his meticulous preparation prior to the 1787 Constitutional Convention in Philadelphia and his influence during the debates are significant enough to merit paternity. Contemporaries described him as "simple, modest, bland, and unostentatious, retiring from the throng and cautiously refraining from doing or saying anything to make himself conspicuous."[32] In comparison to the other convention delegates, he was "young, ambitious, deeply thoughtful, unprepossessing in his personal appearance and manner, and still little known. . . . But more than any other delegate, [he] would provide the combination of intellectual firepower and dogged persistence that animated the Convention."[33] Historian Catherine Drinker Bowen commented, "Long study had given him a prophetic quality. . . . But Madison, enormously pertinacious [opinionated], was also flexible—two qualities not often found together."[34]

Many months prior to the convention, Madison traveled to New York to take his seat in Congress, and he stopped at Mount Vernon, where George Washington and he discussed the upcoming convention to which both men had been named as delegates. Washington was not anxious to attend, but Madison urged him to be there.[35] And for the next six months he laid out his thoughts for constitutional reform in letters to Washington, to Thomas Jefferson (who was then America's ambassador to France), and to other political friends that sharpened their thinking as well as Madison's.[36]

After returning home from the Congress, Madison devoted the spring and early summer of 1787 to studying a number of books sent to him from Paris by Jefferson (in return, Madison sent him grafts from American trees to impress the French). In these books Madison found information on almost every experiment in republican or federal government of which there was any historical record. From them he compiled a lengthy essay that outlined the structure and history and political strengths and weaknesses of the confederacies of ancient Greece, the Holy Roman Empire, the Swiss Confederation, and the United Provinces of the Netherlands.[37] All of this colored his thinking about the upcoming convention, and he did little else during this time but ponder the middle ground between the two extreme political poles of a strong central government and jealously sovereign states. Historian Clinton Rossiter described him as "a single-minded political monk in these months of study and maneuver."[38]

Madison's devotion to the convention was demonstrated when he was "the first of the out-of-state delegates to arrive in Philadelphia."[39] His example of punctuality proved to be infectious for the other delegates as they slowly arrived in the city—it took eleven days for enough delegates to arrive before they could open the proceedings. During this time, Madison organized daily conferences of the Virginia delegates to draft some proposals based on his six months of letter writing and research. In the evenings, he would dine with the other delegates, and the table talk always turned to their ideas of reform. Madison shared his thinking as well as heard his fellow diners' ideas. When Benjamin Franklin hosted the first twenty delegates in town for the convention, the discussion quickly turned to their political ideas, and Madison found that he had another friend in his corner.[40] When the time came for the convention to begin deliberations on May 14, the first draft of governmental reorganization was formally submitted by the Virginia delegation, and it had Madison's fingerprints all over it.

After three and a half months of debate, the framework of the final document still bore a strong resemblance to Madison's early proposals. He viewed the changes as refinements of his thoughts with those of his colleagues. Biographer Ralph Ketcham noted: "In attending to every detail of this structure [of the Constitution], and in being sensitive at every point to the effect of blending the various parts, Madison played his most critical role."

As soon as the delegates adopted and signed the Constitution, Madison was off to New York to take his seat in Congress, where the Constitution would next be debated. For three days the congressmen studied the document, and Madison played a key role in preventing them from reworking the structure of the government as outlined in the manuscript. Thus Congress decided not to vote on the Constitution but to send it to the state legislatures for ratification.

The Constitution was eventually ratified by the states on March 4, 1789. In New York the process was considerably aided by the publication and distribution of a series of eighty-five essays that came to be known as the Federalist Papers. They appeared under a fictitious pen name, but Madison, Alexander Hamilton, and John Jay were the authors. Madison's months of study and preparation prior to the convention brought life and substance to these essays. To this day, the Federalists Papers still are a primary source for interpreting the Constitution.[41]

It's no accident that the Constitution reflects so much of Madison's influence. He earned his credibility. He did his homework. His early draft became the framework of our much-admired Constitution, which has since served as the template for over 120 other democracies. Madison lived the adage that "Preparation precedes success." Today, our nation and many others stand as benefactors of his efforts.

Closure

This chapter began with referencing knowledge and how important it is to this particular mind-set. Then, through illustration, the ways in which many different professionals brought their all-important knowledge to life through their *actions* were spotlighted. Let's now make the implicit explicit: knowledge by itself is insufficient, or as they say in Texas, it's all hat and no cattle. Absent action, knowledge is merely an intellectual exercise.

As President Herbert Hoover alluded, "winning the day" is all in the *doing.* That, as we've seen, often involves personal change. Jeffrey Immelt, CEO of GE, said, "I recognized that if I wanted the company to change, that I would have to change myself." It's all about leading yourself, walking your talk. It's about credibility. And in the end, it's all about trust.

SUMMARY

- This mind-set transcends the traditional idea of personal growth. It's about *being* better, which ironically proves largely to be a by-product of investing our energies and resources in things other than ourselves.
- Being emotionally invested in one's work is perhaps the most important attribute in ensuring that professionals consistently get better.
- Professionals are natural learners—sometimes out of necessity, sometimes out of curiosity. Successful professionals have learned how to learn.
- Persistence is arguably the greatest attribute in enabling things to get better. Persistence trumps talent, education, or personality, whether this involves meeting an important deadline, forging a complicated deal, or developing a breakthrough product.
- Hope and your best thinking are needed for things to get better. This is why professionals are willing to explore what's possible (hope) and share their point of view (best thinking).

CHAPTER **NINE**

MIND-SET **4**

Professionals Have Personal Standards That Often Transcend Organizational Ones

Any time you sincerely want to make a [personal] change, the first thing you must do is to raise your standards.

—Tony Robbins

Best-selling author David McCullough, a two-time winner of the Pulitzer Prize, is a master of the art of narrative history. His books are considered masterpieces. Some of his best-known works are *Truman, 1776, The Path Between the Seas,* and *John Adams.*

David regularly receives inquiries from movie producers to do his books, to make them into documentaries or feature-length films. His biography of John Adams, for example, drew an exceptional amount of interest. As McCullough knows only too well, these types of collaborations are less like blind dates and more like marriages.

The typical conversation with a wannabe producer starts something like this: "I loved your book." Five minutes into the conversation, however, it's clear that the moviemaker hasn't read much more than the book's dust jacket. So much for trying to woo the nation's foremost celebrity historian!

While McCullough has generally been open to such proposals, he's also understandably dubious. "You're [potentially] turning your creation, your child, if you will, over to people," he commented. "[After all] what are they going to do with it?"

The child metaphor may seem far-fetched until one considers that McCullough invests a minimum of four years into each of his books—some even longer. *John Adams* took six. With that level of sacrifice, that level of commitment, prudence suggests you don't hand off your baby to just anyone.

McCullough has had forty years of bliss as an author. He loves what he does. Interestingly, he won't name any of his books as his favorite. That's a lot like asking which child is your favorite. However, he readily acknowledges that his happiest, most fulfilling years were those invested in writing *John Adams.* He said, "It was a privilege to keep company with those people. They set such a high standard for us."[1] McCullough speaks openly and generously of his admiration for Adams (plus Adams's wife, Abigail), noting, "Character is what counts, above all."

Enter Tom Hanks, Oscar-winning actor and film producer. McCullough recalled: "We met in a little cafe in Ketchum, Idaho, for breakfast one morning. I had never met him before in my life, but greatly admired his work. He had a copy of the book in which he had underlined scenes—pages after pages, and he had written marginal notes. The thing looked like an autumn-leafed blizzard of Post-its all the way through it. He not only read it, he had studied it. . . . He wanted to go over scene-by-scene on how he anticipated shooting certain aspects of the film. So I knew he had really done his homework and that he knew exactly what he hoped to achieve. I knew right then, this man will do it right—what integrity!"

Hanks did, indeed, do it right. HBO ran *John Adams*—starring Paul Giamatti and Laura Linney—as an eight-part miniseries to rave reviews. What made this possible? The trust McCullough had in Hanks. The standards he saw in Adams (the ones that drew him so fervently to him) were the same ones that attracted him to Hanks.

Hanks is like so many trusted professionals who hold themselves to exacting standards. And while it helps that their organizations also have standards, these professionals aren't necessarily dependent on them to do a good job, to be responsible, or to be respectful to others. Their standards are integral to their character. Professionals who hold this mind-set:

- have personalized a core set of values.
- do what's right over what's expedient by taking a long view.
- rise above the fray, stay focused, and avoid pointless drama.

For clarification, personal standards can mean a myriad of things when referenced in this chapter. When I use the term, I mean one's personal values, one's moral compass (one's definition of right and wrong), or one's core beliefs.

Have a Personalized Core Set of Values

At a general membership meeting of the Investment Company Institute in 1993, Harvard professor Michael Porter, one of America's preeminent experts on global corporate strategy, chastised his audience of mutual fund executives for what he perceived as stagnation throughout the industry. Companies were acting much like one another, with each firm vigorously exercising a me-too attitude and making very few attempts to distinguish one company from another. After painting that picture of ordinariness, however, he pointed to a single firm that was not part of this homogenization: the Vanguard Group. Porter applauded Vanguard's "genuine, unique, sustainable competitive advantage"—something that had served it well since its inauspicious founding in 1975.[2]

Vanguard's most unique characteristic is its structure: it is owned by the shareholders of its mutual funds. This arrangement allows Vanguard to operate on an at-cost basis, extracting no profits for outsider owners. Additionally, in a total departure from other investment management companies that offered only actively managed mutual funds, Vanguard created the world's first index mutual fund in 1975. The roots of both of these attributes can be traced to a Princeton undergraduate thesis in which the author noted that mutual funds "can make no claim to superiority over" the S&P 500 stock market index and that future growth "can be maximized by a reduction of sales loads and management fees." The impetus for the company's founding was one man's personal value of managing his company "solely in the interest of our shareholders" in a way that was "economical, efficient, and honest." Since 1975, Vanguard has realized remarkable success and is now the second largest firm in the mutual fund industry.

Who was the source for the ideas that became Vanguard? John Clifton "Jack" Bogle.[3] He grew up during the Great Depression and earned his bachelor's degree at Princeton, earning high honors. Beginning in the early 1950s, he pursued the conventional business path and scaled the corporate ladder at one of the mutual fund industry's oldest firms, Philadelphia's Wellington Management Company, to become the company's leader in 1965 and its chief executive in 1967. A poor merger decision, however, led to his being fired. That wasn't the end of his career, though. Bogle told *Fortune* magazine, "The great thing about that mistake . . . was that I learned a lot."

He began anew with the founding of Vanguard in 1975, implementing his insights into index funds, but also incorporating his personal values, including a profound emphasis on trustworthiness and accountability. While many investment firms seem more than cavalier about handling other people's money, Bogle viewed his relationship with his investors as a sacred trust, and he held himself personally accountable to them. He knew that nothing builds confidence in a leader more than a leader's willingness to take responsibility for what happens during his watch. Years later Rudy Giuliani summarized this philosophy in this way: "Nothing builds a stronger case for holding employees to a high standard than a boss who holds himself to even higher ones."[4]

In his book *Enough,* Bogle emphasized that companies need to "stand for something." He added: "My own goal has been to build a company that stands for *stewardship.*" This is not hollow rhetoric. "Let me be clear," he said, "this goal is not without a self-serving aspect. For only to the extent we adequately serve the human beings who have entrusted us with the management of their wealth will Vanguard itself survive and prosper." Because Bogle was the company's founder and chief executive, his and Vanguard's values are closely aligned. My interviews[5] with John revealed the tried and true (some might say unyielding) principles that traditionally are only found amongst the most revered professionals—ones that are at the top of their game.

John's thinking about what constitutes a profession and, by default, a professional also represents that same tradition.*

John based Vanguard "on the sound implementation of a few commonsense investment ideas, an enlightened sense of human values and ethical standards, and the bond of trust between our firm and its clients." He emphasized that these qualities "must be built into the character of the enterprise, not grafted onto its exterior." His goal was not just to build a successful company but one that *deserved* to succeed.

So many companies, especially financial services companies, live and die by their metrics, obsessing in the short term on share price, market share, etc. They do so largely because their metrics are synonymous with their business objectives. Such is not the case for John Bogle. He measured Vanguard's success in terms of the clients' level of trust in the firm.

Consider his approach to numbers: "We place far too much trust in numbers. *Numbers are not reality.* At best, they are a pale reflection of reality. At worst, they're a gross distortion of the truths we seek to measure."[6] This is a contrarian viewpoint from a guy whose industry is smothered in an endless array of metrics.

John believes that the most important things in life defy measurement, things such as character, wisdom, trust, and integrity. A recent personal experience reinforces this premise. A client asked me to help with an important change initiative. By way of introduction to this thousand-member organization, I was given some background materials, including a recent departmental survey. A great deal of time and effort (not to mention money) had been invested in the report. It

---

* Bogle considers professionals as those who are associated with a traditional profession: physicians, lawyers, teachers, engineers, architects, accountants, clergymen—plus possibly journalists and trustees of others' money. He notes a profession has the following six traits: (1) a commitment to the interest of clients in particular and the welfare of society in general, (2) a body of theory or special knowledge, (3) a specialized set of professional skills, practices, and performances unique to the profession, (4) the developed capacity to render, (5) an organized approach to learning from experience, both individually and collectively, and thus growing new knowledge from the context of practice, and (6) the development of a professional community responsible for the oversight and monitoring of quality in both practice and professional educators. This strict view differs from the one I advanced in chapter 2.

attempted to measure employee perceptions about how the business was being run and to gauge their satisfaction with management, and it also offered an opportunity for the employees to offer suggestions for improvement. The instrument used to form the basis for the report was comprehensive. Over sixty questions were incorporated.

The results (in terms of numbers) revealed a moderately impressive department. The answers to the questions (which were largely tactical in nature) demonstrated a respectable level of job satisfaction and the usual grumblings about the brass (we always expect some of that). The customary areas needed to be shored up, but there was no major flaw in the department that could be described as catastrophic. Statistically speaking, at least from the survey results, the department was solid. The problem was that the numbers (borrowing Bogle's words) "were a pale reflection of reality." There were serious cooperation issues across divisions, major challenges with meeting production targets, and significant morale problems that the survey instrument did not adequately detect.

In a closed-door meeting with the leaders, I asked, "On a five-point scale (one being low and five being high), how would you rate the level of trust within the department?" After I deflected a few superficial answers, they glumly agreed on 1.5! The formal survey results had offered the leaders only a glimpse of a few isolated trees and failed to help them to focus on the forest—in this case, trust. In large part, the organization's problems stemmed from a stunning lack of trust. (At this stage of the book you probably don't find that to be surprising.) The employee survey—no matter how well intended, no matter how much was invested in it—failed to measure what mattered most.

This illustrates two of Bogle's points: (1) stakeholder trust should be a north-arrow objective (one that matters most), and (2) many current attempts to gauge organizational health (which tend to focus exclusively on numbers) can be misguided and misleading.

Bogle differentiates companies between "those that count" and "those that trust." He made sure that Vanguard was rooted in trust. John believes that what your clients think of you is far more important than any set of numbers you can claim to represent the health of your organization. He observed that Vanguard's growth strategy "comes from putting the horse of doing things for clients ahead of the cart of earnings targets." During his tenure as CEO, he deplored bureaucracy of any kind that might tarnish a client's experience.

When Vanguard offered its first index fund, its initial public offering attracted only eleven million dollars in assets. Industry insiders ridiculed the offering, deriding it as "Bogle's folly" and wondering why on earth investors would want to settle for "average" returns. Ten years later they were trying to copy it. Why? Because the fund was based on what Bogle calls the "relentless rules of humble arithmetic," which dictate that the less investors pay, the larger their share of the market's long-term returns. That's putting your clients first.

Currently Vanguard manages more than one trillion (yes, *trillion*) dollars in assets, and the firm's index fund offerings have grown from a single fund to eighty-nine index and virtual index mutual funds. Such funds now constitute nearly 90 percent of the assets under Vanguard's supervision.

The funny thing about John Bogle and Vanguard is that this approach is not as unique as it appears; it's really a return to the past, a revisiting of the tried and true. Bogle avoided the trendiness of financial engineering and kept his business model simple—some industry insiders even call it boring. But in the end, Vanguard and its investors are winners. For nearly four decades Bogle has pressed Vanguard to stay on that path, demanding that Vanguard remain a place "where judgment has at least a fighting chance to triumph over process." While every company has a measure of bureaucracy to it, Bogle has fought to keep bureaucracy at bay and paid attention to common sense and personal judgment and the primary character traits of integrity, imagination, intuition, and diligence. "All seasoned with," he candidly points out, "a little foresight and a lot of luck."

John Bogle is the antithesis of Bernie Madoff and Jeffrey Skilling. Bogle has been called the "conscience of Wall Street."[7] He speaks often and passionately about the ills he perceives in the financial services industry. While this outspokenness doesn't always endear him to his colleagues, more than a few industry leaders hold him in the highest regard. For example, Cliff Asness of AQR Capital Management noted, "Capitalism has too many characters and not enough men of character.

When one of the few tells us that the system he loves is ailing, and how to fix it, we had best listen."[8]

Certainly John is ambitious, but he believes that companies "must have values and a purpose beyond just making money." It was his personal values that prompted his aspiration to have Vanguard "stand for stewardship." As important as his insightful analytics were to Vanguard's successful market strategy, it was ultimately John's personal values that made the difference in Vanguard's unrivaled business success. Said another way, his personal values and how he applied them to Vanguard's business practices proved to be the things that mattered most.

Bogle's philosophy of stewardship isn't limited simply to his professional life. A wealthy man by any standard, for many years he has donated half of his income to various philanthropic causes. "I don't look at these contributions as charity," he wrote. "I look at them as an attempt to repay the enormous debts I've accumulated over a lifetime." Two of his major causes are the National Constitution Center in Philadelphia (where he served as chairman of the board of trustees for seven years) and his high school, Blair Academy (where he has served on the board for nearly forty years, including fifteen years as chairman). Other beneficiaries include his alma mater, Princeton University, and various Philadelphia-based hospitals, churches, schools, and service organizations.

The core values that permeate John Bogle's personal life are identical to the values he demonstrated in his professional life. They are the kind of values that make Vanguard successful as well. And this illustrates how pervasive our core values are to everything we touch, everything we do, and everything we say.

Do What's Right Over What's Expedient by Taking the Long View

Too frequently people take shortcuts, take the easy way out, or sell out. Fortunately, we have many stellar examples who don't.

Consider a decision by Gen. Richard Myers. The publisher of the general's memoirs, *Eyes on the Horizon,* wanted to stage the book's release just prior to the 2008 presidential election. The idea was purposeful, as it would surely guarantee heightened book sales due to the inevitable political inferences from Myers's days as chairman of the Joint Chiefs of Staff. The general, however, objected to the idea, believing that, although retired, he continued to have a commitment to the high office he formerly held. His paramount commitment was to remain apolitical.

Even as a civilian, Myers continued to honor this sacred responsibility he felt he held to his former office as the nation's highest-ranking military officer. This shouldn't be surprising coming from a man who elected not to cast a ballot in national elections as part of his effort to remain apolitical—something he believed was essential for a military professional—as soon as he reached a senior flag rank. While this was required neither by mandate nor statute, he chose to relinquish his right to vote because he believed doing so would enhance his objectivity in dealing with congressional leaders—thus enabling him to more effectively represent all branches of the service.[9]

Peter G. Peterson is an investment banker, author, and public servant. In the early 1970s he served as Richard Nixon's secretary of commerce. Later he was chairman of the Council on Foreign Relations until 2007 and the senior chairman of the Blackstone Group, a private equity firm. In 2008, he was ranked 149th on the "Forbes 400 Richest Americans" with a net worth of $2.8 billion. In 2008, he established a foundation with a $1 billion endowment.

Peterson is also a first-generation American. In the 1920s his parents immigrated to the United States from Greece, and his father ran a diner in Kearney, Nebraska. For his part of the American dream, Peterson graduated from Northwestern University in 1947 and was hired by a market research firm in Chicago. While there he earned a graduate degree from the University of Chicago and returned to the market research firm as an executive vice president. He quickly outgrew this company. In 1953 he was hired as a director at the prestigious McCann-Erickson advertising agency, and the next year he was named the head of the Chicago office—remarkable for someone who at the time was only twenty-seven years old! Within a year the Chicago office was bringing in three-quarters of all of McCann-Erickson's new accounts. Two years later he was tempted with an offer to be a coordinator of half the country, with personal offices in New York and Chicago, and to be one of five on the board of directors. Peterson was poised to be one of two directors immediately beneath the head of the company, the renowned Marion Harper. And Peterson was still not yet thirty years old. But something happened that caused him to hold back from taking that step at McCann-Erickson.

As Peterson was poised to hit the big time, the halcyon days of the mid-1950s evaporated. Ad firms took a big hit in the ebbing economic climate. Cost-cutting measures were adopted and layoffs ensued. Even more belt tightening lay ahead for the industry, but McCann-Erickson CEO Marion Harper was focused on expanding the company, and he made some risky and questionable choices. Peterson viewed many of Harper's fiscal decisions as reckless, though he could do nothing to stop them.

While Peterson was a workaholic who paid dearly for his professional advancement with two divorces (one already before he joined McCann-Erickson), his workload did not lead him to do the unthinkable (namely, leave McCann-Erickson). Instead, it was a shocking lack of integrity shown by his boss. While one can abide occasional questionable decisions involving judgment from one's bosses, there comes a time when a line is crossed and there is no way back. For Peterson, that line was plagiarism.

In the course of doing his job, which included writing and speaking commitments, Peterson wrote an article on the future of advertising as he saw it. He speculated on how ad agencies should address the developing economic situation, particularly emphasizing how McCann-Erickson should move forward. In his 2009 autobiography, Peterson said, "I saw an increasing consumer-driven market economy, in which ad agencies needed to grow far beyond writing copy and producing TV commercials and get into things like product development, package design, and sales promotion."[10]

Prior to publication, Peterson sought feedback from his colleagues and distributed copies to peers. Naturally, he submitted a copy to McCann-Erickson CEO Harper. His co-workers quickly replied with positive reviews, but Peterson heard nothing from Harper. "I thought he might want to put it out under his own name," Peterson said. "He was the boss, after all, and it was his role to define the mission of the enterprise, as this piece tried to do."[11]

Still, he heard nothing from the CEO's office, even after seeking a response numerous times. "I began to believe he rejected the thinking in the piece, and just didn't want to hurt my feelings," Peterson commented.[12]

A few months later, Peterson saw his article in print in *Advertising Age,* an industry journal, with Harper's name as the author of the piece. Nothing had been changed in the article; it appeared word-for-word with only the author's name changed.

"I was appalled," Peterson wrote. "To have him do this—without the candor or courtesy of discussing it with me beforehand—was simply unacceptable. Marion Harper was a brilliant man, but I was convinced now that he lacked integrity. I knew I could never trust him again."[13]

After discussing the matter with his wife, Peterson decided to leave McCann-Erickson and informed Harper to expect his resignation. The timing was awkward because a major planning meeting was about to convene. When Peterson arrived from Chicago, Harper immediately ushered him into a private room. With no mention of the plagiarism incident, Harper praised Peterson for his accomplishments and informed him that he planned to make him the company's president, the number-two man in the firm. Despite the fact that this was his dream job, Peterson declined.

When the planning meeting convened, something astonishing happened: Harper announced that Peterson would be the president of McCann-Erickson! He then proceeded to have Peterson take a few bows in front of his peers. "I thought that his announcement displayed a fundamental character deficiency yet again," Peterson recalled. "His ego was so great that he could not imagine failing to get what he wanted."[14]

A short time later, Peterson left McCann-Erickson—his personal standards intact. "I'd never again work for a boss I did not both trust and admire, and with whom I did not share fundamental values," Peterson said.[15]

Standards can work both ways. Tom Hanks's standards attracted David McCullough, but Marion Harper's lack of standards repelled Peter Peterson. McCann-Erickson lost a major talent in Peterson, who proved to be one of the most respected and sought-after business professionals of his time. At the time of his departure, Peterson was like a young, unbridled thoroughbred with unlimited potential. How much farther this overachiever could have taken McCann-Erickson is anybody's guess.

It takes discipline to take the long view, as both General Myers and Peter Peterson did. It's a trait that you typically find in professionals—avoiding short-term expediency, always looking over the horizon. "We [at Blackstone] don't give a damn about quarter-to-quarter earnings," Peter Peterson said in an interview with Charlie Rose.[16] Blackstone refused to artificially manage its business to meet short-term targets—a very common (but often problematic) industry practice. Because of Peterson's high standards, smarts, and discipline, he won the trust and respect of some of the best talent in the industry and ultimately recruited them to Blackstone. Today, Blackstone is the world's largest private equity firm.

Like Peter Peterson, Kathy Ireland stands for something, namely, building a brand that families (busy moms especially) can trust. In chapter 8, I sketched out the story behind her company, kathy ireland WorldWide (kiWW), a design and marketing enterprise, and highlighted some of the successes she has achieved as an entrepreneur. When Kathy and I talked about her experiences at the helm of kiWW, she said, "I'm so proud of what our team has accomplished. So much of the credit for our success belongs to them. They work with me, not for me."[17]

Cynics may cringe at a statement like that, but this is no empty platitude. Company president and COO Stephen Roseberry has been with Kathy for more than twenty years. He noted, "Kathy has a servant's heart. She's completely authentic. There's not a phony bone in her body." Yet mistaking her authenticity for weakness would be a mistake. Roseberry, a savvy and hardened veteran of the rough-and-tumble retail scene, added, "For me, Kathy has redefined what it means to be tough. She knows what she wants for the business and passionately pursues it. She runs a tight ship, one's that very disciplined and based on her values and expectations. Believe me, those expectations cascade throughout the whole organization."[18]

At the same time, Rocco Ingemi, vice president for brand management, observed, "Kathy cares deeply about the organization and our people. We do everything as a team. Kathy sets the tone for that, and when there are problems, she has a unique ability to correct without criticizing. She's inspirational, supporting not only the greater organization, but showing care and concern for every member of our team. Kathy holds the belief that the organization is family."[19]

Roseberrry recalled a time when kiWW had encountered an inevitable rough patch. "We were brushing up against bankruptcy, and without a successful resolution, Kathy's Santa Barbara home was at risk. The staff was on edge. Undaunted, she gathered everyone together and reassured the staff that the company's best days lay ahead. That proved prophetic. Kathy has a gift for being able to bring people together during good times and bad. As a leader, she operates in rarified air. I'm constantly emulating what I learn from her. But as a leader, I won't reach her level. Few do."[20]

From the beginning, Kathy knew what she wanted to do: to build a powerful brand that would flourish over time. She took the long view and did not merely rely on her celebrity panache. It's working. Kathy has built a brand that has proven it *deserved* to win in the marketplace. Kathy, like John Bogle and Peter Peterson who have been chronicled earlier, knows that to build something truly special requires exacting standards of yourself and of your team.

Rise Above the Fray, Stay Focused, and Avoid Pointless Drama

The old adage says that we have two ears and one mouth and should use them in that proportion. I hear *lots* of stories in my line of work, and they are mostly about the especially maddening aspects of running a business. Few of them are about skirmishes in the marketplace; most of them are about skirmishes in the workplace. People issues mainly. And inevitably almost all the stories have an element of high drama: Stephanie was wronged, John and Judy aren't getting along, Tim undercuts Megan. After a while, I can even close my eyes—regardless of the industry, regardless of the firm, regardless of the geographic locale—and finish the stories myself. They're all so similar. There are two reasons I hear these stories so frequently. First, they're so prevalent. Second, they're especially maddening for senior leaders.

Recall the story that opens chapter 8 (Mind-Set 2): the CEO whose team was debilitated by internal contention. From the CEO's perspective, it was a pointless drama in that it robbed precious energy from more important priorities. The drama was an indicator of how far the *team* had strayed from the professional principles he expected from them. In addition, the unnecessary drama also was an indication that the *individuals* themselves did not consciously view themselves as professionals. Paraphrasing John Bogle, they had merely grafted their professional ideals onto their character but had not made them an integral part of their character. When professionals make professional ideals an integral part of their character, they are able to maintain their focus (especially when the heat's on), avoid the pointless drama that can accompany such situations, and rise above the fray when it matters most to handle things as a professional should.

John Adams: Visionary

Among our Founding Fathers, I find that John Adams demonstrated this mind-set at a critical time in the struggle for independence.[21]

When we think of the beginning of this country in Philadelphia in the summer of 1776, we think of the special generation of leaders who convened at Independence Hall. We call them the Founding Fathers, and we regard them as of one mind in their thinking and singular in their accomplishments. But this was not the case. In the fall of 1774, fifty-six of the most influential men in the colonies convened as the First Continental Congress to compile and submit a list of grievances to the British Crown in the hope that diplomacy would resolve the ten-year tension between the colonies and the mother country. No satisfactory response came from the other side of the Atlantic. So the Second Continental Congress (consisting mostly of the same men who had met in 1774) convened in May 1775, soon after the fateful shots were fired at Lexington and Concord, and a very slow course toward independence was charted, obstructed at first by the urgent need for congress to manage the war effort.

Independence was not a forgone conclusion, however. The firebrands for separation came mostly from New England (not surprisingly, since this was the scene of the Boston Tea Party and the armed confrontations at Lexington and Concord). Other parties counseled patience and further negotiation. Among their ranks were Pennsylvanians with pacifist Quaker backgrounds and Virginians who, as representatives of the largest and most profitable colony, were regarded as the appropriate congressional leaders.

Whose voices were foremost in the clamor for independence? Among the New Englanders was John Adams, the most eloquent and outspoken advocate of liberty to hold a seat in the congress. With him stood Pennsylvania's avuncular Benjamin Franklin and the tightlipped Thomas Jefferson of Virginia. When the topic of independence was occasionally mumbled in the hall, Adams saw that the congress was "about one-third Tories, and [one] third timid, and one third true blue." Indeed, six delegations had specific instructions from their governments not to vote for independence. The independence issue was further suppressed by those who continued to believe that the colonies could be reconciled with Britain. Yet Adams was steadfast on the issue of independence, having jotted it down among his priorities for the congress during his journey to Philadelphia prior to the first gavel.

Against these odds, Adams saw himself as the right man at the right time in the right place, and he decided to play out his role with all his intellect and energy. At no time, however, did his zeal reveal itself as anger toward his philosophical opponents. He charmed those he could, following the counsel of Franklin, since his seventy-year-old colleague cast a giant (but quiet) shadow among his colleagues. Initially Adams held back, wishing not to prejudice the issue of independence prematurely. Still, he lived by the view that all should "avow their opinions and defend them with boldness."

For the first few months Adams focused on the work of several committees to which his colleagues appointed him. They recognized "his integrity, his intellect, and [his] exceptional capacity for hard work," observed biographer David McCullough. So Adams bided his time.

Events slowly thinned the ranks of the timid until there were mostly advocates for independence and champions of reconciliation.

In January 1776 Thomas Paine's *Common Sense* helped many to distill their thoughts on independence, but Adams saw that this was not enough. In a letter he addressed his thoughts on the government that would come with independence and victory over Britain to a fellow congressman and then provided copies to others on request (particularly delegates from North Carolina and Virginia). One of the Virginia recipients had the letter published as a pamphlet. When winter turned to spring, three southern colonies sent instructions to their delegations to vote for independence.

On May 8, 1776, two British ships attempted to break through the river defenses thirty miles from Philadelphia. The two-day attack failed. On May 10, Adams knew the time had come. In concert with Richard Henry Lee of Virginia, he submitted a resolution that the colonies assume all the powers of their own governance. Three days of fierce debate followed. On May 15 the resolution was approved. On the same day the Virginia legislature sent instructions to its delegation at Philadelphia to support independence. Thus, on June 7, Lee of Virginia presented the resolution to the congress, and Adams seconded. Debate began the next day, with the few still in the timid camp succeeding in delaying a vote on the resolution for twenty days, which was to allow the middle colonies time to instruct their delegations. In the meantime, a declaration of independence was to be prepared by a committee of five that included Adams, Franklin, and Jefferson, with Jefferson preparing the first draft.

While the Virginian worked on the declaration, Adams attended to his duties with twenty-six committees, not the least of which was the board of war and ordnance, that is, keeping the armies supplied. David McCullough commented, "No one in Congress had worked harder or done more to bring about [independence]." The fruit of his labor was borne on June 23, when Pennsylvania instructed its delegation to support independence.

Still, the battle had to be waged on the floor of the Continental Congress on July 1. One last time Pennsylvanian John Dickinson opposed the resolution for independence. Speaking for independence was Adams. Debate began at 10 a.m. In keeping with the agreement that all congressional sessions were to be conducted secretly—because of the numerous British spies in Philadelphia—neither man's speech was transcribed. Dickinson's notes survive, however. In summary, he likened independence to a paper ship on a stormy sea.

When Adams rose to respond, the light rain tapping on the windows of the hall slowly grew into a storm of lightning and thunder. He spoke without notes, as was his habit, so that what we know of his speech comes to us only as he and others recalled it. But rather than his words, many recalled mostly the force of his delivery. McCullough described it as the "most powerful and important speech heard in Congress since it first convened, and the greatest speech of Adams's life."

He gave the speech not once but twice. Three delegates were an hour late in arriving and asked Adams to repeat his argument for them. At first Adams refused, but another delegate pointed out that only Adams had in mind the necessary bullet points for independence. Thus he presented his case a second time until the tardy gentlemen were satisfied. All in all he spoke for two hours and then yielded the floor to another seven hours of debate. That night a preliminary vote was taken, but four of the thirteen colonies held back. Rather than declare independence on the basis of the nine-vote majority, the delegates agreed to take a final vote the next day.

At the appointed hour, gentlemanly diplomacy swayed the final vote to a unanimous decision (with one colony abstaining). Adams's dogged determination for American independence had prevailed. Deliberations over the specific wording of the declaration occupied July 3, with Adams and Franklin sitting beside Jefferson, sometimes consoling him but always "fighting fearlessly for every word," recalled the Virginian. Thus congress did not approve the final wording until 11 a.m. on July 4.

The bottom line: Adams rose above the fray to tell his colleagues that the moment had come to recognize that the American colonies had, in fact, already separated from Great Britain. There was no going back; there was no status quo for them to return to. It was time to forge a new national destiny, not a colonial existence. The time had come for the American states to succeed or fail on their own terms. Thus, independence was the only option. Of course, independence came with a steep price. But they could settle for nothing less. He argued that this fight was necessary. It was a fight about destiny. And on that issue, they had to be resolute, steadfast. They had to prevail. In the end, his fellow delegates agreed.

Adams's argument carried the day. Imagine what might have happened if he had failed. How different would this country be today from what it is? Adams demonstrated that he could separate the essential (the opportunity for independence) from the trivial (settling for the status quo). He saw what a unique opportunity this was, and he was able to rise above the fray, consistently advancing his position and keeping his focus on independence amid the turmoil of debate. He never lost sight of what was most important. How important his actions were, we'll never truly understand nor fully appreciate.

Never Settling On Things That Matter Most

You may be thinking, what's the difference between Mind-Set 4 (personal standards) and the upcoming chapter on Mind-Set 5, which is about personal integrity? After all, wasn't Peter Peterson acting with integrity when he walked away from his dream job? Wasn't General Myers acting with integrity when he refused to have his book potentially impact the outcome of a presidential election? The short answer is, yes, both men were acting with integrity.

But what made these two stories so illustrative and impactful was the mind-set held by both men that *preceded* their tough calls. Their actions are consistent with their north arrow, their standards, which is an important measure of integrity.

However, as vitally important as integrity is, one must have standards *before* they can be acted upon—before you can actually live them (or defend them). So while personal standards and personal integrity clearly go hand in hand, standards precede integrity.

Thus, while inseparable, Mind-Set 4 (setting standards) precedes Mind-Set 5 (having the integrity to live by those same standards). And setting high standards is critical—at least if one desires to make a difference. Demonstrating integrity consistent with low standards is not terribly impactful—integrity with high standards is. **Have you ever**

noticed that when one speaks admirably of someone who has integrity, it's almost always someone with high standards?

Each individual highlighted in this chapter held themselves up to exacting personal standards, which, after all, is consistent with their mind-set. Each demonstrated why holding high standards and then living them is such a big deal. Our history books are replete with such difference makers—people who changed countries, industries, and societies.

What do others say about your standards? Are they weak-kneed or stellar? From your point of view, do your standards reflect mediocrity or excellence? How do you feel about your standards: ambivalent or proud?

In his blockbuster bestseller *Good to Great,* Jim Collins describes his discovery that great companies consistently hired the "right people on the bus" as a crucial starting point. In other words, first start with the right people (regardless of whether you know precisely what you're doing, let alone know how you'll go about doing it). From that crucial juncture, Collins suggests, you can figure out the rest.

When it comes to building a great company, one that truly represents excellence, Collins believes that the right people simply "won't settle for anything less."[22]

I began this chapter with a quotation about personal change from Tony Robbins, a well-known performance coach. Here's the complete quote: "Any time you sincerely want to make a [personal] change, the first thing you must do is to raise your *standards.* When people ask me what really changed my life eight years ago, I tell them that absolutely the most important thing was changing what I demanded of myself. I wrote down all the things I would no longer accept in my life, all the things I would no longer tolerate, and all the things that I aspired to becoming."

"Not settling" captures the essence of the standards mind-set. The standards one holds are an important measure of who you are. It signals to the world whether you're willing to settle or soar. After all, second-rate standards will not suffice in meeting first-rate objectives.[23] As we've learned, high standards attract other like-minded professionals. In an era of declining standards, you'll stand out by raising yours.

SUMMARY

- In an era of declining standards, people really stand out by remaining true to their highest standards. This involves taking the proverbial road less traveled.
- For leaders (anyone with a formal title) to build efficacy in conjunction with this mind-set, they must stand for something and have a purpose beyond just making money.
- One's standards often prove to involve the things that matter most to people. These include the most important things in their life (this includes one's values), and they often defy measurement (for example, character, wisdom, trust, and integrity).
- Professionals who have very high personal standards find it difficult to work with people (bosses especially) they don't both trust and admire or with whom they share certain fundamental values.
- This mind-set acts like a magnet for attracting talent. Likewise, the absence of high personal standards repels top-drawer people.
- Character and all that goes with it are what matters most when it comes to Mind-Set 4. Not surprisingly, character is also integral to Mind-Set 5 (the integrity mind-set covered in the next chapter).

CHAPTER **TEN**

MIND-SET **5**

Professionals Know That Personal Integrity Is All They Have

Integrity commits itself
to character over personal gain,
to people over things, to service over power,
to principle over convenience,
to the long view over the immediate.

—John C. Maxwell

Pro golfer J. P. Hayes's first disqualification of his career turned out to be a doozey—it left him ineligible to play full time on the PGA Tour in 2009.

While playing a sport that is self-policed, Hayes penalized himself out of a job at the 2008 PGA Tour Qualifying School (Q School) in McKinney, Texas. His error? Inadvertently playing a nonconforming golf ball.

On a par-three twelfth hole, Hayes asked his caddy for a new ball. After an uneventful tee shot and chip, Hayes marked his ball and picked it up. To his chagrin, he realized the ball in his hand was different from the ball he started play with—a clear violation of PGA rules. Hayes immediately called a penalty on himself. Consultation with a tournament official resulted in a two-stroke penalty.

Even with the two-stroke penalty, Hayes shot a 74. His 71 the next day put him in good shape to finish among the top twenty and advance to the Q School final a month later. For Hayes, a former PGA regular,

Q School represented his only chance to earn his exempt status and once again play with the big boys.

Unfortunately for Hayes, his troubles had only just begun.

After finishing his second round, and with a little downtime under his belt, it dawned on Hayes that the ball he played on the par-three twelfth might have been a nonconforming golf ball—a PGA no-no.

"It was a Titleist prototype, and somehow it had gotten into my bag," he said. "It had been four weeks since Titleist gave me some prototype balls and I tested them. I have no idea how or why it was still in there."

He could have said nothing. After all, the new prototype had not proven markedly better than the tried-and-true Titleist he was accustomed to playing.

But he didn't. The forty-there-year-old Hayes called a PGA official in Houston that night. They indicated that they would touch base with Titleist the following day.

"I pretty much knew at that point I was going to be disqualified," Hayes said. True to form, the PGA bounced Hayes from further competition.

Needless to say, Hayes's actions speak volumes about his character. After all, no one would have been the wiser had he remained silent. Plus, using the Titleist prototype provided no competitive advantage. Why let an arcane rule get in the way of realizing one's dream? Yet he spoke up. As desperately as Hayes wanted to play again on the PGA tour, he was unwilling to compromise his integrity.[1]

Many will find Hayes's story remarkable. Fifty years ago far fewer would have been surprised. Over the past half century, cultural standards have fallen like a rock. Conscience today is too often considered old-fashioned. Ethical shortcuts are commonplace. Winning often becomes the be-all and end-all.

Personal integrity involves doing what is difficult but needful. It's having the discipline to ensure that one's deeds match one's words. It's avoiding the temptation to communicate different messages to different audiences. It's having the humility to admit when we're wrong. It's having the courage to stick to your beliefs, even in the face of adversity. It's having the fortitude to walk away from a bad business deal even when you have a lucrative commission riding on it. Integrity requires action. It's not simply about holding high-minded values.

It has been said that integrity is the mother of many virtues. How true! For those holding this mind-set it's more about who they are as individuals and not about having to think about doing the right thing. In other words, people who hold this mind-set act naturally (and usually quickly) when faced with having to make a tough call. After all, it's who they are, and it's consistent with their character.

This chapter focuses on three important underpinnings of integrity:

- Authenticity and honesty
- Delivering on one's commitments (both explicit and implicit)
- Refusing to violate the trust others have extended to us

Perhaps more than any other mind-set, the integrity mind-set has the greatest potential to inspire trust.

Authenticity and Honesty

Professionals know that ethical standards (which are typically established by one's industry or by one's company or firm) have their place. They're quite useful, but they're the floor, not the ceiling, when it comes to how professionals conduct themselves. After all, there are not enough ethical standards in the world to stop the truly nefarious individual from acting out. Surely by now we've learned that no one can legislate virtue; ultimately, it comes down to the individual.

For instance, the practice of law has (at least on paper) an exceptionally high threshold when it comes to ethical standards. Some of these standards are set by individual firms, but many more are set within the profession's governing bodies. Yet, today, the public opinion of lawyers has never been lower—hovering at only 19 percent—just a notch above the bottom-dwelling media at 14 percent![2]

Former congressman Amory Houghton recalls the advice he received prior to taking over as CEO of Corning Glass: "Think of your decisions as being based on two concentric circles. In the outer circle are all the laws, regulations, and ethical standards with which the company must comply. In the inner circle are your core values. Just be darn sure that your decisions as CEO stay within your inner circle."[3]

Trusted professionals never rely solely on ethics to guide their actions. They never forget that it's how they individually show up that determines their credibility. What's ultimately at stake, of course, is whether or not they can be trusted. Will they practice situational ethics or hold themselves to a higher standard, one in which their integrity isn't compromised?

Acting from one's core values is being who you are. It's not about image or persona or the so-called personality ethic.[4] Bill George, former chairman and CEO of Medtronic, wrote a wonderful book titled *Authentic Leadership* about the power of authenticity. His book is directed at leaders, but its core principles are universal. Bill says: "Authentic leaders genuinely desire to serve others through their leadership. They are more interested in empowering the people they lead to make a difference than they are in power, money, or prestige for themselves. They are as guided by qualities of the heart, by passion and compassion, as they are by qualities of the mind. They lead with purpose, meaning, and values. Others follow them because they know where they stand."[5]

Authenticity inspires trust.

Honesty

We all know too well that honesty is the best policy. Our mothers knew why. Honesty enables clarity. Honesty diffuses contention. Honesty builds rapport. Honesty prevents suspicion. Honesty enables productivity. Honesty brings peace of mind. Honesty avoids confusion. Honesty eliminates clutter. But, most important, honesty inspires trust.

During his second term, President Ronald Reagan's administration was tarnished by the Iranian arms-for-hostages controversy. For weeks Reagan fervently denied that he had ever authorized trading arms for the release of six American hostages being held in Lebanon—a practice he stated he was vehemently against. However, he later learned that some members of his administration failed to follow that policy and did, in fact, trade arms for the hostages' release.

In a March 4, 1987, address to the nation, the president stated: "First, let me say, I take full responsibility for my actions and for those of my administration. As angry as I may be about activities undertaken without my knowledge, I am still accountable for those activities. As disappointed as I may be in some who served me, I'm still the one who must answer to the American people for this behavior. . . . A few months ago I told the American people I did not trade arms for hostages. My heart and my best intentions still tell me that's true, but the facts and evidence tell me it is not. . . . It was a mistake."[6]

Many consider this address to be one of the defining moments of Reagan's presidency as it revealed both humility and integrity. Coming clean in such a manner defuses tension and helps cut through the clutter of an otherwise contentious situation. It turns negative energy into positive energy.

On a much smaller scale, I had a similar experience. An important client—a senior executive at one of the world's largest accounting firms—asked me to address his extended team on some key points of my first book, *The Big AHA!* Given the strife and contention within the department, which principally involved some nasty personal issues, the senior executive hoped that my presentation would help their many corrective measures. My address was to be a part of the department's two-day offsite event designed to tackle these issues head-on.

The Big AHA! illustrates how each of us is susceptible to developing an emotionally supercharged view (something I call a telescopic view) of someone that contributes to another's failure. The phenomenon is insidiously subtle; it is a trap that virtually everyone (no matter how smart, how sophisticated, or how well intended) falls into. Realizing that you've fallen into the trap is, for most, a humbling experience as you recognize you've contributed (usually unknowingly) to a colleague's downfall.

Emotionally supercharged views permeated this particular department, many of which were directed at the senior executive himself. This was a result of some necessary but unpopular decisions rendered by the executive during a rough patch the business experienced. The churn within the department, though, had gone on far too long—nearly eighteen months. My message was ideal for this audience. But there was a question as to whether they would respond.

The address went well enough. For forty-five minutes we had a thoughtful, lively discussion, which wasn't so simple, considering that 125 people were involved. During my remarks, it became clear that the attendees had, at one time or another, fallen into the trap I was describing. In some instances this concerned family members and neighbors as well as co-workers. There were plenty of aha's—many of which were linked to heartfelt business issues. (I love when that happens!) We achieved traction.

In closing, the senior executive joined me on the platform and said: "When I became familiar with Bill's work, I dug in and really learned a lot. I thought you would too. You obviously did. Thank you for your honesty and thoughtful comments. I gained some new perspectives."

"I must tell you—and I'm ashamed to admit it—what you heard about this morning, what Bill referred to as a telescopic view, I've done that. I've fallen into that trap. In fact, I've compromised several of you. At some level I suspect this has contributed to some of the problems we currently face. I am truly sorry. Please forgive me. I promise it won't happen again."

This senior executive acknowledged before 125 people that he had failed several of them. The acknowledgment was out of character. I didn't know this was coming.

After he finished speaking, you could have heard a pin drop in the room. It was a little like being at your first boy-girl dance: no one knew what to do. Finally, he and I exited the stage, as there was a natural break in the program.

Then something remarkable happened. People inundated this senior executive with handshakes, backslaps, and other expressions of admiration. Within five minutes of our leaving the stage, it was difficult to carry on a conversation over the din in the conference center.

The logjam had broken. The event proved to be the catalyst for the department to begin healing. Honesty (along with its ability to diffuse contention and build rapport) had won out again. Most important, though, honesty inspired trust.

Please note that I had not coached the senior executive to say what he did. He did it on his own. His message was heartfelt. He was being authentic. He revealed his strength of character by publicly correcting a private wrong. And his people responded.

This story also helps us answer the question, How does one know when the integrity mind-set has really become a part of who we are? A big clue in answering that question resides in the speed of one's decisions involving this mind-set.

For instance, the senior executive sized up his situation and decided on the spot to say what he did. He didn't go through a lot of mental gymnastics or engage in endless self-debate about what he should do. Rather, he did it, and he did it quickly. It showed that the integrity mind-set was a part of who he had become.

Likewise, consider my colleague from chapter 5 who turned down a lucrative last-minute assignment with a A-list client after having previously committed to another client for the same dates. That decision took only ten seconds for her to make. She knew immediately what she needed to do, which was to honor her original commitment. Such decisions are not merely an intellectual exercise. She felt compelled to honor her original commitment. Her ten-second response time was validation of her integrity mind-set.

Honesty can also bring a much-needed element of reconciliation between individuals. Consider this interaction between two heads of state.

Harry S. Truman succeeded Franklin D. Roosevelt as president upon the latter's death in 1945. Truman, a simple, plainspoken man from Missouri, was considered by many to be an inadequate choice as president—especially when he was contrasted with the iconic Roosevelt. Unbeknownst to Truman, Winston Churchill was one such detractor. Imagine Truman's surprise in 1952 when Churchill acknowledged these early feelings and said, "I must confess, sir, I held you in very low regard. I loathed your taking the place of Franklin Roosevelt. I misjudged you badly. Since that time you, more than any man, have saved Western civilization."[7]

Talk about actions speaking louder than words. Truman's administration shaped world events for the next fifty years by focusing on containment rather than confrontation. And in the end, the small man from Missouri cast as large a shadow over the globe as did the magisterial

Churchill who had guided his country through the tumultuous years of World War II. The British prime minister realized that he had misjudged his American counterpart, and a friendship ensued as close as that which he had enjoyed with Roosevelt.

Delivering on One's Commitments (Both Explicit and Implicit)

The senior partner stressed the importance of client trust to the younger men and women of the law firm. When one ambitious lawyer asked how to go about winning trust, the senior partner said dryly, "Try being trustworthy." This story, shared by John W. Gardner, really captures the essence of the subject.[8]

Such a big part of being trustworthy is keeping commitments. Whether it's living up to the terms of a contract, meeting a critical deadline in support of a colleague's project, or coming through on a promise made to a client, it all reflects our trustworthiness. It's walking the talk. Saying you'll do something (think: explicit commitment) is an easy way for others to keep score as to whether we're credible (and trustworthy).

Implicit commitments, on the other hand, are much more subtle and not so easy to keep score on. Whenever

- a leader says, "I believe that business development is our ticket to a brighter future,"
- the company's value statement says, "We trust our employees to do the right thing,"
- an IT manager says, "This initiative is the department's foremost priority,"
- an individual contributor says, " My most important developmental area is interpersonal communication,"

it's implied that an appropriate commitment will follow. Lofty statements plus commitment ensure validity. Too often I've heard similar assertions (especially from leaders) that simply never result in action and are ultimately received by employees (or clients) as meaningless platitudes. An explicit commitment is to a full-blown chorus of New

Zealand tuis (unbelievably impressive songbirds) what an implicit commitment is to a gaggle of hummingbirds. One gets your attention; the other doesn't.

It's about living the rhetoric. It's about follow-through. Individuals (especially leaders) who don't live up to their implied commitments will ultimately pay a steep price for their hollow words. For an implicit commitment to carry any weight, time and energy (and sometimes guts) are required to show others that you're invested in the process.

Was That Mark Zuckerberg Crying in the Men's Room?

When Facebook's membership reached a half million users in 2004, the company's twenty-year-old CEO, Mark Zuckerberg, realized they'd have to raise some serious money to keep up with the company's growing infrastructure requirements. The short-term thinking of Silicon Valley's venture capital moneymen—likely candidates to provide Facebook's funding—bothered him to no end.[9]

Enter Donald Graham, chief executive officer and chairman of the board of the Washington Post Company, who was introduced to the social-media pioneer by one of Zuckerberg's Harvard classmates. Graham and Zuckerberg quickly struck up a friendship in spite of a significant difference in their ages. After concluding that Facebook was "simply a stunning business idea" and learning about their need for capital, Graham made Zuckerberg "an investment offer more spontaneously than any he has made before or since."

Zuckerberg was blown away by Graham's approach because it was so different, influenced largely by Graham's long-term perspective. And it was so unlike Silicon Valley's hard-nosed venture capital community—one whose thinking was too often short-term in nature. Graham's thinking was larger than life, epic in scale and game changing in magnitude. The difference in culture was palpable. Zuckerberg, speaking of Graham, commented, "Wow, I want to be more like this guy."

Zuckerberg and Graham had a handshake deal. Trouble was, Zuckerberg was about to get a better offer—a much better offer. The dilemma was twofold. First, the offer came from a dreaded venture capitalist, and second, he had given his word to Graham about the deal. Zuckerberg grew uneasy over dinner the night the venture capital deal was presented. He excused himself and went to the rest room—and stayed there for an uncomfortably long time.

Finally, Matt Cohler, a Facebook executive, went to check on Zuckerberg and found him sitting on the floor of the men's room and crying. Cohler said, "Through his tears, he was saying, "This is wrong. I can't do this. I gave my word!"

Cohler calmed down Zuckerberg and suggested he call Graham in the morning to talk it out. He did. "Don," he said, "I haven't talked to you since we agreed on terms, and since then I've had a much higher offer from a venture firm out here. And I feel I have a moral dilemma."

Graham, while initially taken back, was also impressed. "I just thought to myself, 'Wow, for twenty years old, that is impressive—he's not calling to tell me he's taking the other guy's money. He's calling me to talk it out.'" Graham knew he was already at his limit, and he was not willing to sweeten his offer.

"Mark," he asked, "does the money matter to you?"

It did. The extra capital ($6 million) would keep Facebook in the black without having to borrow money. That was good enough for Graham.

"I'll release you from your moral dilemma," said Graham. "Go ahead and take their money and develop the company and all the best."

It was a huge relief for Zuckerberg. He eventually asked the publisher to take a seat on the Facebook board, having even greater respect and admiration for Graham than before.

That capital infusion enabled the company to hire new staff and add new features that attracted millions of additional users. As of the summer of 2010, Facebook had nearly five hundred million users.

Zuckerberg proved himself trustworthy in Graham's eyes by avoiding the temptation to simply take the money and run. As CEO he had to do right by his company, but he also had to live up to his earlier commitment to Graham—a delicate balancing act for a seasoned executive, let alone for an overwhelmed twenty-year-old being courted by some of the world's biggest business moguls. Despite his initial angst (and with the help of some coaching), Zuckerberg eventually dealt with the issue head-on and consistently with his earlier commitment. Echoing Graham's sentiments—yes, that's impressive indeed!

A Diminutive World-Beater

Frances Hesselbein's Park Avenue office is a patchwork of eye-catching wall-mounted memorabilia: cherished photos, world-class awards, twenty honorary degrees, and other impressive certificates. While Frances's physical stature is diminutive, her interpersonal stature is off the charts. The memorabilia—principally representing more than fifty years of involvement in the nonprofit sector—represents her association with U.S. presidents, champions of industry, renowned leadership gurus, and world-renowned universities.

Frances has unparalleled credibility. Peter Drucker once called her the greatest executive he has ever known. Frances knows a thing or two about commitment. Her longtime friend Marshall Goldsmith notes: "I have seen her turn down an invitation from the Chief of Staff of The U.S. Army because she promised to give a talk (at no fee) for a nonprofit organization in a small town. When she makes a commitment, if it is humanly possible to be there, she delivers. It doesn't matter that a better deal came along later." Credibility indeed!

Frances has a unique appreciation of the important role culture plays in an organization's success. She describes it as "the beliefs and values practiced by an organization." She also knows that an organization's avowed beliefs and values are tantamount to an implicit commitment of support for those same beliefs and values on a much larger canvas. For Frances, anything short of that support is a breach of organizational trust and a demonstration of a lack of integrity on the part of the organization's leadership.

In Frances's world, living up to her beliefs and values is a requirement, not an option. As CEO of the Girl Scouts of the U.S.A., Frances believed strongly that preparation in crisis management could help to avoid an all-out catastrophe that might mortally injure an organization. An episode during the 1983 cookie drive illustrates just how prescient she was.

Soon after the cookie drive began, a man went on local television in a mid-west community and claimed to have found a pin in a Girl Scout cookie. When asked where the cookie was, he said that he had eaten it. When asked if he still had the box for the cookies, he said that he had thrown it away. Nevertheless, he was given air time to tell his story of the pin in one of the cookies. It was a hoax. But within a week, there were three hundred stories of people who claimed to have found a pin or needle in their cookies.

Product tampering burst onto the national scene in 1982 and received massive media scrutiny when seven people in Chicago died after cyanide-laced Tylenol appeared on some store shelves. While the case has never been solved, one outcome was the development of anti-tampering packaging. Thus began a series of name-brand tamperings that threatened to destroy the reputations of the companies involved. Shortly after news stories appeared with a new tale of tampering, a spate of allegations followed, and company spokesmen appeared to address the public's fear and explain the steps being taken to resolve the situation.

When allegations were made about the pin in the Girl Scout cookies, Frances contacted Jim Burke, the CEO of Johnson and Johnson who had so effectively handled the 1982 Tylenol crisis. She said to him, "You've given all of us inspiration by the way you handled your crisis. I was wondering if you could give me some advice." Burke replied, "I'll do better than that. I'll send you the three vice presidents who were responsible for the handling of that crisis," and he asked who she was using to address the public relations aspect for the Girl Scouts. When she told him, he said, "You don't need my people. He's the best in the world."

Coincidentally, months before and for reasons she can't remember, Francis had organized a crisis-management session for the organization. "Don't ask me why I did it at that time rather than later that year," she said, "but I trained 335 local council executives and 100 national staff members in crisis management. When this crisis hit only a few months later, we all knew what to do. For three days the FDA inspected the five factories where the cookies were made, and the FDA's findings gave us a clean bill of health, stating quite bluntly that the alleged pins could not have come from the cookie factories."

Despite the FDA's findings, more claims of pins in cookies were made. So the FBI made a public service address to inform everyone that the penalty for copycat crimes of this nature was five years in jail and a $25,000 fine. Immediately the claims stopped, but the damage had been done.

"This all had occurred at the height of our cookie sale, yet we continued with the sale" Frances recalled. "The next year cookie sales were down and membership was down a little. But two years later, we had huge increases in both cookie sales and membership. I attribute this remarkable jump to our efforts in crisis management."[10]

As the organization's leader, Frances had told her people that sooner or later they would come face to face with a significant crisis, something that could easily shake the organization to its core. Thus it was imperative that they address the issue of crisis management. And then she followed through on her implicit commitment and scheduled the training. As it turned out, this was well in advance of the season of product tamperings that occurred in the mid-1980s. The Girl Scouts were well equipped to handle the crisis without suffering a massive decline in the organization's reputation. Her follow-through is a sign of her integrity.

Professionals demonstrate their integrity surrounding commitment in the following ways:

- They do not abandon a commitment—even in the face of political expediency or a better deal.
- They are just as committed to please a small client as a prestigious one.
- They conscientiously deliver on their professional commitments, even when it's personally inconvenient.
- They don't expect others to bail them out from the consequences of their own sometimes ill-advised actions.
- Their public declarations of merit translate into commitment, meaning that time, energy, and resources are appropriately prioritized and invested in.

Refusing to Violate the Trust Others Have Extended to Us

Professionals refuse to violate the trust others have extended to them. They know that any violation (1) takes advantage of the vulnerability of the person or group who invested trust in them and (2) it dishonors the goodwill on which trust is based. This is important to everyone, but it is especially critical for leaders.

Sometime ago my wife and I set up a family trust. As part of the process, we selected an executor—someone who would faithfully attend to our affairs (as outlined in the trust) should we be unable to do so. This includes handling all of our finances as well as custody issues involving our children. For my wife and I, we're imparting to a third party the most important things in our lives and hoping that our wishes will be honored in our absence. In short, it's vulnerability on steroids. No wonder it's referred to as a "trust." After careful consideration, we chose an executor who we believed would honor the extraordinary trust we placed in him.

To a lesser degree, all of us do this all the time. We all need people to do the things that we can't do for ourselves because we lack the opportunity, influence, expertise, temperament, time, or authority to do so.

At a hospital, we approve a doctor's treatment recommendations for a very sick family member. At a repair shop, we hire a mechanic to maintain our technologically advanced car. In civil affairs, we collectively grant representation privileges to our politicians.

Details aside, what we're really doing is extending trust. We're asking someone to do for us what we cannot do for ourselves. In doing so, we're vulnerable because we've become dependent on others. Along with that vulnerability comes an implied expectation that we won't be exploited. In other words, we expect to be treated fairly and, in the end, that we won't ever regret extending trust in the first place.

Years ago, for instance, I retained counsel for an obscure legal matter. Because I had no knowledge of the law, I had no idea whether my attorney's approach to settling the case was taking an express lane (minimizing my legal fees) or taking a slow boat to China (padding his billable hours). Of course, I expected that he'd successfully settle the case and minimize my cost. To this day, I have no good sense of whether his fees were reasonable or not. The fact that I raise the question, however, suggests I have my doubts.

It's one thing to extend trust; it's another to be the recipient of it.

My promotion to director quite early in my corporate career was an unexpected but pleasant surprise. Two of us were finalists: the natural (a guy with more experience and better suits) and me (the upstart). The executive who hired me went with his instincts. I knew he took a big chance, politically speaking, in picking me. Talk about extending trust! I was confident in my capabilities but nervous about letting him down. I quickly vowed I'd never give him a reason to regret his decision. He never did.

Each of us is the recipient of extended trust. In the workplace, managers extend trust by providing special assignments to employees, leaders extend trust by supporting a struggling employee, and colleagues extend trust by sharing confidences. To be considered trustworthy, it's imperative to honor those who extend trust to us in the first place. It's what professionals do.

Today, unfortunately, trust seems to be violated much more readily and to a greater degree. Each day's headlines seem to bring yet another salacious tragedy of people who proved themselves untrustworthy. Such violations are commonplace:

- Consultants who maximize a client's billable hours rather than minimize them.
- Managers who play favorites and ignore merit.
- Politicians who kick national problems down the road rather than act responsibly.
- Educators who teach students what to think instead of how to think.
- Journalists who slant their news stories through the lens of their personal bias.
- Salesmen who push products that bring the largest commissions rather than meet their clients' real needs.
- Attorneys who use the law as a weapon rather than a tool.
- Colleagues who fail to keep confidences rather than honor them.

In fact, those who violate the trust that has been extended to them (as in each of the examples above) undermine their own credibility and breed cynicism in others. Trusted professionals use their knowledge, power, and influence to advance the needs of their clients or organization, not to inappropriately line their pockets, perpetuate their power, advance a personal agenda, or enhance their ego. The trusted professional, as the saying goes, "does well by doing good."

A word of caution to leaders: you hold a vital (and in some cases sacred) trust, so live up to it. This is especially important because, for many of you, the people you're leading did not choose you to lead them. Never forget that a governing board, a senior executive, parish or council chose you. They extended trust to you. The people you're supposed to be leading are desperately hoping (and sometimes praying) that you are worthy of the trust you've been granted. And it's not always a unanimous decision. Some of those so-called followers will extend their trust to you (think: goodwill), others won't (think: show me).

In discharging your responsibilities, you'll have access to a great deal of confidential information; information you're not at liberty to talk about publicly. You'll make decisions that aren't (and often shouldn't be) immediately transparent. You can make or break people's lives and careers. Because of this vulnerability, some of the people you'll be leading will be dubious of your leadership. Outwardly, they have to go along with you, but surreptitiously they may hold back or even work against you. Remember, they don't know what you know. As a result, you'll have to earn their trust.

In the case of my attorney, I selected him. As such, any violation of trust by my attorney also was (to some degree) a personal indictment of me as well. After all, I had hired him. I could have hired someone else—someone who would prove to be more trustworthy.

It's bad enough when *we* extend trust to someone who violates it. But worse yet is a leader who violates the trust of his followers who, in the first place, had virtually no voice in selecting the leader. This is a betrayal of the worst kind and cannot help but evoke powerful feelings of helplessness among those who follow. It's no small wonder that betrayals of trust are one of the most egregious ways to impugn one's own integrity.

Frances Hesselbein shared with me her observations on the general temperament of the country today. She said: "Today we are experiencing the highest level of cynicism and lowest level of trust in my whole lifetime. A democracy becomes unsustainable under such conditions!" She's right, of course. A democracy's financial, political, and legal institutions all depend on trust. Without trust, a democracy's future is in peril.

Contrast today's cynicism against the awe-inspiring contribution Alexander Hamilton made to our nation's founding. Of the pantheon of Founding Fathers, Hamilton stands out to me. A while ago I came across a George Will column that helped me put in context Hamilton's impressive contributions to our country. Will pointed out: "There is an elegant memorial in Washington to [Thomas] Jefferson, but none to Hamilton. However, if you seek Hamilton's monument, look around. You are living in it. We honor Jefferson, but [we] live in Hamilton's country, a mighty industrial nation with a strong central government."

Hamilton was not born in this country, but rather on the island of Nevis in the Caribbean. Thus, when the founders gathered in Philadelphia to craft a national government, Hamilton could do so without the baggage of exceptional preference for the legacy of his colony or state. Instead, he could envision the priority of the federal government over the states and also see the states as creators of the federal government.[11]

Hamilton's stateless heritage and non-landholder status allowed him to maintain a wide-ranging perspective on the scope and powers of a strong central government in balance with the sovereignty of the individual states. He had seen the chaos of the Articles of Confederation and knew that the federal government needed to go far beyond states' rights while at the same time respecting those rights. And he knew that the greatest problem the states faced was the debt each had incurred during the Revolutionary War.

After the adoption of the Constitution in 1788 and the election of George Washington to the presidency in 1789, Washington selected Hamilton as the first secretary of the treasury. One of Hamilton's initial proposals was that the federal government absorb each state's debt in addition to the national debt incurred under the Articles of Confederation. This was a boon to many, but there were a few—mostly southern—states that had retired most of their war debt. To persuade the South to accept this idea, Hamilton agreed to relocate the national capital from New York to Philadelphia to the Maryland-Virginia border. Again, Hamilton had no favorites in this action, even though by then he had married into a wealthy New York family.

(Interestingly, Hamilton was no freeloader. He declined his father-in-law's offers of financial assistance and insisted that he alone provide for his family. It helped, of course, that he practiced law in New York City before and after his term as secretary of the treasury. But he never made a tremendous amount of money.)

Hamilton's next hurdle was the idea of a central bank and a slate of taxes and tariffs to fund the federal government. Thomas Jefferson was an outspoken opponent of a central bank, and he based his argument on a strict interpretation of the Constitution. Jefferson had an agrarian view of the future of the country, which is fine if you happen to be one of the landed aristocracy with thousands of acres and a huge labor force to maintain everything. Hamilton countered that, although the Constitution did not define a national bank, neither did it define the construction of the national economy. The need existed, and the Constitution empowered the federal government to address it. The bank was created—but it did not last very long. (Jefferson's administration quashed it, Andrew Jackson's administration eliminated it, it was briefly revived in the 1850s, and then fully reestablished in the 1860s.)

This economic friction involved the growing divide between the agricultural southern and the burgeoning industrialization of the northern states. Hamilton viewed commerce and urbanization as the country's future. Plus it carried the added consequence of benefiting the majority of the people, not just the landowning class. This greater good was his goal.

He also proposed protectionist laws to aid the growth of fledgling industries. Congress, however, did not implement them.

Of course Hamilton had his imperfections, but even his detractors agree that Hamilton possessed extraordinary administrative abilities and that he had no peer in understanding financial systems in the 1790s. As secretary of the treasury, he outlined the structure of the nation's banks, commerce, and manufacturing industries. For his many contributions to the economic structure of the country, Hamilton is called the father of American capitalism and the patron saint of Wall Street. Jefferson, perhaps Hamilton's greatest adversary, said of his esteemed colleague, "We can pay off his debts in fifteen years, but we can never get rid of his financial system."

Still, despite his legacy, you'd think that someone with Hamilton's access and influence as the primary architect of the U.S. economy could easily have been one of the wealthiest individuals of the founding era. After all, he advocated the idea of patronage and endorsed speculative practices, all of which tolerated certain elements of corruption and favoritism (think payoffs). But the only fortune Hamilton knew was that which came from his law practice. In short, he was no Bill Gates or Warren Buffett—financially speaking.

Contrast that against what so many so-called public servants do today. After leaving office (or sometimes during), they reap a financial harvest, benefiting from rules and regulations with their fingerprints on them. Perhaps more than any public official in our history Hamilton could have reaped a king's ransom from his knowledge of the financial system that he devised. Yet, remarkably, he did not personally take advantage of his position (nor violate the trust that was extended to him)—a lesson that many latter-day politicians would do well to emulate.

When Hamilton resigned as secretary of the treasury, George Washington expressed his thanks in a letter dated February 2, 1795, which included this observation: "In every relation, which have borne to me, I have found that my confidence in your talents, exertions, and integrity, has been well placed." Nice praise from the first president of the United States, who himself knew a little something about integrity.

Hamilton's legacy remains all around us: America's status as the world's leading commercial superpower. In tribute, his image appears on the ten-dollar bill.

Integrity Rules

When one thinks about the seven mind-sets of the trusted professional, the integrity mind-set is perhaps the most intuitive and the most obvious.

It's easy to trust someone who has integrity. Hamilton is a case in point. Yet with today's declining cultural standards, it's proving increasingly difficult to count on people to act with integrity consistently. Perhaps that's why our era is called one of distrust. Fortunately, we have a host of current and historical examples from which to draw inspiration and important lessons.

Gen. Richard Myers recently told me about Gen. Henry H. "Hap" Arnold. The general pointed out that the U.S. Army has produced only five five-star generals, and Hap Arnold was one of them. (The others are George Marshall, Douglas MacArthur, Dwight D. Eisenhower, and Omar Bradley.) Few would have predicted that Arnold—a major in the military doldrums of the 1920s—would ever attain that rank. It wasn't as if Arnold did not have talent. He had plenty. He was a pioneer of aviation, an aeronautical whiz kid, and he had even trained under the tutelage of Orville and Wilbur Wright.

Arnold's military service had been stellar. In fact, Hap was chosen to attend the prestigious Command and General Staff School (CGSS) at Fort Leavenworth. At the time, to advance in the service, one had to attend CGSS. Not many did. "Attending CGSS was a big deal," General Myers emphasized. "Only one thing stood between Arnold and CGSS: Billy Mitchell. In the early 1920s Mitchell was a passionate, outspoken brigadier general who was politically sideways with the army brass and eventually faced court-martial for his efforts to promote air power among the branches of service. The charge? Truthfully, he was viewed by his superiors as a heretic!"

When Mitchell was court-martialed in December 1925, his staff officers were warned not to support Mitchell's claims. General Myers added: "Arnold's superiors said, 'Listen, if you testify on behalf of Billy Mitchell, you'll lose your slot at CGSS, and we'll send you somewhere else.' Arnold knew that Mitchell, whose call for the dramatic expansion of America's fledgling airpower antagonized many senior military leaders, was anything but a heretic. Instead of doing the politically correct thing—one that would ensure his slot at CGSS—Arnold testified based on what he knew to be true about Mitchell. His testimony, in effect, supported Mitchell."

Arnold's testimony did not derail the military court's eventual censure of Mitchell. After Mitchell was found guilty, he subsequently resigned his commission. The army, meanwhile, monitored the officers who had vocally supported Mitchell. These junior officers continued to propagate Mitchell's message, and Arnold was singled out as an example and threatened with court-martial if he did not resign. Hap opted for a court-martial, but the army shied away from the threat, given the bad publicity of Mitchell's court-martial. "Predictably," General Myers said, "Arnold's spot in CGSS was withdrawn, and he was immediately reassigned to Fort Riley, Kansas."

Arnold took his punishment and reported to Fort Riley—a cavalry post far from any aviation activity. Although he continued to hold the rank of major, his banishment to the cavalry post and his contrarian reputation with the senior leadership did not lend themselves well to any prospect of enhancing Hap's military career.

In 1927 Arnold participated in the founding of Pan American Airways, and one of the partners pressed him to accept the presidency of the company. General Myers recalled that, without any hesitation, Hap replied, "You know, that's very flattering, but I think there's more I can give to this country."

General Myers observed, "For a major who has just been reprimanded and exiled to Fort Riley, this clearly wasn't the horizon he saw for himself. So Arnold passes on this wonderful opportunity at precisely the time he'd be most vulnerable to jump ship. Rather than waiver, he sticks to his values. Remarkably, he ends up being the chief of the air corps and leading the air forces in World War II. Hap ultimately was the only person to ever be a five-star general in two branches of the service."[12]

Integrity indeed!

SUMMARY

- Ethical standards are the floor, not the ceiling, when it comes to how professionals should conduct themselves.
- Personal integrity and being a true professional go hand in hand. You can't have one without the other.
- The integrity mind-set holds the greatest potential to inspire trust.
- True professionals use their knowledge, power, and influence to advance the needs of their clients or organization, not to inappropriately line their pockets, expand their power, advance a personal agenda, or enhance their ego.
- Honesty is a foundational underpinning of integrity that is essential for cutting through interpersonal and organizational clutter.
- Individuals, especially leaders, who don't live up to their commitments (especially their all too subtle implicit commitments) pay a steep credibility price.
- Betrayal of someone's trust is one of the most egregious ways to impugn your own integrity.
- The speed of your decisions in upholding your values is a key indicator as to whether the integrity mind-set is an integral part of your character.

CHAPTER **ELEVEN**

MIND-SET 6

Professionals Aspire to Be Masters of Their Emotions, Not Enslaved by Them

The only true victories in life are victories over ourselves.

—Paul Orfalea

Some of you may have leapfrogged ahead to this chapter. I'm not surprised. Mind-Set 6 is one of the most difficult, if not *the* most difficult, for people to feel confident in. The smarter you think you are, the more successful you believe yourself to be the more you need to read this chapter.

The first five mind-set chapters dealt with emotions, largely in implicit ways. In this chapter we'll deal with emotions explicitly. That said, I recognize that there have been untold volumes written on the why and the how of managing one's emotions.

Our aim here is to capture the essence of what it means for professionals to achieve mastery of their emotions. Notice I said mastery, not perfection. Mastery of one's emotions produces three especially important by-products. Each is essential in inspiring trust in others:

- Professionals are respecting when it's difficult to be respectful.
- Professionals maintain their objectivity and keep their wits about them.

- Professionals manage their ego and resist the urge for immediate gratification.

Let's be clear, emotions aren't bad. After all, our emotions "wind us up and make us go."[1] Trust is an emotion. Trust is a good emotion. Trust, as we've discussed earlier, is emotional glue.

Some would have you believe that professionals should be dispassionate. Please disregard that notion. The passion you have for your work, your values, your ideas, and your people is wonderful. Keep those emotions alive. Feed them. But keep in mind that emotional consistency is important.[2] People distrust those who exhibit emotional extremes.

Still, you have to watch out for emotions (especially negative emotions) that advance victimhood and promote self-righteousness. As author C. Terry Warner has noted, "One sign of the immature mind is the ease and frequency it feels offended."[3] Emotions, as we have learned through sad experience, can trip us up and make smart people dumb.[4]

There are two important points I want to make here: (1) each of us is responsible for our emotional reactions to experiences and people[5] and (2) we alone are responsible for our external responses to those internal emotional reactions.

Events trigger emotions. This is an automatic reaction—or that's what most people believe. But that's not really the way it works. Rather, emotions are determined by what we think about the event, not by the event itself. In other words, our interpretation of an event ultimately becomes the precursor to the emotion we experience. Simply put: emotions are self-induced.[6]

Thus, to be master of one's emotions is to master one's constructive thinking. As renowned psychologist Seymour Epstein said, "It is one thing to suppress the expression of an unwanted emotion or impulse and quite another not to have the emotion or impulse in the first place." Constructive thinking enables that level of mastery![7] This is what enables especially effective leaders to remain calm in a crisis while others are swept up in the moment.

Regarding our external responses, putting aside for the moment the question of whether an emotion is appropriate or not, how we respond to our emotional reactions often separates the professionals from the wannabes.

Because this mind-set is so challenging, I used the word *aspire* to signify strong and personal intent. Let's face it. This one's tough. Each of us is likely to have occasional trouble with this mind-set, given its nature. Inevitably we'll fall short. But remembering our intent will help us to pick ourselves up and try again.

Professionals Are Respecting When It's Difficult to Be Respectful

In chapter 13 respect will be discussed in some detail, but here I am going to focus on one especially important aspect of respect: the importance for professionals to universally demonstrate respect to all people—even those who aren't worthy of it.

Virtually every organization that has developed a values statement (at least one worth its salt) has included respect as an essential element. Given that respect is a basic human value, it shouldn't be surprising that it shows up so consistently and prominently in so many organizational statements. Yet I believe there's another reason, which is the near-universal lack of respect currently demonstrated in the workplace. Sometimes it's blatant, sometimes it's subtle, but in every case it's a plague.

It's pretty natural to respect someone who sees the world the way you do. It's also natural to be respectful to someone who (1) you think deserves it, (2) you like, or (3) happens to hold common values with you. It's important to remember that respect is an emotion. So having positive, affirming feelings of respect toward someone makes it a natural, effortless experience.

There's no tried-and-true formula to determine whether someone is worthy or not of our respect. Individually, respect is very intuitive and ultimately very subjective. Two people who have had similar experiences with a third person may draw a different conclusion as to whether that person is worthy of their respect.

One would hope there would be some level objectivity in determining whether someone is worthy or not of our respect. For instance, did the individual *earn* our respect? If so, how? In the end, though, there's no guarantee of objectivity when people are involved in making such determinations.

When I think of the people I really respect, they are people I admire. They are people that I want to emulate. They are people I defer to. Why? Because they're capable. They exercise great judgment. They don't try to be something they're not. They aren't sellouts. They have high standards. They're prepared to defend their values or beliefs when the need arises. And if that weren't enough for them to hold my respect, they aren't full of themselves.

These are people who energize me. They enhance my character. I'm drawn to them, and they stimulate my thinking. Because they have earned my respect, they deserve my respect. What they do for me is truly a gift.

And I don't necessarily have to agree with someone to respect him or her. Consider a local politician with whom I'm familiar. He wants what's best for people, he's not lining his own pockets, he walks his talk, he's consistent, he has admirable intentions, and overall he's a good guy. He's arguably an admirable public servant. But when it comes to especially important public policies that impact business, there's very little on which he and I agree. Yet I respect him. I won't vote for him, but I really admire him.

For me, being respectful to such people is second nature. It requires no thought, demands no pretense, extracts no price. It's a completely natural experience. But what about those who don't meet such exacting standards? As a professional, how do you demonstrate respect to:

- those who hold biases against you?
- those who have proven themselves untrustworthy?
- those who work to undermine you?
- those who have demonstrated questionable character?
- those who have wronged you?
- those whose conduct you disapprove?
- those who have proven themselves incapable?

Let's face it, there are days when you'd just as soon tell Judy what you really think of her after she talked smack about you to others. Likewise, you'd have no problem seeing John be demoted for undermining the new customer loyalty initiative. And you'd just might smile if Fred were to fall flat on his face after blowing up the department's budget.

Sometimes the last thing in the world you feel like doing is to demonstrate respect to such people. Clearly, these are people who have not earned respect. Yet, emotions aside, how we treat such people reveals a lot about one's level of mastery of this particular mind-set. Professionals find it within themselves to demonstrate respect to others even if they haven't earned it and even if they are unworthy of it. For instance:

- Professionals don't respond in kind when things don't go their way.
- Professionals don't attempt to silence those who disagree with them.
- Professionals don't attempt to intimidate those whom they perceive to be threats to them.
- Professionals don't subscribe to the philosophy that the ends justifies the means.

Let's be clear. That doesn't mean that there aren't consequences for poor performance or bad behavior. But professionals don't make it personal. So what do you do?

Be respecting! (Note the difference between *being respectful* (to someone who has earned our respect) versus *being respecting* (to someone who hasn't earned our respect).

For example, a police officer is an eyewitness to a horrific crime against a child. After a brief chase and a heated altercation, the suspect is apprehended. The suspect has clearly not earned the respect of the officer, but the officer is respecting of the suspect. After cuffing the suspect and reading him his rights, the officer places her hand over the suspect's head as she places him in the backseat of her patrol car so as to prevent an accidental head knock. Arguably, the suspect is being treated better than he deserves. In spite of her emotional reaction to the suspect, the officer is respecting of the suspect.[8]

In effect, the suspect has received an undeserved gift from the officer. It's a gift that can never be repaid. Ultimately, it can only be passed on to others. During the suspect's arrest, the officer gave the suspect a little piece of her character.

What prompts the officer to act in such a manner? She discharges her duty in this way because of her view of herself as a professional. Her primary focus wasn't on the human tragedy perpetrated by the suspect, but rather on the professional ideals by which she aspired to be defined. That's an important distinction. It takes the spotlight off the negative emotions associated with bad actors and places it on the affirming, positive emotions associated with professional ideals.

FBI agent George Piro's experience reinforces this point. As he was getting Saddam Hussein ready for his trial in Iraq after months of interrogation, he gave Saddam a suit and arranged for him to get a haircut. Certainly he had no obligation (implied or otherwise) to do so. After all, the former dictator was an admitted mass murderer. He had done nothing to earn Piro's respect.

By any measure, Saddam was undeserving of the generous pretrial treatment afforded him by Piro. But Piro later made clear that his actions weren't about Saddam. These steps were taken, he noted, "not because of who [Saddam] was, but because of who we are." In other words, George wanted to show the world how they, as professionals, had been respecting of Saddam.[9]

For most of us, there's times when we feel like dropkicking someone to Mars, wringing someone's neck, or throwing someone under the bus because of something they did. Yet, as professionals, if we're going to "create more value than we extract," it's important to take the high road. Vindictiveness, pettiness, vilification, and the like are the antithesis of professionalism. As professionals, the value we seek to create is largely dependent on our character, especially when dealing with those who haven't yet earned our respect.

In chapter 1, I said, "to be a trusted professional is to master life's lessons in personal leadership." Notice how both the police officer and agent Piro maintained their professionalism by leading *themselves* first. They exemplified the adage "Remember who you are." Their self-image as professionals became their north arrow, enabling them to maintain their composure at a time when acting on their emotions would not only have been the wrong thing to do but would have clearly been counterproductive.

This raises an important point that I covered in *The Big AHA!*—namely that you can't always trust your emotions.[10] And because our determinations about people (which ultimately deal with questions of respect) are influenced by strong emotional undercurrents, it's clear that our determinations about people aren't necessarily always objective. If we're being honest with ourselves we'll own that distinct possibility.

For instance, it's really challenging to make such determinations when it's someone:

- you personally dislike
- you're frustrated with
- you're envious of
- who is undeserving of the position they hold
- who poses a political threat to you
- whose tribe is different than your own
- whose core values conflict with your own
- who holds a worldview that is contrary to your own
- who makes you uncomfortable

Most of us regularly find ourselves in situations where we have to deal with people who have a knack for raising our blood pressure. We have to decide how we'll treat those who give us such an emotional jolt. Perhaps the earlier examples reminded you of specific individuals who give you such a jolt. *The Big AHA!*'s signature story was about my experience with someone who gave me this kind of emotional jolt.

Todd was a teenager, and I worked with him in a leadership development program.[11] By any account, Todd was a hellion. Yet on one special day when he did something marvelous, I was blind to it. The problem wasn't within him; it was within me. Todd taught me a powerful lesson about my personal bias against him—one I was unaware of. My emotions clouded my view of him and ultimately how I treated him.

Certainly mitigating the impacts of personal prejudice and bias help all of us to be more respecting of others. Interestingly, one of the meanings of the word *respect* is "to look anew" (*re,* which means "anew," and *spect,* which means "to look"). With the insight I learned from Todd, I was able *to look anew* at him—this time without the clutter.

I'm not here to question your judgment about the views you hold about people. That's a related but peripheral point. For our purposes, it doesn't really matter whether you're right in your views or not. The basis for your views may be real or imagined, delusional or objective. What does matter is how you deal with the people who give you an emotional jolt. How do you treat them? How do you deal with them? Are you more inclined to trash them or attempt to be respecting? For instance:

- The boss who thinks he's got to act like a tough guy in order to get results, but in reality he's only being a jerk.
- The peer who masquerades as a team player publicly but demonstrates extreme hypocrisy in the shadows by taking credit for the work of others—including yours.
- The high-maintenance staffer who adds a lot less value than she thinks she does.

Demonstrating respect to such people, while certainly an admirable goal for professionals, can sometimes be tough to pull off. But it's what's expected of us as professionals. As we noted previously, how we deal with our emotional reactions often separates the professionals from the wannabes, regardless of how tough it might be. The lesson is this: when dealing with bad actors, if you can't be respectful, at least be respecting. Don't make it about them; make it about you—the professional.

Professionals Maintain Their Objectivity and Keep Their Wits About Them

My friend and colleague Stewart Emery was one of the authors of the blockbuster book *Success Built to Last,* which chronicles the practices that are common among highly successful people—the result of hundreds of high-profile interviews. The authors learned that "many high achievers cherish a dogma with which we disagree, and some that were even offensive to us. We hope you can't tell who they are."[12]

I couldn't. Their displeasure did not bleed through in their writing. To their credit, the authors maintained their objectivity. They didn't let the *personal* influence the *professional.* That's a hallmark characteristic of being a professional.

Financial gain is an obvious temptation to which people succumb, their diminished objectivity blurring the line between the personal and the professional, compromising the efficacy of their professional conduct. Yet money is but one temptress. Power, ego, and status can be just as tempting.

Being objective is becoming an increasingly rare experience as exaggeration, disparagement, and sensationalism have seemingly taken its place. As Senator Daniel Patrick Moynihan once noted, "You're entitled to your own opinion, but not entitled to your own facts."

Objectivity is principally the absence of bias and prejudice. Its aim is to define reality, at least as a professional understands it, and it brings about focus while deferring to impartiality, balance, and fairness.[13]

It's so refreshing when people are objective. You feel like you know where they're coming from. You get the sense that you're dealing with someone who is credible, a straight shooter who isn't trying to advance a personal agenda. Someone who is intellectually honest. Someone who gets it. Someone you feel you can trust. Isn't that what you expect from professionals? But too frequently we experience situations like these:

- Bob says, "We should bring in Acme to rebuild those boilers next year." He fails, however, to mention that his brother-in-law is Acme's general manager.
- Sandy promises to finish a three-week project in two. She is often wrong but never in doubt. Sandy finishes the time-sensitive project four weeks later.
- Cliff declares, "Give me Tom's head on a platter! Last week's accident demands accountability!" But Cliff refuses to acknowledge he has a personal disdain for Tom.
- Audrey mercilessly chastises Judy—one of her best people—for paying a premium to a vendor on a rush job for their department's top client. Audrey knows the price of everything and the value of

nothing.[14] She later expresses astonishment at the news that Judy has accepted a position at another company.

- Ted proclaims, "Of course Steve is the best person for the job." He fails to disclose that Steve was his best man at his wedding.

No objectivity translates into no credibility—along with no trust.

Succumbing to temptations (we all know how effectively the emotional pull of temptation works on us) is easy to understand when your ego, status, or security is involved. That said, understanding those tendencies doesn't make it acceptable for professionals.

Objectivity goes hand in hand with being a professional. Recall our earlier description of professionals from chapter 5: "Trusted professionals use their knowledge, power, and influence to advance the needs of their clients or organization, not to inappropriately line their pockets, perpetuate their power, advance a personal agenda, or enhance their ego." Their self-interests trail the process; they don't lead it. One's emotions can dramatically skew objectivity, although lapses in judgment can do as much damage too.

When you aren't objective, it naturally raises questions. At best, your competence or judgment may be called into question:

- "Wow, he really didn't see the forest for the trees on this one! How much are we paying him?"
- "Unbelievable! She overpromised and underdelivered *again!* Is she really up to the job?"
- "Unacceptable. He created a crisis where none existed. Just how many hundreds of thousands of dollars is this going to cost us in bad PR?"

At worst, one's character might be called into question:

- "Oh boy, from looking at the billables, I'd say it looks like just another consultant lining his pockets. Has he no shame?"
- "Why weren't the financial overheads explicitly disclosed in their proposal? What else are they trying to hide?"

- "I'm disappointed that the vendor wasn't more forthcoming about his relationship with our prime competitor. After all, the vendor has complete access to our proprietary cost structure for project planning."

When we haven't been 100 percent forthcoming and haven't avoided the appearance of impropriety, serious trust questions are asked.

Have you noticed how so many people don't know what (and especially who) they can trust anymore? The dogged pursuit of self-interest—even when weighed against the potential stain against one's character—will produce an overwhelming level of cynical distrust.

Objectivity is an elixir that put self-interests in their place. Note I said we should put self-interests in their place, not *eliminate* them. It simply puts them in a subordinate position—where they should be. Objectivity is also a powerful agent to help restore trust. Consider:

- A senior director who self-selects himself out of an interview process over concerns about his inability to maintain impartiality toward a candidate's pending promotion.
- An account executive who recommends reassigning an especially important account to one of his peers after months of unsuccessfully attempting to develop chemistry with an especially difficult client.
- A senior executive who acknowledges management's missteps of the past—steps that, while well intended, later proved to be detrimental to the firm.

For service providers, objectivity builds customer loyalty like mad. For instance:

- An associate at a hardware store who recommends a fifty-cent solution and steers the customer away from the ten-dollar solution he thought he needed.
- An attorney who recommends a potential client consider using a different firm to handle her case, citing concerns over his firm's ability to do a quality job, given the firm's current caseload.

- A dentist who prescribes a nominal level of dental treatment for a frail, elderly patient, contrasted against the gold-plated level of treatment earlier recommended by a well-known dentist in an upscale practice.

Providing such deferential treatment to customers and clients in this way builds tremendous credibility in the service provider. Such treatment, however, is a rare exception, certainly not the rule. It is easy to see how firms that take this approach wind up with a loyal following when these practices become part of their competitive advantage.

This brings us to the idea of objectivity: what it is, what it aims to achieve, and the disciplined process required to make it work.

Objectivity is a complex skill requiring one part constructive thinking, one part discipline, and one part integrity. Foremost, however, is the realization that objectivity demands mastery of one's emotions. It's about not disadvantaging people and/or organizations whom the professional is committed to serve. This is analogous to a medical professional's "do no harm" directive found in the Hippocratic oath. At the same time, this is not always about playing defense; there also is a proactive element aimed toward creating opportunities (think: creating new markets, mergers and acquisitions, etc).

When we speak of fairness, we mean fairness in treatment, thus fulfilling the universal need for all parties to be dealt with equitably. Fairness is another way of demonstrating respect, whether you're an employee, a consumer, a member of the media, or a board member.

The *Star Trek* character Spock exemplified an individual's struggle to be thoroughly objective. As a Vulcan, Spock allegedly was devoid of emotion, but his human DNA was not completely quashed. For him and other mortals like you and me, total objectivity is arguably impossible, because we're human. We are equipped with powerful self-images and bundles of emotions, some of which are associated with biases and prejudices. And when it comes to business, as René Descartes said, "A man is incapable of comprehending any argument that interferes with his revenue."

This is why we can't *be* objective until we *see* things objectively. Borrowing a medical analogy, successful treatment depends on an insightful, unbiased diagnosis. Individuals who become wed to a solution or a certain way of thinking risk losing their objectivity. In addition, groups who fall victim to groupthink are likewise at risk. And providing an unbiased diagnosis is tough to do when you're potentially working against your own self-interests—at least in the short term.

As a professional services provider, I pose the following questions either to myself and/or my potential client to move toward an unbiased diagnosis. Thus the client realizes the greatest value from the ensuing solution. These diagnostic questions are:

- Is the problem the client believes to be the issue the real problem?
- Is there an alternative that the client hasn't considered that may be a better fit? (This may include not using my firm's services.)
- Is the client wasting her money by pursuing this course of action?
- Are my firm's capabilities a good fit for the client's need?
- Aside from capability, is there anything that might impede my ability to do the best job I can for my client? (For example, workload.)
- Is there anything that might sway my judgment that would disadvantage my client if my solution is implemented?
- Would I inappropriately realize a greater benefit than my client as a result of this engagement?

I've found these questions and others like them to be especially helpful in doing my due diligence before engaging a client. The questions aid me in (1) assessing what the real problem is (diagnosis process) and (2) determining who, in the spirit of avoiding bias and prejudice, is best suited to bring the greatest value to the client (treatment process).

I'm fond of the old adage, "Just because you *can* doesn't mean you *should.*" Even though I may be capable of doing the work, it doesn't mean I should do the work. For instance, should a conflict be revealed, it's important that I withdraw from the process and either recommend another firm or explore an alternate solution.

If the diagnosis isn't right, naturally the treatment is going to be of little help. That's why the diagnosis is so critical. The diagnostic process, regardless of what process is used or who utilizes it, inevitably produces a conclusion.

Not long ago I realized that a potential new client didn't need the communication training they were asking for. What they needed instead was a shift in one of their long-standing cultural norms, a dysfunctional norm that was the root of their problem. In their case, the treatment worked because the diagnosis was right.

Notice I didn't say either "facts" or "the truth." I said "conclusion."

Friedrich Nietzsche noted, "There are no facts, only interpretations." The point is this: our conclusions reflect reality as we understand it or wish to understand it. Conclusions may be influenced by a wide array of assumptions (hopefully good ones) along with an undercurrent of impressions from one's personal beliefs and values. All of these are laced with emotions. Some we recognize, others we don't.

A conclusion is usually a precursor to some sort of action. Thus our conclusions are especially important, because the inevitable actions that follow carry significant consequences. Our conclusions form the basis for:

- a recommendation—provided to others, which may or may not be acted upon
- a decision—made by a third-party or by the individual who originally formulated the conclusion
- a personal opinion—that may or may not be shared with others

Hopefully our conclusions are objective, minimizing bias and prejudice to the greatest possible degree and making sure that the interests of our clients or organization is foremost. Yet our emotions sometimes get the better of us. Consider these instances:

- A vindictive decision by a middle manager to hire a high-potential candidate for a backwater operation rather than allow a rival manager to hire the candidate for his team. Meanwhile, the talented candidate finds the work boring and becomes apathetic. Ultimately, the organization fails to benefit from his real skills and capabilities.
- An executive assistant recommends a lesser candidate to her manager to fill a vacancy in the support staff. Later the recommendation is shown to have been motivated by jealousy and fear. The assistant felt threatened by a rising star with superb

qualifications and capabilities and feared she would be displaced. The manager, however, went along with the recommendation, and the department ultimately suffered as a result.

- A director decides to consolidate two operations into one because she is more motivated by kingdom building and grabbing power than doing what is best for the firm. The consolidation subsequently proves to be ineffective.
- A project manager fires a popular journeyman, not for cause, but because of a personal dispute. The manager's action results in a slowdown by the workforce, and the project's completion is delayed an additional month. The bottom line: the firm's interests were compromised as a result of someone's personal power trip.
- A CEO and the board initiate a hostile takeover of a competitor in order to create the industry's largest company. The so-called merger, however, proves to be a flop. Later the move is seen as having been motivated by the CEO's ego rather than the idea of advancing the interests of the company.
- A crew leader allows two linemen to haze an apprentice. The crew lead, who himself had been hazed as an apprentice, believes that hazing—despite a company policy prohibiting it—was a right-of-passage that, despite some short-term drawbacks, makes the long-term environment of the crew better. The apprentice, however, does not see it that way. He quits, thus wasting the company's eight-month investment in his training.
- A manager decides to reorganize her department rather than reset the leadership team's expectations in an attempt to deal with the organization's dysfunction. The change proves only to redistribute the problems, instead of dealing with them at the root level. The decision, presumably, was based on the assumption that the new reporting relationships would solve the problem. Later the manager's rationale is seen as a maneuver to avoid conflict rather than contend with her leadership team's expectations.

Notice the motives, the absence of objectivity, and the unfortunate consequences for the businesses. In every instance, the businesses' interests took a backset to the personal interests of a decision maker. Instead, emotions determined what actions were taken. And don't think this occurs exclusively in the for-profit world.

Anyone with any experience with volunteer organizations serving youth knows that the most difficult aspect of the work can be dealing with the parents, not the kids. I've had my share. Once, in the throes of a particularly sticky situation with several parents, one of the kids approached me. She wanted to know what was holding up the final plans for summer camp. I answered her as tactfully as I could, indicating that there were a number of options that the parents hadn't been able to agree on. The truth was that the volunteer parents had turned dysfunctional. They exhibited unattractive control issues and struggled with hurt feelings over unresolved issues from prior years. I couldn't share this, but the girl picked up on my frustration.

She sighed and said, "You should be doing what's in the best interests of the kids." Wisdom from the mouths of babes!

You would think it would be easy to keep the interests of a volunteer organization—one that serves the needs of kids—front and center without the unnecessary distractions of drama queens and machismo power trips. After all, these kinds of organizations have admirable goals and lofty ideals. Plus, virtually all the kids involved are the children of the adult volunteers. In the end, people are people. But mastery of our emotions can help us to maintain our focus and stay on track.

Nietzsche also said, "The most fundamental form of human stupidity is forgetting what we were trying to do in the first place." Too often, emotionally, we get in our own way—even within an organization that's filled with well-intended volunteers.

Keeping on track is not just a nice thing to do, it's essential in getting results, especially when the stakes are high. It's about keeping our wits about us while Rome is burning. Consider this perspective from FBI agent George Piro.

"In the FBI's world, objectivity ties directly into getting results, or to put a finer point on it, the right results. We take on a case because something's happened or about to happen, usually something pretty bad, and if you let it, it'll eat at you. We're talking about real human tragedy, but we're charged with getting to the bottom of it, objectively. So we're after the truth. Yet people typically aren't forthcoming, and the work can be tedious, frustrating at times.

"Despite that, we absolutely have to get it right. There's just too much riding on it. Our conclusions form the basis for decisions from our leadership that impact essential aspects of homeland security and international relations. If we get it wrong, people die. In our world, there are huge costs when you lose your objectivity.

"That's why we must allow the evidence to make the case. We can't allow preconceived notions or personal feelings to overtake our objectivity. Otherwise, you'll make the evidence fit your case. Objectivity enables us to absorb *all* the available information, especially pertinent information that seemingly doesn't fit. Without objectivity, you'll miss something—often something really important. The right result is dependent on our objectivity."[15]

Delivering meaningful results—whether at the FBI or at a for-profit company—is essential for professionals. It enables constant reality checks on an organization's strategic objectives as well as its tactical targets. This is largely accomplished by what well-known author Jim Collins described as "dealing with the brutal facts." Culturally speaking, this makes it safer to bring up tough issues and reinforces focus on the organization's priorities. Also important, it helps us to avoid huge missteps.

Objectivity, as a concept, is easy to understand, but some of its nuances are less so. In the end it's personal. It's what we do when we're tempted to let the personal violate the professional. There's something special, even Zen-like, about people who have mastered this ability. Plus, have you noticed how it attracts like-minded people? Their admiration is a by-product of the trust and respect they hold for one another. Plus, like-minded people prefer and expect the work to be conducted in this manner. It's really pretty simple, paraphrasing George Piro, "It's all about the work."[16]

Professionals Manage Their Egos and Resist the Urge for Immediate Gratification

During the course of running a workshop or working with an intact team, it's not unusual for someone to pose what I call an "A-Rod" question. Its namesake (the iconic and egotistical New York Yankees shortstop) tempts one's narcissistic tendencies. It enables the person responding to show how smart they are, to name-drop, and to feed their ego.

So when an A-Rod question gets posed, I respond in one of two ways. I either tell an entertaining story that is off point that makes me look good and is likely to throw the group off track, or I boomerang the question back to the group, which helps the group to move forward. Interestingly, the group (at least in the short term) rarely recognizes the difference.

Sometimes number one is *really* tempting. And on more than one occasion I've succumbed.

Each of us faces the task of managing our ego. Out-of-control egos are, among other things, at the foundation of salacious media stories on corporate malfeasance and personal excess. I'll spare you the stories, because you're surely already all too familiar with them.

Steven Smith, co-author of *Egonomics,* notes, "Over half of all businesspeople estimate 'ego costs' their company six to fifteen percent of annual revenue; many believe that estimate is conservative."[17] Smith believes that managing ego is *the* most important among all the so-called management capabilities. I'll leave the quantification to Smith, but in my mind, ego is way up there.

An unhealthy ego has a strong association with one of the most unattractive human traits: arrogance. This is because arrogance is largely interpreted as superiority.[18] Overconfidence such as this puts people at the center of their own universe. They lead cheers for a team of one—themselves. Normal rules don't apply to the arrogant. After all, they're special. But that may also mean having disdain for authority and what that authority represents. The egoist's favorite pronoun is "I." And because egoists know best, theirs is the only way. So deception, manipulation, and intimidation are prevalent in their organizations, because they can't imagine not getting what they want.

A healthy ego is about having genuine confidence, which is defined as confidence without attitude. People find self-confidence attractive. Professionals with healthy egos demonstrate respect. They aren't coercive by arm-twisting you to their point of view. They aren't interesting in making you wrong. Their favorite pronoun is "we." They're not overly enamored with themselves. They're comfortable in their own skin and consistent in their behavior. These are the signs of a contented ego.[19]

So, between the two, who are you more likely to trust? Everything being equal, the healthy ego wins every time. Someone with an unhealthy ego may talk a good game, but he will consistently keep his organization's (or his clients) interests as an afterthought. For the unhealthy ego, self-interests predominate. These are largely influenced by an obsession with winning, a sense of entitlement, the intoxication of success, a feeling of invulnerability brought on by overconfidence, and a sense of self-worth tied to money, title, fame, being in the know, or being in the club.

Consultant Michael H. Smith reminds us, "We like big egos as a culture. Ego-driven behavior is rewarded and rewarded well."[20] True enough. This is why organizations must be vigilant in appropriately rewarding behavior consistent with a healthy ego.

Washington: The Epitome of Someone with a Healthy Ego

George Washington is a wonderful example of someone with a healthy ego. He chaired the Constitutional Convention—the successful outcome of which was attributed to his strong leadership. Yet during the convention, he engaged in debate only once. While Washington was revered by his peers, as president he refused to surround himself with worshiping sycophants.[21] There were no yes men in his cabinet. Rather he assembled a team of brilliant men whose intellectual prowess outshined his own.[22] During cabinet meetings, at Washington's encouragement, his advisors advanced divergent positions that often proved contentious. All the while Washington carefully weighed the opposing positions and kept an open mind about the benefits and costs of each. As I outlined in chapter 6, Washington shattered the assumed premise that he would be an American monarch. Instead, after two terms in office, he stepped down, surrendering power to the people, and returned to his farm as a commoner.

Washington had tremendous but not overbearing self-confidence. He felt a tremendous responsibility to the fledging nation, and the success of the nation was his life's work. At the same time, Washington had a healthy ego.[23] He realized the significant place in history he would likely attain, and he hoped he would be favorably and fairly portrayed (probably not unlike the rest of us would). Yet he kept things in perspective. For Washington, it was duty first, and if he were successful in making the country successful, his legacy would take care of itself.

Let's face it. People aren't naturally drawn to people with big egos. Too often frequently painful interpersonal dynamics overwhelm prudent decision making. Decisions should be in the best interests of the enterprise, rather than being a monument to someone's ego. And when there's a collection of big egos (think: senior teams), the dynamics and risks become even greater, because collaboration, teamwork, and innovation all take a hit. It's been said that we're beginning to get a big head when we start believing our press clippings.

Marshall Goldsmith told me about an experience at a dinner with one of the top officers in the U.S. Army. "At the table were seven newly minted generals (all men)," he said. "The senior officer laughed as he looked at their shiny new stars, and he started to reflect back on his own promotion. He joked with the new generals, 'Have you noticed lately that when you tell a joke, everyone laughs? You aren't that funny! Have you noticed lately that when you make a comment, people nod in agreement. You aren't that smart! Have you noticed lately that women seem to be more attracted to you? You aren't that charming!' The general grew serious, sighed, and continued, 'Always remember, they are not saluting *you.* They are saluting that star on your shoulder—all that it stands for—and all that it has stood for over the years. Never let admiration go to your head. When you quit wearing that star, they won't be saluting any more.'"[24]

Of course, there are few of us who have press clippings to gloat over. However, each of us has "interpersonal press clippings" that we're constantly reviewing. For the new generals (or any leader for that matter), they anticipate the predictable kiss up—especially from those in the lower ranks. My point is: getting a big head from counterfeit groveling is a failure in personal leadership because it isn't about you; it's about the power you hold over someone else's life. Taking the bait and believing that it's all about you only leads to a loss of respect and a diminished ability to lead others.

Big Egos: Big Problems, Lost Opportunities

W. Edwards Deming became a world-renowned consultant through his teaching of statistical process control techniques to industry and governmental entities. His early forte—quality control—played an essential role in the manufacture of the hardware (planes, tanks, ships, etc.) that helped win World War II.

Deming, someone clearly ahead of his time and despite making such a significant contribution to the successful war effort, was largely ignored in the United States for nearly four decades after the war. Ironically, in Japan (a country he played a significant role in defeating) he really made a name for himself. After adopting Deming's methods, Japan leapfrogged the United States in manufacturing prowess and made "Japanese management" all the rage in the mid-1970s and early 1980s.

James O'Toole, Daniels Distinguished Professor of Business Ethics at the University of Denver's Daniels College of Business, has long been puzzled by the surprising avoidance in the United States of Deming's methods—especially after Deming's methods have been proven successful in Japan. Professor O'Toole, who wrote about Deming in his landmark book *Leading Change,*[25] has long been an admirer of Deming and has been sympathetic to this plight.[26] He attempted one last time after Deming's death to revisit the resistance to Deming's work with a few managers who had personal dealings with Deming.

"Several common themes ran through their replies to my questions," he said. "First, they all respected Deming's genius. Second, they all volunteered that he had been right all along and that America had paid a high price for resisting the changes he advocated. Third, none of the companies used his methods today. Why? One manager explained, 'Deming insisted on doing things his way. If managers made a slight change in Deming's way to tailor it to their needs, he dismissed everything they did as unworthy. It was his ideas, and never ours.' Said another: 'It wasn't simply that he was insulting and impolitic; I think we were big enough to discount that. The problem was that he had "the truth." He didn't listen to us, to our needs, to our concerns. He was a nonstop lecturer. Worse, it felt like he was always trying to shove his ideas down your throat. After a while of being ignored, you just turn him off.'

"When Deming first dealt with the Japanese," O'Toole said, "he listened to them, showed them respect, and couched his ideas in terms of their needs. But later, when he came to deal with Americans many years later, he was imperious and arrogantly demanded that they swallow his philosophy whole (doubtless because he was bitter at having been ignored for so long in his own country). It took his death to open my eyes to the fact that, when it came to U.S. managers, he wasn't advancing their agenda, he was advancing his. It was then that I started to hear what the managers had been telling me for twenty years."[27]

Even though he had admirable intentions, Deming was viewed by U.S. managers as arrogant and an out-of-control ego.[28] Deming said, "We are here to make another world." This is consistent who desired to craft large-scale transformative change on their own terms.

Whether success changed Deming to the point of his getting a big head is debatable. What isn't debatable, and is really the bottom line, is that U.S. managers perceived Deming as having an air of superiority and wanting to advance *his* agenda—both of which are consistent with a big ego. They wanted no part of him. Professor O'Toole added, "I do know that [later in life] he was convinced he had been right, and he felt that American business had been foolish in not listening to him as the Japanese had done. He was both arrogant and angry in his old age."[29]

In fairness to Deming, O'Toole noted, "Deming was charming and friendly and open (even a little humble) to those who showed him respect." We don't know whether Deming was aware of the negative impact he was having on U.S. managers, all we know is that he did.

Deming, no doubt, was well intended. The irony, of course, is that, when it came to U.S. managers, Deming, in many ways a U.S. patriot, got in his own way. He had been proven right, but this isn't a story about a business prophet's message being rejected in his own land. It's about the business prophet himself. It is a story about lost opportunities and the high costs associated with them when the messenger is rejected.

In Deming's case, it was about the opportunity one country (Japan) took advantage of while another (the United States) didn't. That choice enabled Japan to surpass the United States in manufacturing prowess, outdoing the very country that, having adopted Deming's methods earlier, had defeated it just a few years earlier. By deselecting Deming's methods, the United States paid a hefty price.

Big egos come with a big price. It elicits the disdain of others. Some people won't do business with you. If they are forced to do business with you reluctantly, they will rejoice when you fail. And it they are given the opportunity, some may even work toward that end for you.

Managers with big egos regularly make decisions by decree or, when they wish to be seen as inclusive, via manipulation or intimidation. Just because they can doesn't mean they should! This translates into big losses and lost opportunities—lots of them.

Dr. Paul Nutt has conducted extensive research at Ohio State University on why business decisions fail. He concluded, "Over one-third of all failed business decisions are driven by ego."[30] From Nutt's perspective, about half of all business decisions are failures,[31] which means that approx 17 percent of *all* business decisions (1) are failures or (2) became failures because of ego.

Think about it: the successful outcome of every job interview, team meeting, contentious conversation, board decision, contract negotiation, vendor selection, etc. is subject to the whims of ego. Succumbing to the whims of ego is not in keeping with our aim to be better professionals. Instead, we should aspire to keep bias and prejudice at bay. We should aim to do what's best for the firm or organization. According to Steven Smith, Paul C. Nutt, and from my own observations, we've all got a long way to go.

Humility to the Rescue

The antidote for big egos is humility. A great deal has been written about the importance of humility in business leaders in recent years. Perhaps most notable is the conclusion advanced by Jim Collins in *Good to Great* that humility was one of two characteristics (professional being the other) that separated leaders who ran great companies from those who ran good ones.

Others have written, although with less specificity to quantifiable business outcomes, about the compelling benefits leaders (and by default, their businesses) enjoy when they conduct their affairs with greater humility. That's all well and good, and it's something that I not only agree with but advocate, but the principle of humility transcends leaders. It's applicable to *anyone* at any level in an organization for all the same reasons and benefits originally ascribed to leaders. My point is this: you don't have to be in the club to benefit from this virtue. So let's broaden the discussion.

The problem with humility is the perception often held against the term and, in some cases, a bias against those who exhibit it. Weak and wimpy and subject to abuse by the higher-ups are only a few of the uncomplimentary connotations attributed to humility. However, demonstrating humility does not mean a lack of confidence, settling for mediocrity, becoming roadkill for the big dogs, or blindly conforming to the orthodoxy of the day. Far from it! Never mistake self-effacing modesty for weakness.[32]

Humility should be viewed as a paradox. One shuns public adulation while calling a supplier on the carpet for nonperformance. One avoids self-promotion while forcefully but diplomatically correcting a faux pas by a uncooperative department that threatens the viability of a make-or-break contract. It means that you aren't full of yourself, you acknowledge you don't know it all, your commitment is to the work, and you recognize and acknowledge that your success is attributed to factors beyond your own efforts—even allowing for luck[33] to play a part.

As Olli-Pekka Kallasvuo, CEO of Nokia, noted: "Having humility does not mean that you are quiet or that you lack the courage to say what you think. Courage and humility are more complimentary than contradictory. Humility is a vital quality."

Humility enhances:

- Listening
- Curiosity
- Teachability
- Empathy
- Likability

Listening

When each of us thinks there's nothing left to learn—whether it be from clients, colleagues, industry experts, or whoever—we stop listening. Or at least we stop listening with much depth. Also important, we stop asking questions. That's a big ego at work. The trouble today is there's too much know for any one person to think he or she has a handle on it.

People with healthy egos realize there's much more that they don't know than they do know, especially now, when change occurs so often. Accordingly, humility heightens their desire to listen, especially to key stakeholders. This is especially important, because as listening is interpersonal communication's most important and powerful skill. Over time, better listening tends to become a habit, helping individuals to identify emerging trends in markets, recognize budding issues and opportunities with clients, validate (or invalidate) key assumptions from which strategic plans were originally based, identify thorny root-cause issues that are integral to contentious interpersonal conflicts, and reveal sources of dissatisfaction among groups of employees before they hit critical mass.

Curiosity

Knowing is the enemy of learning. Knowing also kills one's curiosity. Humility keeps knowing at bay. This very book is an attempt to fulfill my own curiosity in answering a question I had about what it really means to be a professional. British novelist and playwright W. Somerset Maugham said, "It wasn't until late in life that I discovered how easy it is to say, 'I don't know.'" For me, I really didn't know the answer to a question I considered to be especially important, one that I also believed millions of others considered important too. Thus I started this journey to satisfy my own curiosity.

Curiosity is dependent on an inquisitive mind and insightful questions. Curiosity is at the root of innovation, and innovation is now a major driver of the U.S. economy (think: technology advances). Jim Leach,[34] a former member of Congress, believes the "the future is now the province of the curious."

Curiosity usually starts out with a question. Questions like: What are the implications if we could increase battery performance by 500 percent? Why do we do it this way? What's required to be able to reduce the production cycle time by 50 percent? What are the possibilities of incorporating the new disruptive technology into our business? Curiosity enables these types of what-if questions; knowing kills them.

Teachability

Teachability isn't about becoming something you aren't; it's about having the willingness to be influenced by people whose personal traits, capabilities, and knowledge compliment your own. It's about doing better by being better. Humility helps to show us our weak spots.

It's about deferring to those whose knowledge or capabilities are greater than your own, even if that person reports to you. For instance, the leader whose core expertise is finance demonstrates teachability when she defers to her chief lieutenant's advice and recommendation on the organization's marketing strategy. The leader whose initial discomfort stems from his lack of marketing expertise doesn't blindly adopt the strategy. Neither does the leader abandon his accountability or forsake common sense. In the end, the leader defers confidently to someone whose marketing expertise is far greater than her own—to a chief lieutenant who has competently and professionally made his case.

On an interpersonal level, teachability is akin to emulation and imitation. It's genuinely admiring another's gifts and committing oneself to learn from them. An impulsive manager, for instance, wants to emulate a cool-headed colleague who patiently and systematically attacks problem solving. It's not a comparative thing. This is not a competition with colleagues. It's not trying to be better than someone else. It's simply trying to be *our* best.

Empathy

This is the ability to (1) recognize especially important emotional drivers in others and (2) communicate in such a way as to enable the impacted individual to understand, cope, and better self-manage her own emotional reactions to situations and people. In effect, empathy is an effort to experience vicariously another person's feelings specifically for the benefit of that person.

Empathy enables a frustrated senior leader to calm down sufficiently to objectively assess the merits of a merger proposal that has been stymied by pointless legal wrangling. Empathy aids a hiring manager to objectively assess the merits of a technically superior candidate whose values are slightly askew of the manager.

Without humility, empathy is little more than a wish and a prayer. With it, humility enables the recipient to work himself out of some tight emotional jams that threaten important relationships, endanger essential projects, strain long-standing partnerships, and put at risk coveted opportunities. This is the classic illustration of realizing hard business benefits from so-called soft skills.

Likability

First of all, it's more important to be respected than liked, but it's too often a false choice to have to pick between the two. Being liked, which each of us largely controls, makes a big difference in our work life in a number of ways. I'm not suggesting that you pander to people in order to make someone like you. I am suggesting that people are naturally drawn to people who demonstrate humility.

Think about it. If you had a choice between working with someone you liked and someone you didn't (assuming both were equally capable and of good character), you'd pick the person you liked. It's in your best interest.

We've all had experience with people with inflated egos—they're emotional boat anchors. Toby Keith, the well-known country singer, had a popular song, "I Want to Talk About Me," that cleverly encapsulates the problem in a funny, entertaining way. Contrast the big ego against someone with humility—someone who has a genuine interest in others, someone who is self-effacing, someone who isn't trying to show how smart she is, someone whose very approach in dealing with people naturally tends to make others feel good about themselves.

Best-selling author Bob Burg notes, "All things being equal, people will do business with, and refer business to, those people they know, like, and trust." His advice? "Be the person worthy of eliciting those feelings toward you."[35]

In general, most of us overestimate the degree to which our efforts contribute to our success.[36] That phenomenon is more about overconfidence than arrogance, but it's certainly not an awe-inspiring demonstration of humility. Taken to an extreme, however, there are those who attribute their success almost exclusively to their own doing, their own energies, their own insights, their own brilliance, their own imagination, and dare I say it, their own superiority. No one else could have done it as well or accomplished as much. Many consider themselves indispensable. Some would have you believe that they are the father of the discipline that sustains their ability to make a living—but what they're really doing is standing on the shoulders of the giants who went before them.

What self-centered egoists conveniently forget (or discount) are the efforts of their colleagues (their support staff), their company's stellar reputation built on years of hard work, their company's generous resources, their supportive boss who put them in a position to succeed, and their visionary mentor whose advice led them to this career path. My point is this: regardless of how hard we work or how smart we are, there's a variety of important factors that contribute to our success that we have had nothing to do with.

Vanguard's John Bogle is fond of asking people with big egos who demonstrate such ingratitudes, "So just how did you arrange to be born in the United States?"[37] After all, the United States offers unparalleled opportunities.

Alex Haley, author of *Roots,* had a logic-defying picture of a turtle atop a fence post in his office. Whenever anyone asked him about it, Haley would say, "If you see a turtle on a fence post, you know that he had some help. Any time I start thinking, 'Wow, isn't this marvelous what I've done?' I look at that picture and remember how this turtle, *me,* got up on that post."[38]

The Ultimate in High-Stakes Group Dynamics

I've done a lot of work with senior officer groups. Typically, everyone in attendance is a leader in his or her own right. The issues before them are heady, and coming to an agreement (at least one that can be successfully implemented) is tough. Self-interests, egos, and group dynamics all come into play. The emotional demands are far greater than the intellectual ones. It's art, not science.

The Constitutional Convention represents the ultimate in high-stakes group dynamics. The Constitution, considered by some to be one of history's crowning achievements, didn't start out that way.

In May 1787 delegates from twelve of the thirteen states arrived in Philadelphia and convened at Independence Hall, the same venue where eleven years earlier many of these same individuals had adopted the Declaration of Independence and drafted the Articles of Confederation, the first organizational document of the United States. For almost a decade the country had limped along as best it could under the severe limitations imposed by the Articles on the central government, which was designed to be subservient to the individual states. The states, meanwhile, were anything but united. Each had its own currency, taxes, post office, and militia. The states felt free to ignore or implement whatever Congress deemed to be in the national interest. When the delegates arrived in Philadelphia, each owed allegiance to his state first and the country second.

Quarrels between the states, however, had led to a 1786 meeting in Annapolis, which authorized a convention to amend the Articles. Most of the representatives knew that the Articles were beyond mending, since all their proposals would require unanimous acceptance by the states, and the past few years had shown that such unanimity was unlikely. Thus Congress amended the purpose of the convention and allowed the Articles to be revised completely.

Many of the problems involved in governance under the Articles had been argued in this very same room by many of the same men who now met to correct them. They faced a rare do-over situation, and now they had the added benefit of hindsight. This is not to say that those who earlier had won an argument over a point of governance now capitulated or conceded the point to their opponents. There was little doubt that the forthcoming debates would be as heated as they had been years prior.

With the benefit of hindsight, we know that no single personality dominated this convention. Neither John Adams nor Thomas

Jefferson was present; both were serving as ambassadors in Europe. Patrick Henry of Virginia decided not to attend because he believed the outcome of the convention would be a monarchy, and he wanted no part in such a process. Avuncular Benjamin Franklin was eighty-one years old, and he projected a subtle calming influence over some of the deliberations. And it was no surprise that George Washington was unanimously selected to preside over the convention, but he did so with a very light hand.

Before the representatives convened, the primary battle lines had been drawn between the states in terms of size and slaves. Many of the larger states believed they should have a greater say in the conduct of the federal government, and the majority of the states that condoned slavery believed that the federal government should not have the power to regulate or abolish the practice.

The most hotly debated issue, however, focused on the idea of how the states would be represented in the federal legislature. Should it be based on population or should it be proportional? Various plans were proposed, but none of them satisfied the majority of the delegates. For two months the question tortured the proceedings. As the rhetoric became more heated, the outside temperatures were also rising—a fact not lost on the delegates since they had decided to keep the windows shut to prevent outsiders from overhearing the debates. The summer heat and humidity made the atmosphere within Independence Hall completely stifling, which was hardly optimal working conditions for the delegates, given the gravity of the task before them.

The future of the country rested with the delegates. One newspaper noted, "Such a body of enlightened and honest men perhaps never before met for political purposes in any country upon the face of the earth."[39] But despite the country's vote of confidence, they certainly felt the weight of the nation's anticipation breathing down their necks, plus the pressure of representing their own state's interests.

Failure was unthinkable. Yet the delegates were not sure that the convention would produce a conclusion. "No delegate confessed it in his letters home," observed historian Catherine Drinker Bowen, "yet there was an ever-present danger that the Convention might dissolve and the entire project be abandoned."[40]

Throughout four months of debate and compromise, delegates came and left—after all, they had their own concerns to manage as well as obligations in Congress, where business continued to go on as before. Sometimes they returned, and sometimes others came in their place. Sometimes their seats were left empty. All the while, the country awaited an outcome. Would the result be a representative republic or a dreaded monarchy? One newspaper reported, "Anticipation has brought the country to a virtual standstill."[41]

The implications were enormous for non-Americans too. Should a new federal government be adopted, many anticipated that thousands of oppressed and persecuted Europeans would embark immediately for the United States.[42]

Meanwhile, the pressure on the delegates was tremendous. Each topic's deliberations were passionate and frequently heated. Most were resolved with compromises by every side. When the focus fell on slavery, however, tempers flared to a boiling point. At this juncture, Franklin addressed his colleagues: "We are sent here to *consult,* not to *contend* with each other; and declarations of a fixed opinion, and of determined resolution never to change it, neither enlighten nor convince us."[43]

It certainly helped that the discussions and deliberations remained confidential between the delegates. They did not have to fashion their words to fit a position or posture for the public. Each delegate was free to change his mind and to even reverse his position on an issue without facing a public inquisition. Even so, the stakes couldn't have been more daunting.

After the delegates had worked all summer, unspoken fears still remained that the convention might not reach a successful conclusion. During the first week of September, three months into the proceedings, things heated up in earnest. Earlier Franklin had counseled his colleagues about the importance of "harmony and union are extremely necessary to give weight to our councils, and render them effectual in promoting and securing the common good."[44] (Sounds a lot like Mind-Set 2, doesn't it?) On Monday, September 17, 1787, thirty-nine delegates endorsed the final document.

From experience, I can tell you what an important role the "something bigger" mind-set plays in aiding executives in reaching consensus on tough issues. It's huge! It helps to frame the big picture and assists one in mastering his or her emotions during critical times of stress. It helped the Founders too!

We know that each delegate to the Constitutional Convention held passionate points of view—that's why each one was there. But while they fervently advanced their views, they didn't let their emotions get the better of them. We also know that every delegate considered the final document to be imperfect. Yet they were able to see beyond their self-definitions as New Yorkers, Georgians, and New Englanders and glimpse what it meant to be Americans. They were satisfied that the document represented extremely high standards (see Mind-Set 4), but they did not allow the idea of perfection to hinder its adoption. In other words, they didn't throw the baby out with the bathwater.

Even after all their labor, formal ratification by the states was not a forgone conclusion. In fact, several states approved the Constitution with the tacit understanding that a bill of rights would be forthcoming. In the end, the Constitution was ratified, and the rest is history.

Success Factors

Earlier, I defined a trusted professional as one who has mastered life's lessons in personal leadership. Mind-Set 6, perhaps more than any other mind-set, challenges us to live up to that definition. It requires restraint, discipline, patience, forbearance, and compassion. It means that we cannot expect things to be fair. It means that a short-term win isn't the primary goal. You're doing well with this mind-set if you're able to:

- Admire the messenger while disagreeing with the message.
- Hear another person's point of view while avoiding the need to defend your own.
- Support professional initiatives you disagree with.
- Avoid being distracted by someone who wants to draw you into a contentious confrontation.
- Validate someone else's point of view without their knowing what yours is.

- Receive candid feedback without becoming defensive.
- Have the maturity to learn from another's experience, not just your own.
- Be respecting of someone who doesn't deserve it.
- Resist the temptation to pull rank.
- Have the temperament to put opposing ideas into play without being paralyzed by fear and anxiety over the result.[45]
- Not surround yourself with yes-men.
- Resist the temptation to one-up others.
- Remain intellectually honest in the face of adversity.
- Refrain from using expediency as a *means* to conveniently justify a tempting *end.*
- Appreciate that you wouldn't be where you are today without the help of others.
- Resist the urge to intimidate or silence those whom you disagree with.
- Demonstrate excellence, without making anyone feel inferior.
- Separate the essential from the trivial.
- Avoid talking down to someone who may not be your favorite.
- Refuse to use someone's values or beliefs against him.
- Resist the urge to cherry-pick information out of context in order to denigrate or mislead others about a view or person you disagree with.

None of these things is easy or pleasant. It means taking the high road often when we'd rather not. But as Paul Orfalea reminds us, "The only true victories in life are victories over ourselves."[46] It means being better and being a better you.

SUMMARY

- Trust is a good emotion. Professionals need not be dispassionate. The passion you have for your work, your values, your ideas, and your people are wonderful.
- Emotions are self-induced. Thus, we are personally responsible for, not only our interpretation of experiences and events, but how we respond to them.
- Not letting your emotions get the better of you—especially in a pressure-packed situation—is a sign of a real pro.
- The degree to which we remain respecting of others who are not necessarily our favorite people often reflects the degree of development we have achieved with this mind-set.
- For aspiring professionals, the absence of objectivity consistently translates into a lack of credibility.
- Professionals manage their ego, ensuring that it's an asset and not a liability.
- For most people, this mind-set is one of the most difficult to master. It often becomes a canvas for self-development over a lifetime.
- Perhaps no mind-set more exemplifies the challenge to master life's lessons in personal leadership than this one.

CHAPTER **TWELVE**

MIND-SET **7**

Professionals Aspire to Reveal Value in Others

You'll have more fun and success helping other people achieve their goals than you will trying to reach your own.

—Dale Carnegie

It's 5:30 a.m. It's dark. It's damp. It's cold. And officer candidate Amanda Myers (no relation to Gen. Richard B. Myers) is nervous. It's crunch time for seventy-six candidates at the officer candidate school (OCS) at Fort Benning, Georgia. Twenty-seven-year-old Myers and her colleagues are just moments away from an all-important event: the timed five-mile run.

Getting into OCS is a very selective process. Standards are high; slots are few. For these seventy-six candidates—there were ninety-six in the beginning, but twenty have since washed out—becoming a commissioned officer is the fulfillment of a lifelong dream of challenging leadership opportunities in sixteen career fields. Now it's week twelve in the fourteen-week program, and the timed five-mile run represents one of the last obstacles to the successful completion of the OCS program. Failing to meet or beat the required time means not graduating.

Two weeks earlier Myers fractured a toe at the one-mile mark of a twelve-mile march. She was loaded down with thirty-five pounds of gear, and the agonizing pain from her wounded toe increased with every step over the final eleven miles. She toughed it out, drawing on a special kind of grit that it takes to achieve such a monumental task under near-impossible circumstances. Since then her foot has been in a therapeutic boot, and she can barely walk. Yet OCS required every participant to complete every event. Myers's injury warranted no reprieve.

She knows the five-mile run will make or break her chance for success in the program. More than distance, the five-mile run is also about speed. Unlike many of the earlier events, which involve teamwork, this is an individual test. Fortunately for Myers, her conditioning is top-notch—at least it had been up until the twelve-mile march. Would the severity of her injury be her undoing?

Out of the gate, Myers's pace is substantially slower than the pack, due to her throttling back to reduce the pressure on her toe. Mile one proves uneventful, but mile two finds her falling appreciably behind and dealing with increasing pain in her toe. A quarter mile later everything changes. The pain is over the top. Not even halfway through the run, the throbbing is getting the best of her. She slows to a kind of limp walking. Things look bleak.

"I really thought it was the end of the line," she said. "As painful as my injury was, the mental anguish was far worse. Here I was in the last major field event, so very close to achieving the most significant professional accomplishment of my life, and it was all going up in smoke. I felt angry! Angry that I had come so far and now this course was challenging my resolve."

She couldn't see anyone else on the path ahead. There was no one around. The rest of the runners were far ahead of her. Moments later, though, she received the surprise of her life.

"Two other officer candidates appeared out of nowhere," she said. "Suddenly they were standing on either side of me. Given my position relative to the pack, they had reversed course and run quite a distance back to me. How they knew I was in trouble, I'll never know."

These guys say that they're going to run with her the rest of the way. Myers tries to dissuade them. "I told them I was really hurting, that I didn't know how this was going to turn out, meaning I probably wouldn't finish within the required time." She insists they not wait for her. "I didn't want them to sacrifice their standing on my account. While I did not say so to them, I had all but counted myself out."

Instead, she sees how focused they are, how unwavering they are in their resolve. "No, Myers," one says. "We're going to run with you. We know you can do this."

Their belief meshes with her determination to finish the run. She finds new resolve to beat the necessary time. Myers picks up her pace and starts running along with them.

If the threesome is going to complete the run within the allotted time, they know they are going to be really close. "While I was hurting pretty badly, I knew I'd be hurting even worse if none of us met the time limit. These guys, after all, were putting their graduation in jeopardy!"

Across the remaining miles, all she hears over their footfalls is "Myers this and Myers that" and a constant barrage of encouragement, humor, and mental distraction. The strategy employed by the two comrades is to keep Myers's mind off her injury. Amazingly, it works. Add the pressure of the time constraint to these conditions, and she discovers a singular focus unlike any she had ever experienced. "I didn't think about my pain," she said. "I just ran!"

Their actions on the trail also allowed Myers to get to know the men who were helping her. You see, these guys aren't from her platoon. She doesn't know either one of them, although they might have casually greeted or acknowledged each other in the chow line once or twice over the twelve weeks they have been in OCS together.

"About a quarter-mile from the finish, I started thinking, 'Maybe, just maybe, we're going to make it after all,'" Myers said. That's a real boost. The three finish the course at 43:40—a minute and twenty seconds ahead of the required time.

"I don't know how we did it," she said. "What I do know is that I wouldn't have finished that run if it wasn't for the two guys who came back for me. To this day, I think of them as brothers."

In the end, Amanda Myers is one of seventy-four in her class to graduate (two more washed out) because she rose to the occasion when it mattered most. With the support of her "brothers," she conquered the five-mile run within the allotted time—and against all odds.[1]

Officer Candidate Myers's 2004 experience at OCS captures the essence of what Mind-Set 7 is all about: aspiring to reveal value in others. It's propping someone up in their hour of need. It's investing in a person's capacity to make meaningful change. It's believing that people can and will do the right thing. It's extending trust in an appropriate way. It's providing meaningful opportunities. In the end, it's bringing out the best in them.

The word *aspire* is especially important and illustrative in understanding this particular mind-set. Aspire suggests intent, priority, and, most important, pro-activity. For those who possess this mind-set, what they do for people is not an afterthought, it's a long-term investment in people. Professionals with this mind-set find great pleasure in the growth and success of others. They're comfortable in their own skin. They aren't threatened by another's success. Some have official leadership titles, some don't. They're helping to advance someone's interests one day, protecting someone's back the next. If you think these people are weak-kneed pushovers, they're not! Their reputation is stellar. Most great leaders, it has been postulated, have a strong affinity to develop people in this way. It's part of their DNA.

Professionals who hold this mind-set:

- readily extend trust
- recognize the value other professionals bring to the table
- aspire to lift others through their demeanor and actions

As you'll see in this chapter, the genesis of this mind-set can sometimes be traced to one's philosophy of life, sometimes to purely practical reasons, and sometimes to altruistic values based on idealism. Or perhaps a combination of these. Regardless of the reason, Mind-Set 7 has an undeniably positive impact on the recipient because it builds confidence and inspires trust.

Readily Extend Trust

There is perhaps no more powerful way to show confidence (and ultimately reveal value) in others than by extending trust to them. Many examples of this have been provided earlier in this book, such as the executive who hired me in chapter 10. Of course, extending trust must be done in appropriate ways.

Paul Orfalea is considered the single-most-successful graduate in the history of the Marshall School of Business at the University of Southern California. Yet many have never heard of him. Those same people, however, are likely familiar with his college nickname: Kinko. Orfalea founded Kinko's (the copy center) in 1970, and it ultimately grew into the dynasty that Federal Express bought in 2004 for $2.4 billion.

Not bad for a guy who graduated with a D average!

Allow me to explain. Paul has dyslexia—the learning disability that carries a powerful social stigma for those who are unable to learn according to today's educational norms. He flunked out of the second grade. As a teenager, Paul was fired from a gas station job for writing illegible receipts. He doesn't really read—at least not in the sense you and I might think about reading. In fact, Paul won't read this book, one in which he is a formal contributor.

While he was growing up, Paul recognized that people didn't listen to him much. "No one knew what to make of me," he observed. His skill sets initially proved limiting when he tried to cope with the nondyslexic world. To survive in school, Paul befriended and won over others on whom he could depend. Most dyslexics' experiences—whether it be in academic environments or otherwise—are similar to Paul's. He said that he learned empathy because he had to.

Paul received D's in school because he didn't test well, not because he wasn't smart. He's smart—plenty smart! Looking back on his formal education, he said, "Other kids studied hard for their A's and then forgot everything they memorized for the test. I took the D, but came away with the concept."

On a very practical level, Paul learned that for him to flourish (and in some cases survive) he had to depend on other people. He did so (especially as a leader) by extending trust. He also successfully learned the how-to's (that is, the skills) of extending trust. He quickly became aware of the strengths of others (especially those who complemented his weaknesses), which enabled them to do what they did best. In doing so, they were able to shine. In other words, it revealed their value.

Few thought he would make anything of himself, much less grow an obscure one-hundred-square-foot copy shop into a thriving $1.5 billion-a-year enterprise. Fewer still envisioned that Orfalea would create a company that would be named one of the best places to work in the country by *Fortune* magazine—three years in a row! Today, California Polytechnic State University has a dedicated business school in Orfalea's name.

Paul is anything but a corporate button-down. As Kinko's CEO, he was about as nontraditional as they come. He's an anarchist of sorts. Paul hates business meetings and would much rather talk shop while doing something fun, like bowling. Throwing cold water on someone in the shower was one of his classic tricks during company off-sites. My interview with Paul was the most uncommon I've ever conducted. Rather than being the usual one-on-one meeting, the interview was a *very* public event because it occurred during an economics lecture, namely, one of the classes Paul teaches for seniors at the University of California at Santa Barbara. One minute he was discussing economic principles, the next minute I was posing an interview question. (The class, no doubt, felt like a Ping-Pong ball between us.) Whenever you deal with Paul, you've got to be ready for anything.

Someone once described Paul as a weather pattern (think: hurricane). I choose to think of him as Wile E. Coyote with his pants on fire. Carrying on a conversation with Paul is like nothing else. It's a multidimensional, multisensory experience. Fortunately 3D glasses aren't required. Paul is usually three steps ahead of you; trouble is, you don't know it.

When it comes to his business philosophy, Paul keeps it simple. He's been successful because he kept it simple. John Davis, a longtime Kinko's board member and a professor at the Harvard business school, observed: "Business to Paul is not mystical. He speaks in a nonliteral, rather circular or creative way, but his thinking is actually very clear. You start to appreciate how clearly he thinks about business. He keeps his eye on the basics at all times. . . . He doesn't get distracted. "

Paul once said, "As a leader, all you do is manage trust." Thus it's no accident that the first chapter in his popular book *Copy This* is entitled "Anybody Else Can Do It Better," an allusion to his obsession about giving near-total autonomy to his store managers.

He knows that there's real value inherent in people, and he's committed to revealing it. He starts by extending trust. All of this has a practical purpose. First, Paul set up a customer-centric business, which simply means that the customer is king. Everything his employees did, first and foremost, was about pleasing customers. Paul commented about Kinko's, "We weren't so much selling copies as we were assuaging our customers' anxiety."

Given the service orientation of the business, Paul knew that his employees (he prefers to think of his employees as co-workers)—the people in the trenches with the customers—either make or break a customer's experience. As so many service companies (for example, Four Seasons, Marriott, etc.) ultimately discovered, happy employees make happy customers. Paul was among the first to grasp this, and for him this insight meant that Kinko's had to be a great place to work. The Kinko's culture became an integral foundation for the company's competitive advantage. For his part, Paul made sure that the culture at Kinko's emphasized trust, and this investment in trust helped the company to accomplish its objectives. As I mentioned earlier, *Fortune* magazine recognized Orfalea's success by three times naming Kinko's as one of the best places to work.

Giving store managers near autonomy was a natural extension of Kinko's investment in trust. It allowed the stores to serve their customers much better and without undue interference from headquarters. Plus this investment in trust avoided the fallout of Paul's 20 percent theory; namely, every layer of management screws up a good idea by 20 percent. Ruining other people's ideas does not engender trust!

Paul often jokes, "I didn't like work, so to get out of work I gave other people a lot of power. I'm really good at doing one thing: getting out of work."[2] Building a billion-dollar enterprise takes a tremendous amount of work, so while Paul effectively delegated many details to others, he certainly did his fair share of the heavy lifting. That's apparent in Kinko's success.

Consider how Paul enhanced trust in corporate governance and within the partner ranks (those who owned stores) at Kinko's. More often than not, corporate boards are the seat of power at any enterprise. That power is jealously guarded and can become a source of distrust, especially when an unpopular or unwise edict is issued from headquarters.

At Kinko's, corporate policy changes required approval from three-quarters of the stores.[3] In standard business practice, that's unheard of. But Paul knew that his people knew things he didn't, and he didn't want to waste time and effort on wrong-headed decisions. "So to do anything of significance," he said, "I had to get buy-in—lots of it. I believe democracy is the best means available to get people to buy-in. That's what we needed, more than anything else, from everybody at Kinko's: partners, co-workers, and customers."

This approach obviously takes much longer on the front end, but it ensures back-end ownership. Most corporate leaders don't have the stomach for such an approach, let alone the guts to relinquish so much power in such a dramatic way.

What was Paul's inspiration for this radical corporate governance model? When I asked him, he simply pointed to the Constitution. Paul loves the Constitution; he draws strength from it. He ran Kinko's like a democracy.[4] He said, "I learned that the Founding Fathers distrusted centralized authority almost as much as dyslexics do. So I was forever protecting the small from the big."[5] Paul knew that for democracies require a huge element of trust in order to thrive. So why not, he reasoned, bring that level of trust to Kinko's?

Ever the independent-thinking contrarian, Paul insisted that his store managers have a representative on the board of directors. He did this despite strenuous protests from his executives. Looking back, Paul noted, "Turns out, the store manager was the most valuable person on the board."[6]

So when Paul says that "trusting people is very emancipating," he knows what he's talking about, because he incorporated the principle of extending trust into every essential aspect of Kinko's. Investment guru Charles Schwab observed, "The Kinko's we've known for all these years would not exist were it not for the exceptional thinking of its founder."[7]

Who would have thought that the youngster who so many had given up on would achieve so much and positively impact so many. The truth is that dyslexics, while often being unconventional, see things the rest of us can't. And Paul is not alone. Richard Branson of Virgin Records, telecom pioneer Craig McCaw, John Chambers of Cisco, and Charles Schwab are all exceptionally successful businesspeople who also cope daily with dyslexia.[8]

Paul's experience also addresses a question I frequently hear: Are the seven mind-sets learned or are they innate?

While Paul is extremely respectful of others, he doesn't have some warm, fuzzy, innate altruistic value driven by compassionate idealism. Paul extended trust because it worked for him. He learned that on a very practical level. His experience shows us that the genesis for one's mind-set can come from a purely practical (and learned) experience—in addition to one's values, philosophy, or idealism.

Recognize the Value Other Professionals Bring to the Table

Each of us has probably been there: attempting to adjust a toilet that just won't stop running. On the surface, it certainly looks straightforward enough. An adjustment here, a tweak there, and everything should be okay, right? Yeah—in theory.

After wrestling with a new-fangled toilet in my own home—investing over six hours of my time, getting a half-baked result, plus creating a disgruntled wife in the process—I finally realized the toilet had won. I called a plumber . . . reluctantly! (There are two plumbers in my family. For me, being able to fix my own plumbing is a badge of honor, something to brag about over a holiday dinner.)

You already know what happened next. The plumber came, and a half-hour later, the toilet is fixed. And I mean really fixed. Not like one of my Band-Aid fixes. And he didn't even break a sweat doing it. I should have followed the adage: do what you do best and leave the rest to others. Rather than reinvent the wheel, when facing tasks that are outside of your expertise, find someone who can use their expertise—someone who can do it in his sleep, someone who can make it look like child's play. You'll save yourself a lot of time and aggravation, plus it will be done right. And isn't this what professionals want: to have it done right?

Professionals don't try to be all things to all people. Bill Cosby noted, "I don't know the key to success, but the key to failure is trying to please everybody." Professionals know their limitations and are comfortable reaching out to others whose expertise complements their own. They're not threatened by someone who can do something they can't.

Many times we're our own worst enemy (men especially) when we're reluctant to ask for help from another professional. Rather than bring in someone with expertise, we try to do it ourselves. Usually it's about something we really have no business attempting. We tell ourselves that we like challenges, but we're just being stubborn. We tell ourselves we're up to the task, but it's only our ego getting in the way. We tell ourselves that we're being financially responsible, but we're just being cheap.

This same thing happens regularly in the workplace. Namely, our egos get in the way of leveraging the expertise of other professionals. We tell ourselves that asking for help demonstrates weakness. We get concerned that we might not appear as indispensable as we believe we are. We obsess that someone might get a leg up on us. What's ominously missing here is the first and foremost question, which is, will involving another professional improve the deliverable? Too often, instead of focusing on the deliverable, our focus is centered on ourselves.

As important as short-term deliverables are, we may want to involve another professional for other reasons. Sometimes involving another professional is about making a long-term investment in people or processes.

Consider:

- the leader who asks her chief lieutenant to make an especially important presentation to the boss—because it's expected the lieutenant will do a better job.
- the project manager who asks a new colleague to develop a critical portion of the department's new operating plan because of the newcomer's expertise and unique skill set.
- the perfection-driven department administrator who has personally organized the department's renowned holiday party for the past ten years but now delegates the full responsibility for that party to a capable department member, because the administrator has finally realized that other people, when given the opportunity, can do things just as well as (and sometimes better than) he can.

- the manager who offers her department's high-potential all-star to take a high-profile special assignment outside the department because the all-star needs the developmental experience.
- the chairman who invites a reclusive board member to chair the compensation committee because the board member feels disconnected—and the board feels the recluse has more to offer.
- the team leader who asks a longtime vendor to the meet with the executive committee that is contemplating a change in an important operating policy because the vendor has an unmatched reputation in such matters.
- the director who asks a performance consultant to help revitalize a languishing operating committee because of the specialist's infectious personality, along with her unique ability to act as a catalyst in jump-starting the group's ownership, collaboration, and results.

When it comes to involving other professionals, the circumstances may vary, but what is common among those who hold Mind-Set 7 is an appreciation of the capabilities of others—whether it's a proven competence or a future capability—and an aspiration to reveal that value. These professionals are people who are secure, comfortable in their own skin, if you will. They're not compromised by another's success. They're willing to share the stage. They aren't trapped by the all-too-prevalent belief that when someone else wins, they lose. They share power. As Charles Schwab commented, "The real test of business greatness lies in giving opportunities to others."

Dave Ulrich observed, "It's unfortunate that so many don't take better advantage of the opportunities they have to collaborate professionally with others. It's obviously good for the person who is being offered the opportunity, but it can also be great for you too. Certainly, you've got to be smart about it, and when you do, you'll find the deliverable is better, the process is easier, and you've forged the beginning of a long-term relationship with another professional. The impact this has on trust can't be overstated! In the end, you'll find you have expanded your own capabilities and opportunities."

Getting Life-Size

Frances Hesselbein recognizes the inherent value others bring to the table. She also knows that personal transformations are powerfully aided by the important aspects of one's self-image.

As the CEO of the Girl Scouts from 1976 to 1990, Frances took an organization in disarray to the heights of success. She achieved this primarily by enlarging and energizing the base of volunteers. Volunteer membership increased 788,000 in an era when volunteerism in most comparable organizations dropped precipitously and total girl and adult membership soared to 3,200,000.

What Frances observed early on was that some executives of the 335 local Girl Scouts Councils didn't see themselves life-size. She committed to change that. Frances wanted the local Girl Scout Council executive directors to see themselves as CEOs in one of the most significant voluntary organizations in the world and the largest organizations for girls and women in the world. She wanted them to see themselves *life-size,* as Frances prefers to describe it.

Frances envisioned the Girl Scouts becoming the country's preeminent organization for girls and young women. Having the council executive directors' self-image become life-size was vitally important for the organization to realize its highest potential. With this perspective, the organization's goals would be achieved. Without it, their success would be limited.

Frances told me, "I spoke with Professor Regina Herzlinger at the Harvard Business School and asked, 'Could you and several professors design a corporate management seminar for our Girl Scout executives?'"

Dr. Herzlinger said, "Oh, we've never done anything like that. Yes, we will do it!"

Five professors designed and presented the seminar. Five hundred staff members and local and national Girl Scouts executives attended the seminar, fifty at a time. "We called it the Harvard experience," Frances said.

"You've never seen such a transformation. They saw themselves life-size," she recalled. "What happens when you do something like this? It sets up a revolution of rising expectations. Instead of just receiving their Harvard certificate and saying thank you, they asked, 'What's next?'"

In response, Dr. Herzlinger set up an asset management seminar just for our Girl Scout executives. After everyone completed the course, Frances said, "You've never seen a more skillful group of financial managers in your life. These were people who were responsible for a $333 million cookie sale every year, for thousands of conference centers, buildings, headquarters, and camps." Such development costs money. "But it was an investment," Frances noted. "An important investment in people. And every year, for twelve years, the Girl Scouts held a conference we called 'An Adventure in Excellence.'" For three days we brought the same 335 council CEOs and 100 national staff members together with great thought leaders such as Peter Drucker, Warren Bennis, Noel Tichy, Marshall Goldsmith, John W. Work III—the great thought leaders of our time. They all graciously agreed, as their contribution, to speak to us. The difference they made was immeasurable!"

As Frances knows very well, you can't get local leaders to see themselves as life-size just by speaking from her office in New York. Thus she also sponsored a world-class developmental plan that was every bit as life-size as the people whose self-image she was attempting to elevate. Seeing oneself as a CEO in the country's preeminent character-building organization for girls and young women is quite a different experience than merely seeing oneself as the executive of a local affiliate program sometimes defined by the annual cookie sale. Her investment in people worked.

If there ever was a leader who elevated the importance and capabilities of others while deflecting attention away from herself, it's Frances Hesselbein. She's not about herself in any way. Rather, Frances shines the light on others, gives other people opportunities, and recognizes the value and potential in each and every person with whom she comes into contact. Her spirit and enthusiasm are infectious. She sees in others what they can't see in themselves.

What made this work? To the local council leaders the world-class developmental effort spoke volumes. It shouted, "You're important! You're integral to our success!" She was teaching the organization's next generation of leaders without herself uttering a word of instruction. The energy she devoted to staff development was a "top of mind" experience, not an afterthought.

Frances and leaders like her are constantly asking probing questions like:

- What natural gifts does she possess?
- What situations or environments can best reveal those gifts?
- Who could enhance this person's using his gifts even more?
- What strengths or potential do I see in her that she can't see in herself?
- What experiences will make him even better?
- What should I personally be doing to support her success?

Aren't these the types of questions we would naturally ask if our intent is to recognize the value other professionals bring to the table? For Frances, it certainly is.

Aspire to Lift Others Through Our Demeanor and Actions

Unpolished, easily rattled, wild, bad mechanics—all of these words were used to describe future Hall of Famer Randy Johnson during the first five years of his Major League Baseball pitching career. "Unrealized potential" was how baseball insiders viewed Randy. But for Johnson, everything changed as the result of a fortuitous encounter with legendary pitcher Nolan Ryan. Prior to a 1992 game, Ryan watched Johnson's throwing motion in the bullpen at Arlington Stadium and observed a subtle but critical flaw in Johnson's pitching mechanics.

Ryan—a Western Division opponent—suggested Johnson land on the ball of his right foot instead of his right heel. Johnson said, "Everything is a chain reaction from there. Your knee falls over the ball of your foot, your body falls over your knee, your arm will be in the upright position on a consistent basis, you'll be able to drive the ball in on a right-hander, you'll have more velocity over the course of the game because you'll have your body behind it, you'll be able to field your position better, and more importantly you'll be a better pitcher."

Johnson faced Ryan in the last game of that same season. He struck out eighteen. Since then, Johnson has been one of the most feared pitchers in the game. He's won the Cy Young Award five times, has over three hundred career wins, and has pitched one of the eighteen perfect games in Major League history. Johnson credits Ryan for the suggestion that changed everything for him.

Ryan, despite being a divisional opponent, encouraged Johnson. He didn't have to do that, but he did. And what he did speaks volumes about him. Ryan said that he had a great appreciation for Johnson's talent and hoped Johnson didn't take as long to figure things out as he had.

Notice how Ryan aspired to bring out the talent (value) he saw in Johnson. Despite Johnson's being on an opposing team, Ryan couldn't help himself. He really didn't have to think about it. He just did it. The impetus? His mind-set![9]

Leadership expert John Maxwell told of an experiment years ago in which people's capacity to endure pain was measured by how long they could tolerate standing barefoot in a bucket of ice water. One critical factor made it possible for some to endure the freezing water twice as long as others: encouragement from others. Support and encouragement from others enabled the volunteers to endure the needling pain much longer than their counterparts who received no such support.[10]

Nolan Ryan's encouragement and support made a difference for Randy Johnson. Co-workers in the workplace constantly do the same for one another. Sometimes their encouragement is subtle; sometimes it is career changing. In any event, what they do hits close to home by helping others to put their best foot forward.

Consider:

- the coordinator who mentors the department's newbie.
- the director who opens up her network to a colleague seeking to find a new job opportunity.
- the sales representative who offers to coach a peer who is struggling to make his numbers.
- the administrative assistant who offers to cover for a colleague during her annual development week.
- the marketing specialist who takes a bullet for an unsuspecting colleague.

Each of these examples is affirming. They are things that professionals do in the spirit of uplifting and supporting others. There are also things that professionals don't do in advancing that same goal. Have you ever noticed:

- how it only takes one person to ruin the atmosphere of a meeting?
- how a group tends to reflect—for better or for worse—the demeanor of its leader?
- how contentious the conversation becomes when you respond in kind to someone who disses you?
- how unproductive problem solving becomes in the absence of objectivity?
- how futile planning becomes when you're stuck in the most mundane details?

Professionals take the high road even when they may be justified to act otherwise. They don't take the bait when someone cleverly attempts to engage them into a contentious conversation. They don't flake out when they're having a bad day. They demand objectivity from others. They refuse to get lost in the weeds when the situation warrants dealing with the big picture.

Professionals know they're part of something bigger than themselves. (Recall Mind-Set 2.) They act responsibly whether they impact an individual in a one-on-one conversation or a five-hundred-member department.

Ben Franklin: Purveyor of Magnanimous Acts

Benjamin Franklin was one of the most influential Founding Fathers and at the same time one of the wealthiest men in America. His beginnings, however, belied these achievements. His father was a maker of candles and soap in Boston, and Franklin was the fifteenth of seventeen children. Ten-year-old Franklin first worked in his father's shop, and at the age of twelve became a printer's apprentice under an older brother. When he was sixteen, he resorted to a pseudonym in order to publish humorous comments on colonial life through a series of letters that appeared in his brother's newspaper. While the letters proved to be very popular, the brother was not amused when Franklin was revealed to be the writer. As a result, in violation of his apprenticeship, Franklin fled to Philadelphia and found work in various printing shops before publishing his own newspaper.[11]

He also wrote and annually updated *Poor Richard's Almanack,* a bestseller for almost thirty years. To fill in the open spaces between some entries, Franklin added numerous proverbs and maxims, which made the work even more popular. He later expanded the adages in a separate pamphlet that he entitled *The Way to Wealth.* Its emphasis on industry and frugality certainly proved to be the way to wealth for Franklin.

But Franklin was more than an entrepreneur. While he proved to be a sound businessman, he was also fascinated by science and math, which led to his well-known experiments with electricity. Franklin was also greatly involved in community affairs. He helped to organize the first fire department, the first hospital, and the first lending library in this country, and he was involved in the founding of two colleges. Franklin's political life was born as well, first serving as a local councilman, then a justice of the peace, then a colonial assemblyman, and then as a deputy postmaster-general for all the British colonies. Some have observed that it was in this last role that Franklin glimpsed the potential national framework that would become the United States. He was a representative at the 1754 Albany Congress that tried to improve relations with Native Americans and also address the needed defenses against the French. Franklin's achievements were recognized with honorary degrees from Harvard, Yale, Oxford, and the University of St. Andrews.

When the tension between Great Britain and the American colonies exploded on the commons at Lexington and Concord, Franklin was in England, attempting to moderate a resolution to the schism. Upon his return to Philadelphia in 1775, Franklin found he had been named a representative to the Second Continental Congress and made chairman of numerous committees, as well as being named to the committee charged with composing a declaration of independence. As I noted before, independence was not a sure thing when the congress first convened, even though shots already had been fired and blood already had been spilt. While British actions throughout 1775 and 1776 slowly pushed Americans toward independence, a single polarizing publication appeared, which was in no small way due to Franklin's unqualified benevolence to a down-trodden man who would come to play an integral role in the nation's independence.

In the fall of 1774 Franklin encountered an out-of-work tax collector whose business and marriage had failed simultaneously. To stay out of debtors prison, the man had sold everything he owned and moved to London. There he met Franklin, and the American celebrity suggested he should emigrate to the colonies and wrote a letter of introduction for him. Within a month the man booked passage for Philadelphia, but the voyage nearly killed him. Fortunately, Franklin's physician was at the dock to welcome him and saw to his treatment and recovery. Once back on his feet, the man became the editor of the *Pennsylvania Magazine,* and he began wielding his pen with fervor. Throughout 1775 he worked on a single pamphlet that was later published in January 1776. It was an amazing success, selling 120,000 copies during its first three months, 500,000 in its first year, and going through numerous editions.

The recipient of Franklin's attention and support was none other than Thomas Paine—who ultimately proved to be one of the most influential Founding Fathers; Thomas Edison regarded Paine as "one of the greatest of all Americans." It was Paine's forty-six-page pamphlet *Common Sense* that played a tremendous role in 1776 in stimulating the debate over reconciliation with Britain and the idea of independence. While the reconciliation-independence debate may not have been determined specifically by Paine's simple arguments, his arguments no doubt influenced the debate by bringing it out into the open at the same time that the Second Continental Congress was weighing which course of action to take and how it would affect the war effort. The timing proved fortuitous. Thus, when independence came to the floor for debate on July 2, 1776 (and Franklin was there too), agreement followed on July 4, and the United States of America became a reality.

Franklin's assistance to Paine illustrates a lesser-known virtue of Franklin: his personal generosity. He cared about people and enjoyed seeing them succeed by their own hard work and ingenuity. Franklin also realized that sometimes people needed someone to help discover their value. In Paine's case, that someone was Franklin. Consider these personal qualities:

- Franklin never sought patents for any of his practical inventions (for example, bifocal reading glasses, lightning rod and other experiments with electricity, etc). He explained, "We should be glad of an opportunity to serve others by an invention of ours; and this we should do freely and generously."
- Contrary to the business model of his day, Franklin initiated a franchising model that enabled interested printers to expand their businesses by assisting them in acquiring capital and equipment. This franchising model often became the key break an aspiring entrepreneur needed to jump-start a successful printing career.

Franklin's paradox was his disdain of waste while being personally generous to so many. Certainly, he was well known for being frugal. Yet when it came to others, Franklin used his money and influence to carry out magnanimous acts for individuals (such as Thomas Paine) for the better part of his life. "I would rather have it said 'he lived usefully,' than 'he died rich,'" said Franklin.

Benjamin Franklin set out to be neither famous nor rich. He believed that a person's net worth was "determined by what remains after your bad habits are subtracted from your good ones." He set out to do what he could to find value in himself and help reveal it in others. For all his publicly based philanthropic efforts, Franklin also believed that "individual endeavor can change the course of history for the better." He walked his high-minded talk. In Paine's case, Franklin's words were indeed prophetic.

Wrap-Up

To say that the people chronicled in this chapter are trustworthy is an understatement. Revered is more like it. Just ask Amanda Myers. People are especially passionate when they talk about people who exemplify Mind-Set 7. It's not hard to understand why. These are individuals who have had the biggest impact on the development, career success, and professional satisfaction of many other colleagues.

Let's face it, many don't come to this mind-set naturally—especially those from Western "me-first" cultures. Plus many corporations—with their use of bell-curve performance assessments, forced-ranked succession planning, and vanishing promotional opportunities—unintentionally work against this mind-set. As well intended as these management practices are, they often produce internal competition that encourages employees to aspire to principally reveal value in themselves, not others.

Organizationally speaking, Mind-Set 7 is a paradox. You hear people speak passionately about those who exhibit this mind-set, but too often their organization doesn't reinforce its practice. When conducting an organizational assessment of the seven mind-sets, it's not uncommon that Mind-Set 7 receives the lowest score relative to the other six.

For instance, I conducted such an assessment in a highly profitable but troubled division at one of the world's largest accounting firms. Personnel turnover was through the roof, morale was low, and recruitment efforts were impossible. Lots of people wanted out, and nobody wanted in—an ominous trend that threatened the division's sustained financial success. Mind-Set 7 easily scored the worst on a one-to-five scale, with five being the highest. Every other mind-set (with one exception) scored at least a three. The assessment proved to be a catalyst for the organization to make substantive changes.

In many ways this mind-set is a mixture of each other mind-set. People who are particularly prone to exhibit this mind-set do so primarily because of their own core values rather than the organizational norms of which they are a part. Certainly this is consistent with Mind-Set 4: professionals have personal standards that transcend organizational ones.

Dave Ulrich notes, "It's funny all the things we tell ourselves that get in the way of collaborating more effectively with other professionals: 'It'll take too long,' 'It'll be hassle,' 'It's too risky,' 'The person isn't good enough,' 'I work better alone,' 'Let them prove themselves first,' 'I can do it better.' There's hundreds more. But these up-front concerns are rarely realized.

More often than not, they're just excuses that serve to keep us in our own comfort zone. That's unfortunate, because the benefits of professional collaboration far outweigh the costs. This very book—with all of its wonderful contributors—is certainly a prime example. The most successful people I know hold this mind-set."

SUMMARY

- Whereas other mind-sets inspire trust, this one *builds* trust (as well as confidence)—fast!
- This mind-set is first and foremost about bringing out the best in others, seeing their potential, challenging them, and elevating them beyond what they thought they were capable of.
- Recognizing the value other professionals bring to the table reflects a deep emotional maturity, one that is requisite for increasing responsibility throughout your career.
- Because the by-product of this mind-set occurs publicly (manifested in our work relationships), it quickly reinforces the efficacy of the mind-set. People who try it find out how quickly it works.
- Those who lack this mind-set are often unable to attract the best talent for their organization.
- Those who have developed this mind-set not only demonstrate wisdom, generosity, and empathy, but also an uncommon sense of personal security.
- This mind-set helps others realize their greatest strengths and untold opportunities in a way that creates a legacy for you.

PART

III

Upgrading the Culture

CHAPTER **THIRTEEN**

Your Competitive Advantage Is Hiding in Plain Sight

One competitive advantage that cannot be readily purchased, copied, or go out of style is the superior management and development of people.

—Howard Gutman

This chapter is directed primarily to leaders, managers, human resources professionals, and organizational consultants, both internal and external—the people who define the atmosphere of an organization. An organization achieves its competitive advantage by culturally reinforcing people's views of themselves as professionals. This is an advantage that is hiding in plain sight. It is available to a mobile work unit, a centralized department, or an entire enterprise. This premise is built upon three conclusions that have been advanced previously:

- Being a professional is synonymous with being trustworthy (chapter 1)
- Being a professional is an equal-opportunity aspiration available to every employee (chapter 2)
- Being a professional is highly motivating (chapter 3)

Organizations achieve a competitive advantage when their employees view themselves as professionals, and this is particularly pertinent now. Thus this chapter addresses three important, interrelated ideas:

1. Professionalism and competitive advantage are inseparably linked.
2. Developing a culture of professionals, by default, builds trust.
3. Trust is the *one* thing you must get right in achieving competitive advantage. It places professionals front and center in a company's culture.

Walking the Walk

In business, people rarely fall short because they lack knowledge, especially technical knowledge. This is especially true in the military. Gen. Richard B. Myers told me, "In virtually all cases where allegations of wrongdoing are brought against a senior officer, it isn't because they lacked expertise or didn't have access to the expertise. Rather, it's either a case of bad judgment or knowingly doing the wrong thing, not because they lacked knowledge or the ability to comprehend." People know what to do, but for varying reasons they do not consistently do what they know they should.

Management guru Noel Tichy told me that when his clients and students too regularly confess that their judgments have fallen short, they frequently add, "I really knew in my gut what I should do, but I didn't do it."[1] For leaders and managers, this is a real head scratcher. Is it little wonder that we often hear the phrase, "Do the right thing"? Consider:

- The senior executive who faithfully resource shares with her peers despite putting herself at risk for not making her own numbers.
- The crew foreman who resists the temptation to haze the new apprentice despite being hazed at the beginning of his career.
- The manager who generously supports a newly approved implementation plan despite arguing against it three days earlier.

It's one thing for an individual to show up in such an exemplary way. Steve was one such individual we met in chapter 1. These kinds of people help to set the standard within an organization. But what if your entire organization collectively raised its level of professionalism? That means having many people with mind-sets like the senior executive, crew foreman, and manager illustrated above. Think for a moment about the pressing issues you regularly face (productivity, organizational cohesiveness, commitment to initiatives). What does your intuition tell you the impacts would be?

Figure 13.1—Competitive Advantage

Individual Potential

VIEW SELF AS A **PROFESSIONAL**

COMPETITIVE **ADVANTAGE**

MIND-**SETS**

BUILD **TRUST**

Delivery Mechanism

Organizational Need

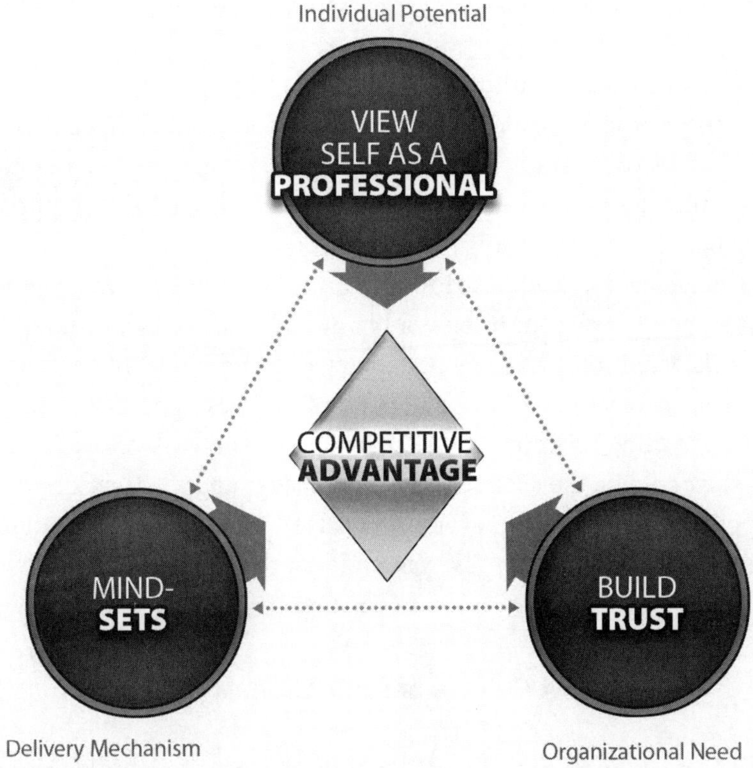

When an organization's culture reflects the highest professional standards, more people will do what they know they should do—and they'll do it more often.

A lineman heard about a job opening at a yard no more than fifteen minutes from his home. If he took the job, there would be no more long commutes in horrific traffic to company headquarters. He would save a bundle on gas and gain nearly two hours of precious time with his family. Surely he'd apply for this position. Wrong!

Despite the compelling arguments to take the assignment at the other yard, this exemplary lineman thought that the prospects of working with a different team were unappealing due to the group's dysfunctional management. The work would be essentially the same, but the environment would be like a war zone. The lineman's current yard and management afford him a great working environment with superior leadership that takes pride in who each man is and what they do. In the lineman's eyes, the difference between the two yards is that one is run by professionals and the other isn't.

One work-team within the same company can have an advantage over another, depending on the degree of professional behaviors and attitudes the team demonstrates. The role that leadership takes in establishing such a professional environment, as well as the positive consequences for the organization, cannot be overstated.

Management consultant Howard Gutman observed, "One competitive advantage that cannot be readily purchased, copied, or go out of style is the superior management and development of people."

Thus, developing professionals—in the very best sense of the word—and establishing a professional environment that will allow them to flourish should be the aspiration of every leader and manager desiring a competitive advantage. An ever-rising tide of professionalism within an organization lifts all boats. The remainder of this chapter explains why.

A Culture of Professionals

When I speak of being a professional, I am not simply talking about taking pride in your work. Many people almost exclusively associate *professional* with the technical aspects of their work, but that's not what I'm talking about here. Neither am I talking about the generic term *professional development,* which to most is a catchall term used to describe any type of development. Recall that six of the seven mind-sets are nontechnical. There's a big difference between what you do and how you do it.

Figure 13.2—Professionalism

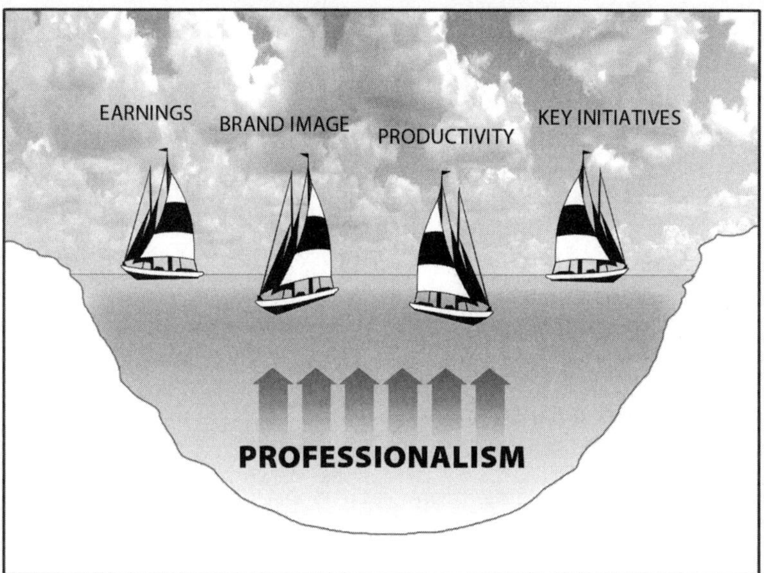

In consultant-speak, I advocate that leaders should create a culture that centers around an organization's professionals. The brand earns efficacy when culture becomes synonymous with professional, thus creating a culture of professionals.

Much has been written on competitive advantage as it relates to strategy. It is not my intent to repeat that here. When I speak about competitive advantage through a culture of professionals, the fundamentals (the right people, a well-thought-out strategic plan, sufficient capitalization, etc.) must already be in place. In short, that means hiring, developing, and rewarding people as professionals. Certainly, that seems straightforward enough, right? It isn't!

Culture as a Brand

Branding answers the all-important question, "What do you want to be known for?" S. C. Johnson, the consumer products giant, for example, prides itself on its powerful brand: "Products you can trust." However, the principle behind branding isn't limited to consumers. Building a premier leadership brand, as GE and others have done, has positive and far-reaching impacts for a company, externally and internally.[2]

The same is true for branding one's culture. In other words, culture as a brand has positive and far-reaching impacts on employee morale, recruiting, and retention, just to name a few. The international biotechnology giant Amgen is a good example. Amgen attributes its marketplace leadership to the aggressive development of cutting-edge products its scientists collaboratively have brought forth. Amgen's culture enables it to compete intensely and win.

What Culture Is and What Culture Does

Mention culture to some senior executives and watch their eyes glaze over. There are various explanations why many here-and-now hard-driving senior executives are uncomfortable about dealing with the important issues involving culture: (1) culture is a somewhat vague and ambiguous term, (2) they can't see it because they're immersed in it, (3) culture changes through influence, not through executive edicts, and (4) changing culture tends to be a slow process.

Many have great difficulty characterizing their own culture. Face it, it's hard to describe something that is as ethereal as culture. You can't see it, touch it, or put it on a balance sheet, but you can *feel* it. Renowned organizational consultant Edgar Schein may have put it best: **"Culture is to an organization what character is to the individual."** This qualitative description may provide the ultimate sniff test when maneuvering around an organization's culture.

The responsibility for shaping a culture of professionals falls squarely upon its leadership. Schein also said, "There is a possibility that the only thing of real importance that leaders do is create and manage culture."

But how much does culture really matter?

Ask Jack Welch, former CEO at GE. Without undue reservation, he terminated employees who brought in good numbers or even great results but failed to live up to the tenets of the GE culture. Welch felt GE's culture was too important to overlook.

Ask Ray Davis, CEO of Umpqua Bank. In 2007 his bank's market capitalization was $7 billion—a substantial sum for a regional bank. But Davis (arguably a numbers guy) felt the value of Umpqua's culture was of greater worth to the bank than its impressive market capitalization.

Ask David Nadler, CEO at Delta Consulting. He said, "Virtually every successful CEO with whom I've worked has viewed culture change as a top personal priority." Delta has succeeded in generating more significant major organizational change projects than any other firm of its type.

So what is this ethereal thing referred to as culture? From a functional point of view, culture is to an organization what DNA is to a cell. A culture's function is to reinforce, drive, and teach.

- Culture reinforces what an organization values, although not necessarily its declared values.
- Culture drives how things get done for better or worse.
- Culture teaches the next generation without a word of instruction.

Practically speaking, you can learn a lot about the nature of your organization's culture by answering questions such as:

- What do people do when no one is looking?
- When something goes wrong, where is management's emphasis? On what or who?
- Is it easier to ask forgiveness than permission or to soothe someone's guilty conscience after not acting at all?
- How large is the gap between how customers are treated versus how employees are treated?
- Are ideas based on incrementalism or on truly novel approaches?
- What gets rewarded: personality or substance?
- Are employees treated as assets or as costs?
- When there's a problem, do people run for the exits or offer to help?
- What's more prevalent: careerism or professionalism?
- Is leadership communication authentic or just so much propaganda?
- To what degree are people proud to be associated with the organization?

- What's more important: who you know or what you contribute?
- Are mistakes opportunities for learning or occasions to blacklist someone?
- When getting feedback, do you get it straight, or do you need a Ouija board to interpret it?
- When a senior leader sneezes, does the entire organization get a cold?
- What's more valued: not rocking the boat or speaking up?

Every organization, regardless of size or type, has a culture just as surely as individuals have personalities. Your answers to the questions above should tell you a lot about the nature of your own organization. What is your organization reinforcing, driving, and teaching?

Three Buckets

In my experience, people characterize their organization's culture in one of three ways:

1. What is despised about it.
2. What needs immediate fixing.
3. What it should be.

What's Despised About It

Disgruntled employees, observant consultants, and occasionally insightful leaders have characterized their organization's culture as one of fear, contention, conformity, avoidance, have and have-nots, or corruption (rarely). These negative characterizations revolve around "what is." They focus largely on people's negative experiences. Thus a culture of this type is defined by those kinds of experiences: the ones people despise. For example, a boutique law firm led by an absentee managing partner and sustained by an overworked staff (a culture of have and have-nots), a state bureaucracy whose annual budget is at risk (a culture of conformity), and a hospitality operation run by an overzealous owner (a culture of fear).

One obvious sign of a despised culture is the complaining of employees that they are not being treated as adults. Almost without exception, this is a red flag and usually symptomatic of a myriad of other problems.

What Needs Immediate Fixing

Nervous leaders, vulnerable managers, and well-intended regulators frequently talk about their desire to create a culture of retainment, production, timeliness, compliance, etc. These descriptions typically focus on needs that require immediate fixing and produce important but largely tactical outcomes. Examples include a retail establishment focusing on retainment (employee turnover is its Achilles heel), the weak production numbers of a widget company threaten its viability, the timeliness required by a telecommunication company to compete effectively for new customer business, and a financial services firm that consistently flounders under the scrutiny of Security and Exchange Commission audits.

In these cultures, a new cultural mantra usually emerges based on whatever new crisis the organization faces. The problems with this approach are reactive in nature, not proactive. A steady stream of new mantras confuses employees about priorities and creates a never-ending series of fire drills. It is rare that this is the only aspect of an organization's culture that needs emphasizing; so many other priorities, by default, go wanting.

What It Should Be

Many proactive leaders want to create what their culture should be. This is to be applauded. Their cultural descriptions, however, are largely aspirational in nature. While the organization hasn't yet perfected collaboration, it aspires to do so, believing that an improvement in collaboration will markedly advance its business objectives. Focusing on the cultural "should be" will usually improve it. Examples include cultures of execution, discipline, collaboration, commitment and performance, trust and accountability, and inclusion.

While cultures that need immediate fixing may be good, and cultures that focus on how they "should be" may be better, I believe that the best, the ultimate brand is a culture of professionals.

The Ultimate Brand

If an organization's culture is analogous to an individual's character, then ideally the description and resulting brand of that culture should elicit the highest standards of excellence. The brand should speak to those who are integral in realizing its potential. I know of no word more appropriate than *professional* and all it represents in achieving that end.

Think of some of the most troublesome problems your organization faces:

- complacency within the ranks
- leadership not being in agreement
- lack of cooperation between key departments

Now consider some of the biggest opportunities ahead for your organization:

- developing a new product line
- hiring a key member of your leadership team
- partnering with another company on a joint venture

How would these problems or opportunities be impacted if your organization's culture truly reflected the highest professional standards? Raising professional standards dramatically impacts all facets and aspects of an organization, because an organization's culture delivers, for better or worse, its results. And trusted professionals deliver the best results. Thus it is natural for an organization's character, or culture, to be synonymous with *professional.*

Trusted professionals show up very differently than the wannabes. The difference? Their mind-sets. They think differently, but it transcends being a mere intellectual exercise. Recall that a mind-set is one part personal values, one part emotional maturity, and one part life's experience. The attributes managers and leaders aspire to—accountability, commitment, authenticity, integrity, etc.—all come with the package. Mind-sets are inherent to the trusted professional. In the end, they are a part of their DNA.

A culture of professionals strikes at the roots of every problem and every achievement. Henry David Thoreau pointed out, "For every thousand people hacking at the leaves of evil, there is one striking at the roots." Organizationally speaking, developing a culture of professionals strikes at the roots. The approach is especially compatible with an organization's values, complimentary to an organization's priorities, affirming to employees, and ultimately becomes an invaluable tool for leaders. Institutionalizing the individual power of the seven mind-sets delineated in part 2 produces desirable characteristics when aggregated into the collective culture.

Figure 13.3—Culture of Professionals

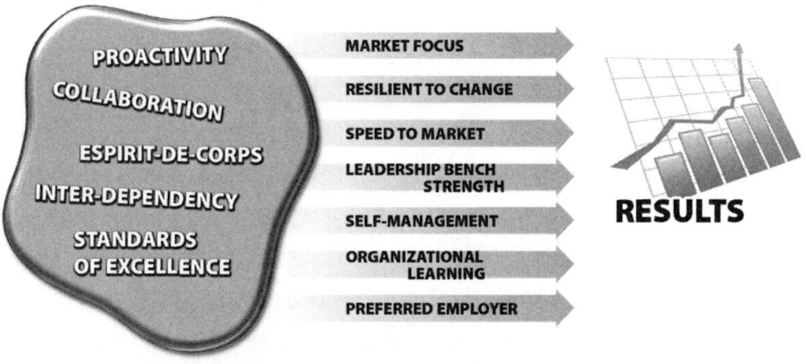

As Figure 13.3 suggests, a culture that reflects the highest professional standards outperforms those that don't. It's a matter of focused energy. People get beyond themselves and generate numerous desirable outcomes. Turf wars give way to collaboration. Power struggles concede to interdependency. An esprit de corps replaces complacency. The culture is enhanced and becomes more change adept and more market focused. The culture is more robust; people become more capable and produce an even deeper leadership bench. **When *culture* becomes synonymous with *professional*, it has greater character, all of which is reflected in higher levels of performance.**

Why is the brand especially compelling?

- It reveals the best in people's character.
- It paints people into the heart of the picture.
- It appeals to an increasing cynical generation of employees.
- It maximizes lost opportunities.

Revealing the Best in Each Person's Character

Recall the lineman from a few paragraphs ago who rejected the opportunity to work in an unprofessional yard even though that refusal entailed continued sacrifices. That is the power of professionalism! It's also seen in a courageous senior leader who authentically and apologetically reveals a personal failing that has held back his team. It can be found in room of senior staff and partners at one of the world's largest professional services firms who recommit themselves as professionals and tackle several organizational issues heretofore believed insurmountable.

Where does the strength come from to take an action that is sure to prove unpopular? to admit to a personal failing? to stick to your standards even if it means sacrifices? to support a decision that you don't agree with? to approach a colleague on a topic you know will be unpleasant?

That strength comes from within individuals. Rarely is this kind of professionalism influenced by the hype organizations generate to motivate their people. Instead, these people are motivated internally and driven by character! They are not just in it for the money—arguably an acid test in determining true professionals. As Dee Hock, chairman emeritus at Visa, noted, "Money motivates neither the best people, nor the best in people." Ray Davis, CEO of Umpqua Bank, added, "If pay is all you've got to motivate people, then you've got a whole bunch of mercenaries working for you." Professionals are many things, but they are not mercenaries!

Here's the ultimate paradox: for trusted professionals, it's personal! It's about who they are. They feel it in their bones. Money is a consequence of what they do—not their express purpose. Professionalism ain't just a job!

An organization's vision should describe what the company is trying to be. Likewise, its culture should describe what its people are trying to be. People must become better *prior* to their organization becoming better. A culture that aspires to have its people be something—rather than simply do something—has the very best chance of revealing the best in them.

But you might ask, Couldn't you bring out the best in people by emphasizing leadership? After all, isn't leadership development the primary mantra that most organizations focus on?

Emphasizing professional development applies to all employees, but leadership development applies only to a select few. People will always desire to be viewed as professionals, but they won't always want to be seen as a leader.

There are marked and important differences between leadership (executive) development and character development (developing professionals). Recall Peter Drucker's observation that the best leadership development program (the U.S. Army) was "about the development of character."

Leadership development is about the outside world: giving leaders experience, further training, etc. Character or professional development, in the truest sense, is about your inside world.

In chapter 1, I said that to be a trusted professional is to master life's lessons in personal leadership. Said another way, trusted professionals are the masters of their inside world. They consistently maintain their standards *and* make the tough calls, sometimes despite their organization. Trusted professionals can be found providing leadership at many levels in a company.

The word *professional* is generally synonymous with the word *trust*, but the same is not true of the word *leader*. This is unfortunate, but to think otherwise is simply naive. Think of Adolf Hitler, Joseph Stalin, and Mao Tse-tung as social leaders; think Jeffrey Skilling (Enron), Dennis Kozlowski (Tyco), and Bernard Ebbers (WorldCom) as business leaders. The Mafia has historically excluded anyone from its ranks whose behavior it deems as inconsistent with moral values. Talk about moral relativism!

Thus, a professional will always be construed as a leader, but a leader won't always be construed as a professional. **A leader who is not a professional is a leader in name only. Leaders who want to make a difference must be professionals and must instill professionalism in their people.**

It Paints People into the Heart of the Picture

How do you define or describe the word *culture*? If you're like me, people come to mind. Culture, after all, is synonymous with the language, customs, and behaviors of groups of people.

As a part of a leadership transition team, Shelly Lazarus, chairman and CEO of the advertising agency Ogilvy and Mather Worldwide, spent three days with the firm's legendary founder, David Ogilvy. Lazarus asked him, "If you were going to say one thing to me, what would it be?" Ogilvy didn't hesitate for a second. "No matter how much time you spend thinking about, worrying about, focusing on, questioning the value of, and evaluating people, it won't be enough," he said. "People are the only thing that matters and the only thing you should think about, because when that part is right, everything else works."

Renowned venture capital investor Arthur Rock echoed that premise: "Nearly every mistake I have made in this business has been in picking the wrong people."

Culture is about people. When people hear descriptions of their organization's culture, they need to be able to paint themselves into the picture. How deeply? Hearing that one's organization has a culture of execution says a lot about the organization and its priorities, but how easy or difficult is it to see yourself in that picture? Just as the word *culture* is so vague to many people, your ability to associate with your organization might also be vague. Consider the following:

"At Acme we have a culture of trust and accountability. I'm sure you're gonna like it here," said the senior vice president to the freshly minted MBA during a new-hire orientation. Setting expectations is a good thing. But employees don't want to see themselves as company drones. Just as employees need to paint themselves into a company's mission or vision statement, they also need to do so within a company's cultural brand.

Which of these is more compelling to you? At Acme we have (1) a culture of trust and accountability, or (2) a culture of professionals committed to trust and accountability.

My experience suggests that individuals, despite rank or responsibility, respond far more favorably to the second option because it honors the professionals most responsible for the company's results. Employees track to the second statement because they see themselves, or hope to see themselves, in that picture. In addition, leaders serious about developing their culture realize that putting professionals front and center marks a significant philosophical shift in their own thinking as well.

Note that trust and accountability, two very important Acme values, aren't lost in their branding statement. Rather *professionals*—the face of the organization—describes culture, while trust and accountability (organizational values) describe commitments made by those professionals. Including both the *who* and the *what* complete a branding statement and make a distinction with substance.

As I mentioned in chapter 1, professionalism is unique. It's the ladder upon which all other organizational virtues mount. It has innumerable rungs, but for our purposes, in Figure 13.4, I've only mentioned some of the foundational virtues: integrity, respect, accountability, etc.

Figure 13.4—Professionalism: The Ultimate Organizational Virtue

Appealing to an Increasingly Cynical Generation

Today, faith and trust in long-standing institutions are at all-time lows, especially with regard to corporations. Employees are frequently more wed to their own aspirations than to those of their organization. Some of the causes for this trend are deserved while others are not. Yet Me Inc. remains dominant. Cynicism is high and employee loyalty is low. Art Kleiner, author of *Who Really Matters,* observed that the oft-stated mantra "Employees are our greatest asset" is one of the great lies of modern organizations. Many employees seemingly agree with him. They feel faceless, like interchangeable parts, even disposable. They are merely workers, a means to their organization's ends.

Most employees perceive that the messaging around cultural aspirations is slanted toward the company. Employees want communication, but they often feel like they're getting propaganda. They know that management's primary job is to increase productivity, and to them the clarion calls of accountability by managers often ring hollow. "Is this merely a guise to extract more work from me?" they ponder. All of this creates the great paradox: American culture exalts individualism, but most organizations revere teamwork. This engenders a never-ending push-pull between the two ideals. In spite of this cynicism, employees respond favorably to an organization that aspires to conduct itself in a professional manner.

Maximizing a Lost Opportunity

In chapters 1 and 3, I pointed out that viewing oneself as a professional is so important that it becomes a part of our identity. For so many, this is a defining recognition. Not seeing yourself as a professional is a significant opportunity lost. But in our world today:

1. Most people don't think of themselves as professionals.
2. Even some of the best leaders and managers don't view their people as professionals.

Given the traditional history of who is and who isn't regarded as a professional (see chapter 2), it's easy to understand why those on the lower rungs of an organization don't see themselves in that light. I'm convinced, however, that most people on the higher rungs of the organizational ladder don't either see themselves as professionals either. Instead, they more often define themselves through their company and/or title. For instance, Jeff Immelt, CEO of General Electric, said, "This company is all I think about, it's who I am." Immelt has a lot of company!

It's only human nature that we're unlikely to reinforce in others what we don't see as uniquely valuable in ourselves. For senior people who define themselves primarily through their company and/or title and all the trappings that go with them, is it any wonder that they don't perceive their people as professionals either?

People are likely to embrace a view of themselves as professionals when their leadership does. Treating people as adults has been the successful cultural mantra that has served companies like Netflix, Seibel Systems, FedEx, Merry Maids, and the U.S. Army. Isn't being an adult a subset of being a professional? What's more motivating to you: being treated as an adult or being treated as a professional? Organizations whose membership views itself as professionals outperform, outsmart, and outlast organizations that don't.

You might think that this would be especially true in a white-collar environment—such as law and accounting firms—especially in comparison to the blue-collar world. Regretfully, it is not. At least, that has been my experience. Apparently David Maister, the world's leading authority on the management of professional services firms, has had similar experiences to mine. He commented, "I rarely meet individual professionals who believe their firm, as an institution, is built on such [professional] principles."

Think You're There? Think Again!

Most organizational cultural norms need to be ratcheted up to reflect a truly professional culture, but so many leaders and managers minimize the fundamental message that positive outcomes follow when people view themselves as professionals. These leaders may downplay this idea because they perceive that their organization is managed well and is successful. They may have a tendency to lessen the importance of branding their culture, because they feel that their people already perceive themselves as professionals. Unfortunately, that does not reflect reality.

When asked, most people consider themselves to be professionals, but few can explain what it really means to be a professional and few organizations reinforce the notion. Ask any starting pitcher how he feels in the late innings of a game, and 99 percent of the time he'll tell you that he feels great. In fact, they don't feel great. They're probably trashed. Pitchers respond the way they think they're supposed to. It's no different with professionals in the workplace. They affirm their desire to be considered a professional because they're expected to, but they have only a vague idea of what that means.

All of this may seem like bad news, but it isn't! The fact that people want to be perceived as professionals is great news. While they may have a lot to learn, we should never minimize or dismiss the impact inherent in this desire. Wanting to be perceived as a professional is the first step toward becoming one. And this aspiration is extremely motivating. Even top performers take it up another level.

I was brought in as a consultant to a financial services firm with exceptional leadership, explosive growth, and unbridled success. If ever a firm epitomized professionalism, this firm did. During my consultations, I thought that these people were teaching me more than I was teaching them. But below the surface I saw stress fractures in their conduct (driven from growth) that prevented them from achieving the next step up. What enabled this superb firm to regain its footing? The answer was, in short, a reevaluation by each member of the firm to be a better professional.

Culture in Action

Imagine investing millions of dollars to develop your brand. Your best thinking goes into it, and your commitment necessitates painful sacrifices. Differentiating yourself within a very competitive industry is difficult at best. Now imagine that the people who are providing the frontline defense of that brand are maids! Welcome to the world at Merry Maids, a company that provides top-of-the-line housecleaning services.

Maids don't seem to fit the image of defending your hard-fought brand. Actually, Merry Maids doesn't refer to their employees as maids. They are called team members (an organizational value), and each one is viewed as a trusted professional. According to former Merry Maids president Joy Flora, this ultimately has customers viewing them in the same way. Not only does the company's marketing efforts reflect this culture, but their people consistently back it up.

Merry Maids centered their brand on three things: the *quality* of their work, providing a *professional relationship* throughout their clients' experience, and guaranteeing *security* to their customers (being able to trust the people who come into their homes). On average, 60 percent of the time, the homeowner is absent while a team member performs the service. Providing a cleaning service with a key to your castle is a big leap of faith. In addition to superior professional service, Merry Maids is selling peace of mind based on trust. Is it any wonder that their marketing mantra is Relax, It's Done? What has this meant to Merry Maids?

- In 2007, *Good Housekeeping* named Merry Maids the nation's best housecleaning company.
- Two out of three people considering housecleaning services call Merry Maids *first.*

The Merry Maids brand is essential to their success. Their mastery in differentiating themselves as trusted professionals in a non-white-collar world is not only instructive but hopefully inspiring for leaders of all stripes, regardless of industry.

Notice the essential element of trust. "Trust is the key value of our times," said James E. Burke, a former chairman of Johnson and Johnson. I cannot stress enough the importance of trust as a key attribute of the trusted professional. Trust sets the bar for the depth and quality of a professional, regardless of the field of work.

Understanding the importance of trust is one thing; building it is quite another. **Build professionals and by default you build trust.** Trust is the one thing you must get right in order to achieve competitive advantage.

What really gets us through those moments when we're most challenged, dealing with a dicey ethical dilemma, working effectively with someone whose behavior we view as especially troubling, extending ourselves on an important but unrewarding assignment? It's not the company vision, our boss, or the work itself. What gets us through is our self-image as *trusted* professionals—and then we act accordingly.

Going Somewhere Fast

Every organization has a culture that drives its people to produce the results. Does your company culture create competitive advantage? To what degree does *professional* describe your culture?

Every year a portion of the workforce retires, and since culture teaches the next generation, a lot of teaching goes on every day. What does your culture teach the newest members of your organization?

Culture is learned. The trick for leaders is to shape the environment in a way that is stimulating. Since people motivate themselves, especially professionals (see chapter 3), it's imperative that a leader creates the right environment and the right assignments, opportunities, and sanctions for professionals to motivate themselves to get the job done. Leaders *can* shape their organization's DNA. David Lawrence, CEO of Kaiser Permanente, observed, "The winners do it less wrong."

Our bias is to create a culture of professionals that is shaped by an organization's senior leaders. Your ideal culture will be the one that delivers the results your organization demands. Regardless of the form your culture takes, it's imperative that its foundation is based on professional standards. David Maister said, "It is easier to find the discipline and motivation to behave professionally if everyone around you is doing the same." But not only does a culture of professionals provide superior competitive advantage, it uplifts and motivates more than any other culture.

While creating a professional environment is no easy task, it raises the bar and expectations. And great expectations are evidence of great respect, which is not lost on professionals. Given the never-ending waves of retirements in the years ahead, and the cultural teaching that goes with them, there's no better time than now to get the lesson plans right.

SUMMARY

- Professionalism and competitive advantage are inseparably linked.
- When an organization's culture reflects the highest professional standards, more people will do what they know they should do—and they'll do it more often.
- Developing a culture of professionals builds trust by default.
- Culture as a brand has positive and far-reaching impacts on employee morale, recruiting, and retention. An organization's culture is analogous to a person's character.
- Raising professional standards dramatically impacts all aspects of an organization, especially its results—and trusted professionals deliver the best results.
- A culture of professionals strikes at the roots of every problem and empowers every achievement.
- A culture that reflects the highest professional standards outperforms those that don't. It's a matter of focused energy.
- Branding is compelling because it (1) reveals the best in people's character, (2) paints people into the heart of the picture, (3) appeals to an increasing cynical generation of employees, and (4) maximizes lost opportunities.
- People are likely to embrace a view of themselves as professionals when they see that their leadership perceives them as professionals.
- Trust is the one thing you must get right in achieving competitive advantage. It places professionals front and center in a company's culture.
- Trust sets the bar for the depth and quality of a professional, regardless of the field of work.
- More than any other culture, a culture of professionals provides superior competitive advantage as well as uplifts and motivates everyone.

CHAPTER **FOURTEEN**

Professional Ideals: The Centerpiece of Success

Culture eats strategy for breakfast.
—Author Unknown

The implications from the previous chapter beg the question, To what degree is *professional* synonymous with *culture* in your organization? The answer partially answers another important question: *Who are we?* For leaders, this is the fundamental question that you must ask in order to assess where you are on the path toward integrating professional ideas in your organization. For conscientious leaders, the question is a humbling one, especially when you consider all the lofty expectations and implications that come with term *professional.* Most leaders know intuitively that they have a ways to go. Some have farther to go than others.

This chapter is designed to help leaders answer this basic assessment question. Included are assessment tools—both big picture and tactical—to aid leaders in the process. Fortunately, culture, perhaps more than any other aspect of business, is far more art than science. My approach here gives you a glimpse of that art.

Assessment questions can be threatening for some. The implications can be interpreted by leaders as a personal indictment of their leadership abilities. Some bristle at the questions, interpreting them as an implication that their organization is unprofessional. Some become overly concerned that questions about their organization's level of professionalism are interpreted by their staffs as a sign that the leaders believe the organization is unprofessional.

Both inferences are unfortunate because they are barriers to an honest evaluation of the effectiveness of the organization they have stewardship over. Most would not define an organization as unsuccessful should it happen to fall short of an especially choice, but challenging goal. Achieving a conference title instead of a Super Bowl victory, for example, does not make an organization unsuccessful. It simply means that the organization has a ways to go to get to the top of the heap. It also means that they are in a high percentile in performance, hardly a record that a reasonable person would characterize as unsuccessful.

Likewise, achieving perfection in fulfilling an organization's professional ideals (an extremely stringent standard) is unrealistic. (No one team wins the Super Bowl every year.) Falling short, however, does not make an organization unprofessional.

Organizations, like people, are unfinished products. The finest leaders I know constantly ask tough questions, and the answers they get might leave them personally vulnerable. But they're not terribly bothered by that possibility, because they have placed their institution above their ego.

I've learned firsthand how sensitive some people can be when they think someone else may view them as *unprofessional.* In chapter 3 my friend Jay was incapacitated after such an incident. The reason? Because it's as personal as you can get. It's about who you are. Leaders, therefore, need to reassure their people that they don't consider them unprofessional, but rather they want to continuously improve the organization. Leaders demonstrate the need to become an even better professional by starting with themselves, which is consistent with Mind-Set 3 (personally getting better) and Mind-Set 4 (high standards).

Figure 14.1 shows the big picture as I see it by illustrating the integration of professional ideals as a function of frequency of organizations.

This figure is not based on an empirical study—I am unaware of such a statistically based study—but rather represents my own observations sweetened with a small dose of academic research.[1]

Figure 14.1—Integration of Professional Ideals and Practices In Organizational Culture

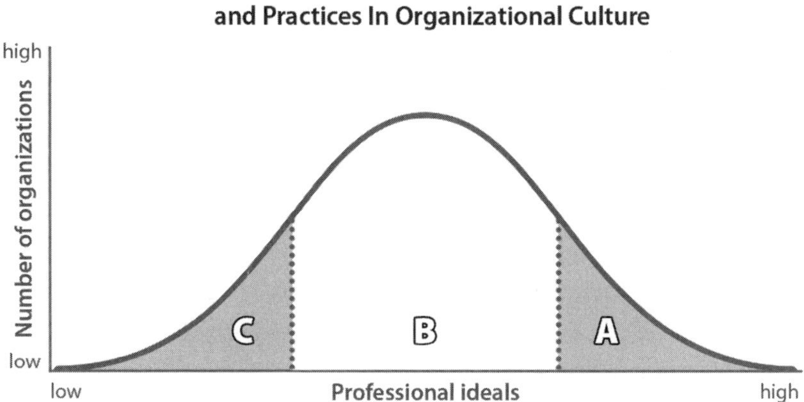

While I cannot defend Figure 14.1 empirically, I have confidence in it. I can defend it anecdotally from experience and through an interminable number of volumes in the business literature on topics relating to this general subject. I believe Figure 14.1 captures the essence of the degree that professionalism has become integral to an organization's culture.

It's important to understand what this figure means and what it doesn't mean. At first blush, it may appear that Figure 14.1 represents a distribution of organizations based on their degree of bottom-line success. That is *not* what this figure represents. Rather, it represents the overall health of an organization's culture based on the inherent assumption[2] that the integration of professional ideals buoys an organization's culture. Recall an earlier point, namely, that a healthy culture alone does not ensure an organization's success. Organizational success also requires an insightful strategy, robust expectations, disciplined execution, sufficient capitalization, and a host of other factors. At the same time, while many successful companies have healthy cultures, there are exceptions.[3] Therefore Figure 14.1 shouldn't be taken out of context.

Note the three different categories—A, B, and C—in Figure 14.1. These represent three natural groupings of organizations with varying levels of professional ideals integrated into their culture. C is the lowest of the three, B tops C by quite a bit, and A is the highest—the preferred state. It's a yardstick of sorts, a way of keeping score. Naturally, conscientious leaders will aspire to the A category.

Recall that numbers can distort reality, especially on things that matter most, like culture. It's something you feel far more than something you can measure. Keep that in mind while making evaluations about your culture.

Before each of the three categories are addressed individually, let's look at some important trends and perspectives that impact all three.

Figure 14.1 represents organizations across a broad spectrum—for-profit, nonprofit, nongovernmental organizations (NGOs), and the like. You might think that organizations that are not based on a profit motive (based more on benevolent ideals) might have healthier cultures. That has not been my experience. You see just as many power struggles and ego-motivated ambushes in nonprofits (academia, government, etc.) as in for-profit groups.

Figure 14.1 is a general guide. Use it as a rule of thumb, not a hard-and-fast rule. CEOs of large organizations (1,000 or more employees) can apply it to the greater organization just as well as department heads representing 150 employees can apply it to their organization's situation. A team-lead of a dozen employees will find it equally useful. The only real difference in each instance is scale. Department heads will likely gain a greater degree of specificity, largely because their departments are self-contained, whereas CEOs will have multiple departments, each having their own cultural characteristics. Because the CEO has responsibility for policy as well as the degree to which professional ideals are formally embraced within the greater organization, they have the biggest lever in shifting the organization to a higher level. But regardless of one's responsibilities, this figure should help assess where the organization stands.

Significant disparities in the degree of the integration of professional ideals can exist within each of the three categories. For example, in category C, a few companies have integrated a few ideals, but at the other end of the C spectrum, numerous companies have integrated many more. Comparing the substantive differences between a high C and a low B is difficult because there are not that many.

An A organization, for example, isn't comprised entirely of A individuals. Some are B's and C's. Some Super Bowl winners, for example, occasionally have a naysayer or two on the team. An A organization has a critical mass of A people. The same principle applies to B and C organizations. For example, a B organization contains both A and C individuals, just in lower proportions than the critical mass of B individuals.

A B-rated organization isn't necessarily destined to stay at B. It may fall to C or rise to A. Categorization is a dynamic that is influenced by the leadership of the organization. The same principle applies to A and C organizations. Organizations are also subject to temporary shifts. For example, a crisis may prompt people to rally around a compelling cause, and a B organization may temporarily jump to A, but the shift typically proves unsustainable. Likewise a B organization may fall to C during a vacuum in leadership, such as the sudden resignation of a prominent leader tainted by scandal. This, too, typically proves temporary, and the organization bounces back after new leadership is established.

As with most studies, people want to know the approximate percentages attributable to the C, B, and A categories. In my experience, it approximates a bell curve. That means that approximately 25 percent of the organizations are categorized as C and approximately 25 percent are rated A, with the remaining 50 percent occupying B status. Given that A is the preferred state, this means that 75 percent of organizations have a ways to go.

In spite of the difficulty in finding a direct correlation between the categories and an organization's level of success, I'm often asked for some general observations. I have confidence in commenting only on the A category. If an organization has achieved A status, there is a 75 percent chance that they are successful in a sustainable way. The B and C categories are much more difficult to assess. B is littered with metrics-driven leaders who often deliver meaningful results for their organization. Their cultures may not be optimal and may have harmful unintended consequences, but they are producing results. C organizations can have scoundrels at the helm, and their conniving ways can also lead to what some might call success. The next section will help put this tricky question into context.

Attributes and Characteristics of A, B, and C Organizations

A Culture

An A culture is a unique experience. Trust is highest in A compared to B or C. Professional ideals—whether they have been expressed implicitly or explicitly—are integral to the organization. Working in an A culture is often a positive defining experience in one's career. It is not necessarily because one's self-interests (money, prestige, ego, etc.) are advanced but because of the degree of personal satisfaction realized. The experience had real meaning, something with a significant purpose, something special about it, a special accomplishment. Perhaps it was building a great company, developing a cutting-edge product, bringing an impressive project to fruition, achieving the top market share in your niche, or turning around an underperforming team into a great one.

When founder and CEO David Kelley of the design and innovation consultancy IDEO started the firm, his objective was to "hang with friends and do things greater than any one of us could do alone."[4] Notice how this idea of accomplishment ties in with Mind-Set 1 (bias for results) and Mind-Set 4 (high standards).

Almost without exception the accomplishment was greater than any one person or even a small group could achieve. This means interdependency. The accomplishment was more strategic in nature, something that brought enduring success. As chapter 7 highlights, people often do their very best work and gain the greatest satisfaction from the experience when they are a part of something bigger than themselves (Mind-Set 2). Author Daniel Pink describes "something bigger" as one of three essential motivational drivers.[5]

Invariably individuals come away from the experience proud to have been a part of it. When asked, they invariably identity a number of professional ideals as key in realizing the accomplishment.

When one looks at the commonalities of an A culture, they are dominated by (1) like-minded people who hold shared values and (2) have embraced something that might best be described as a noble cause.[6] The noble cause need not be solving world hunger or finding a cure for cancer. Sometimes it's as simple as people wanting to do high-quality work (a common value among them) that makes a difference in something they view as important, something as straightforward as serving an underserved market (for example, financial services targeted to minority markets) or as involved as introducing a disruptive technology that changes the face of an industry.

When Nucor, for instance, started steel production with their revolutionary mini-mills in 1969, its aim (noble cause) was to redefine the rules on how steel was made and from what. It situated many of its production facilities in nontraditional areas in small rural communities. Why? The company wanted to recruit farmers with a high work ethic (an essential company value). Today, Nucor is the nation's largest steel producer, and in the process the company changed the way the world views discarded scrap, which is the source of the company's raw materials.[7]

Of course in addition to a strong work ethic, Nucor holds other important values, like teamwork, adding value to customers, etc. These values are not necessarily unique to Nucor; many organizations have similar values. What is unique is that Nucor *lives* them. The company defends its values. A general manager once laid off forty workers, an apparent violation of a Nucor value about workers having confidence in their employment. The employees retained their jobs, but the general manager was fired.[8]

It is no mystery to anyone at Nucor that the company's values mean something. An organization willing to defend its values is an important distinction that typically separates A cultures from B cultures.

Nucor isn't into mind control, but rather it has a singular focus on what the company is about. A cultures demonstrate this trait. Their work is their north arrow. An A culture is a "we" experience, not a "me" experience. Easily the biggest differentiator between an A culture and a B culture is Mind-Set 2 (Professionals realize [and act like] they are part of something bigger than themselves). People in A cultures demonstrate how a singleness of purpose to something bigger than themselves and an unwavering commitment to each other[9] can result in unparalleled success.

Three words characterize an A culture: collaborative, unity, self-less. Nucor certainly demonstrates these, and many other organizations do too. An A culture has power. It exudes energy, optimism, confidence. It is populated with people who are having the best career experience of their life. That it works is self-evident.

B Cultures

Working in a B culture is an experience most of us have had since 50 percent of all organizations fall into this category. Trust can be high between individuals or small groups, but it's spotty across the greater organization. The integration of professional ideals is not an express priority. Most would not consider the word *professional* to be synonymous with their culture.

For most employees, working in a B culture is not necessarily a memorable experience, largely because the degree of personal satisfaction is not terribly high. For conscientious overachievers, the experience is usually a letdown. Short-term profits in the for-profit world usually take priority over other considerations. Short-term thinking and protecting one's parochial interests are common. Hierarchy and politics are particularly prevalent in B cultures. The working environment can prove to be chaotic and unsettling. Working in a B culture is typically a "me" experience, not a "we" experience.

From a financial standpoint, a B culture can work for many organizations. Some positions (high-end individual contributors, professors, researchers, physicians, and attorneys) in fact lend themselves well to a B environment. Individuals who love freedom and independence can flourish in such an environment. "Leave me alone and let me do my work" is commonly heard. It would not be unusual to find many companies with B cultures on lists of the best companies to work for, but that doesn't mean there isn't room for improvement.

B cultures can be characterized by gold stars, mixed values, and flawed processes and practices.

Gold Stars: Individual achievement is the hallmark of B cultures. It's the way to get ahead, an avenue to advance your ambition for personal success, a way to get noticed, a way to be validated, a way to be rewarded. In some cases, it's a way to keep your job. The trouble is, it lends itself to unwanted internal competition (the real competition is across town, not across the hall), self-promotion, an inflated view of yourself, looking askance at others, thinking others are not as good as you (people will pick up on that), and denigrating others in the name of making yourself look good and making others look less worthy.

The desire for gold stars can taint your judgment. A leader buys a competitor company. What prompted the unexpected purchase? Enhancing the parent corporation's competitiveness or looking good by expanding the empire? A sales executive proposes a special deal with deep discounts to a preferred customer. What's the motive? To reward a loyal customer or to win the company's annual sales contest?

Gold-star environments, while having some redeeming benefits, too often unintentionally enable conduct that is antithetical to professional ideals, which works against the professional standards the organization should be aspiring to. A cultures strive to put the organization first; B cultures less so. Mind-Set 2 is far less developed in B cultures.

Mixed Values: This group is less like-minded than an A culture. As a result, people in B cultures have fewer shared values, which can be the result of the absence of a noble cause or the lack of something that prompts individuals to want to be part of something that is bigger than themselves. Thus, people tend to have less of an emotional connection to their work and to each other.

Flawed Processes and Practices: Organizations need processes and practices, especially as they grow. But an organization must either own their processes and practices or their processes and practices will own them. Taken to an extreme, they can strangle an organization. A process or practice is flawed if it doesn't reinforce and sustain an organization's values. When you hear complaints about "the system," that's usually a veiled reference to processes and practices. An organization that operates by committee cannot possibly live up to its value of empowerment when it takes five people to make a decision.

The absence of processes and practices results in a haphazard scheduling of preventive maintenance on essential operating equipment, or the unwieldiness of processes and practices results in a physician having to maneuver through a maze of bureaucratic red tape to get approval for a patient procedure. Mishandling processes and practices will harm the effectiveness of the organization and frustrate otherwise well-intended people. In either case, it detracts from the organization's aim to be construed as professional.

B cultures have more than their fair share of flawed processes and practices. In some cases the organization has become oversystematized, stripping out creativity and zeal and replacing it with robotic compliance. In other cases, processes are missing or inadequate, which requires greater discipline and prudence. The key is to find the right balance—judgment only a professional can bring.

C Cultures

Many of the same issues associated with flawed practices and processes discussed above can also be prevalent in C cultures.

Through informal studies I've found that the ratio of negative expressions articulated through language to positive expressions is 3.88 to 1.00.[10] Simply said, people whine far more than they express gratitude. The types of people in C cultures are what drive that ratio so high! They are people who are beaten down by life, their boss, or themselves.

The C culture could be characterized as a downtrodden people led by so-called leaders who either created the situation or enabled more of their people's innate dark-side tendencies. Even when things go well, people stuck in the C category are reluctant to acknowledge it. They exhibit little accountability and even less initiative. They consistently find ways for things *not* to work. They're not fun to be around. C is not a happy place, despite the faux nice attitudes and painted-on smiles.

Not all C cultures are condemned to stay that way. For instance, organizations can slide into C from B or A due to circumstances (for example, failure to secure FDA approval for a new drug) or hitting a rough patch (a bad economy). Professional leadership, however, eventually pulls them out of their funk, and they ultimately return to B or A status. But there are those organizations that seemingly are terminally stuck at C.

When working in a C atmosphere—one that breeds mediocrity—you find it easy to succumb to. It's like poison. It validates current victims and, by bringing others down, creates more. Compounding the problem, C cultures attract precisely the wrong people, namely, more C players. It's a cycle that's tough to break.

In fairness to the leadership of C cultures, there are often numerous and substantive constraints that you have to deal with. They include incoherent policies, dealing with C bosses, insufferable bureaucratic systems, uninspiring work, etc. Certainly these are tough conditions to work in, but they shouldn't be used as excuses.

Individually, these people can be found in every culture, but when a critical mass comes together, it results in a C culture. The catchphrase "misery loves company" was inspired by these people. It seems as if they're intent on recruiting others to their plight:

- A service representative, when asked by a customer for assistance, acts like it's an imposition.
- The naysayer shop steward who turns every labor grievance into a fight.
- The chief engineer who believes there's only one way to do things—his. He shuts down new approaches and condemns the organization to manage as if in a bygone era.

This points out one of two primary causes for C cultures: what individuals bring to the table. To say that they are short on Mind-Set 3 (things get better when I do) is an understatement. Typically they have defeatist attitudes either because it's innate to their nature or the circumstances at work bring it out. It's true that some have had a rough time of it outside of work. Yet it's incumbent, as a professional, to not drag that into the workplace.

The second primary cause of C cultures is faulty leadership. Some are Machiavellian. Some have good intentions but lead reluctantly. Some are blindly ambitious B leaders who create C cultures. Some are status-quo leaders short on Mind-Set 4 (high standards), which simply means they are not leaders at all. The by-products of their actions are different, but these leaders elevate the misery index inside their organizations.

Jennifer Colosi, principal of Colosi Associates, an executive search firm specializing in A player hires, noted, "We see it all the time, B players hiring C players, believing the C player won't pose a threat to them, enabling the B player to look good—at least relative to the C player."[11] Combine these types of leadership outcomes with someone with a defeatist attitude, and you've got a disaster on your hands.

It's possible, with hard work, to shift a C culture into a B culture, but it takes a leader who believes in the people and their capabilities and wants to build a great organization. Turning Mind-Set 3 (things get better when they get better) from a weakness into a strength is an important initial step.

A Reality Check

Perhaps this has given you a better idea of where you stand personally as well as where your organization stands in the A-B-C assessment model. To further help your evaluation process, peruse the three tables below that will drill down with even more specifics. All of this is to help you answer the question, To what degree is *professional* synonymous with *culture* in *your* organization?

The first of the three tables shows a comparison of what you see people doing in the three cultures. The second table illustrates defining characteristics. The third table reveals important perceptions of leadership. For leaders, it's a long look in the mirror. The source of the information comes from years of anecdotal conversations with clients and their teams, my own conversations as well as those of my colleagues. In essence, this table lets leaders know what perceptions their people have of leaders in each of the three categories on the most foundational, bare-naked aspects of their stewardship. While some may take exception to the methodology used to identify the information, I believe this table captures the reality of the situation.

A few cautions:

1. Keep in mind that you're trying to answer the question about how synonymous *professional* and *culture* are in your organization. You'll find areas where your culture has strengths and where it needs improvement. You may find that some aspects of your culture are B in nature and others are A. Try to look at the big picture.

2. Many have never experienced what it's like to be a part of an A or even a B culture. So it's difficult to make accurate assessments when you don't know what you don't know. B leaders particularly tend to believe that their cultures are A when they're not.
3. Self-diagnosis can be a tricky thing. Most of us tend to overestimate our strengths and our contributions. Plus, we all want to look good. This contributes to the dilemma that the quality of one's culture is a direct reflection of the quality of one's leadership. So in the spirit of the earlier example, it's important to realize your perception may be very different from that of a third-party or someone on your staff. Thus, people tend to rank the quality of their culture higher than it really is.

Table 14.1: What You See People Doing

	C	B	A
Taking Responsibility	Accountability applies to actions, not results.	Uses the formal leader to act as sheriff in ensuring organizational accountability, both for individuals and their colleagues.	Individuals are self-accountable for own results. In a supportive way, individuals hold their colleagues accountable for their results.
Degree of Unity	Low. Compliant when forced to be. Subversive when allowed to.	Too often supports initiatives in public, but subverts them in private.	Fully supports initiatives, even ones they don't agree with.
Demonstrations of Caring	Speaks up, typically voicing complaints about the organization without suggesting solutions and resulting in contentious debate.	People speak up when it's safe. They go along to get along.	Take personal risks by speaking up on matters of substance.
Expending One's Energy	Too often spends energy to ensure the status quo. Plays too many political games. Avoids work.	Too often people attempt to earn gold stars by outperforming other individuals within their own organization.	Competes to win institutionally, often to prove superiority in the marketplace or to other departments internally.
Who Gets Hired?	More C players, often hired by blindly ambitious B leaders.	More B players. The accidental A hire won't last, eventually seeking an A culture and/or an A leader.	The best talent available. A players compatible with an A culture.

Table 14.2: Telling Characteristics

	C	B	A
How People Are Feeling	Powerless, unimportant, disengaged, uninformed, victimized, disconnected, disappointed, angry, second-class, envious, violated	Challenged, accomplished, unsupported, prideful, unappreciated, insecure, disappointed, isolated, fatigued, overwhelmed, disheartened, dubious, let down, constrained	Trusted, challenged, respected, confident, valued, grounded, hopeful, energized, professional, grateful, appreciative, satisfied
Degree of Ownership	Tends to have more of an entitlement mentality. People take more than they give. They leave the place worse than they found it. If they were let go, they'd see it as a sign of validation for what they've claimed all along.	Has more of an employee's mentality. Too often people care only when it's convenient. People grudgingly tolerate of ineffective leadership, largely because it's in their best interests to do so. If they were let go, they'd be sad to be leaving their friends, but often they are relieved to be leaving an unsatisfying environment.	Has more of an owner's mentality. Emotionally connected. People will make sacrifices (e.g., take pay cuts) to be a part of the group. If they were let go, they'd be devastated, primarily because of the loss of the work they enjoyed so much and the sense of accomplishment they felt.
What Drives Them	Security. Validation of their victimhood. Affiliation with people who see the world much the same way they do.	As an individual overachiever, to show the world how great they are. Seeking opportunities to perform quality work. Meeting a significant challenge.	Working with accomplished professionals who share like-minded values. Using the shared values of their team to accomplish something special. To show the world how great their team is.
What You See/ What You Get	Surprisingly, has the ability to perform like an A culture in a crisis, only to revert after the crisis has subsided.	Is chameleonlike in ability to look like an A culture. But regretfully, it can have the form of an A culture but not the substance.	What you see is what you get. Plays politics when it's necessary to benefit the organization.
What You Hear	"Look at what they did to me."	"Look at what I did."	"Look at what we did."
What People Take Pride In	Being an organizational contrarian.	Their own accomplishments.	The group's accomplishments.

Table 14.3: Perceptions of Leadership

	C	B	A
Aspirations for the Organization	What aspirations?	The words may be right, but too many question the sincerity. Leadership's actions often reinforce the status quo. Keep the goose laying the golden eggs.	Wants to build something great that transcends them, something they alone couldn't build.
Attitudes About Money	Anything for a buck.	Money is the first and last measure of success for the organization.	Money is a consequence of success, not necessarily its express purpose.
How Success Is Defined	Machiavellian-type power. Live to fight another day.	Money, ego, prestige, influence. Being in the "club." Winning on a personal level.	Professional reputation. Succeeding the right way. Winning on an institutional level. Being deserving of success.
Level of Commitment to "the Work"	Too often an afterthought.	Can fall victim to careerism and ego.	The north arrow. Puts the organization and what it's attempting to achieve first.
Commitment to Their Group	The group is a means to the leader's ends.	Displays commitment only when convenient or expedient.	Consistently puts the group first.
What Has Leadership Earned?	Cynicism, a vote of no-confidence.	Few true followers.	Loyalty, respect, admiration, benefit of the doubt, credibility.

Perhaps you now have a better sense as to where your organization stands, whether you're mostly B, solidly A, or strongly C but approaching B. As a reality check, you may wish to have others in your organization do their own assessment as well. But heed these three important cautions:

- Remember that it wasn't a fish that discovered water. Internal assessments (or self-assessments) can miss things—big things. People are sometimes too close to see the situation clearly. I'm not saying this because I'm an external service provider who's fishing (no pun intended) for your business; I'm saying it because people typically rate their organization's culture higher than it is.

- Labels can stick. C organizations or individuals can be viewed by others through the C lens, much to the organization's detriment. C's are likely to be viewed negatively by others, just as A's are likely to be viewed positively. But one's level can change—up or down. Organizations are *at* a level, not *in* a level. They shouldn't be defined by their level, but rather assessed by the characteristics associated with that level.
- Being A doesn't mean that B and C are unprofessional. It simply means that the A organization has made more progress in having every individual in the organization become an even better professional.

While this is not a how-to book, here are three things to consider implementing that constitute a digest of how to more effectively integrate professional values into your organization.

Start with Yourself

The laws of credibility demand that we walk our talk. This prompts a thorough look in the mirror. Realize that this is not about leading others; it's about leading yourself. It's what Kim Clark, former dean of the Harvard Business School, fondly describes as leadership with a little *L*.

Leaders must embrace Mind-Set 3 (things get better when I get better). Where are my strengths? my gaps? You soon realize that to be a trusted professional is to master life's lessons in personal leadership.

Leverage People's Natural Motivations

With *professional* being synonymous with *best,* who wouldn't want to be considered a professional? Equally important, who wouldn't want to avoid being considered unprofessional? Experience has shown me that despite the apparent costs, people willingly embrace the mantle that comes with being a professional. It proves to be a free and often untapped source of motivation.

I beta-tested a workshop for fifty blue-collar utility crew foreman, emphasizing the *nontechnical* aspects of what it meant to be a professional and what it meant to them as individuals. Beforehand human resources and industrial resources warned that this would not work. "You'll never keep their attention for six hours. Besides, these guys don't respond to that kind of stuff." After the workshop, when most attendees scramble for the exit, many more of the foremen wanted to talk than made a beeline for the door. The workshop proved to be an overwhelming success. The foremen, while having a completely new perspective about what it really meant to be a professional, were willing to embrace the responsibility that comes with being a professional, even with the newfound responsibilities inherent to it. The workshop was later rolled out to eight hundred crew foreman in the business unit. Being a professional has little to do with the color of one's collar.

Be Persistent

It is surprising that so many talented, successful, experienced people fail to see themselves as professionals,[12] but I've seen this too many times to discount it as incidental. Because there are so many people like this, and it's going to take some time to bring about this kind of culture change. The good news, though, is that people are proud to associate with an organization they deem professional. Given the opportunity, they will welcome the prospect to make it so.

Professional Ideals

The priorities that are of utmost importance to the leaders of virtually any organization are all driven by the degree of professionalism achieved by leaders, managers, and employees. The higher the degree of professionalism, the better the attainment of priorities, all of which drives better results. This is the underpinning of my advice to every leader: build your culture around professional ideals.

This is especially important because culture is to an organization what character is to an individual. And organizations whose culture encourages its members to practice the seven professional mind-sets will have a competitive advantage over those who don't.

Clearly leadership holds the biggest lever of all when it comes to driving professional ideals deep into an organization's culture. This is why one shipping company flourishes while another flounders, why one call center excels while another languishes, why one division's executive team is stellar while a comparable one stumbles. In each case, the work isn't different, but the culture is,[13] and that's what makes the difference in outcomes. Work methods, processes, business models, procedures, and the like can be copied, but culture is unique. Culture is difficult, if not impossible, to copy. Likewise, there are limitations to copying best practices. Adopting a world-class best practice into a dysfunctional culture does not ensure superior results. While you can copy a successful business model, if you lack a culture populated with the seven professional mind-sets, you will likely be disappointed in the outcome.

In a survey of more than four hundred prominent CEOs and other successful leaders, Geoff Smart and Randy Street asked what factors contributed most to business success. Management talent rated 52 percent, which was head and shoulders above execution (20 percent) and strategy (17 percent).[14] This mirrors what Jim Collins advised in *Good to Great*: "First, get the right people on the bus."[15] Smart and Street and Collins advocate that leaders surround themselves with what Smart and Street refer to as A players,[16] ones who fit well within—or will positively help shape—your culture. These are people you can trust. And you'll know you can trust them because (1) they have the kind of proven competence that produces results, (2) they exhibit great judgment, and (3) their character is beyond reproach.

These three characteristics are discussed in great detail in chapter 5 and they're emblematic of trusted professionals. While Smart and Street and Collins don't literally say "surround yourself with trusted professionals," that's the reality they describe.

Aaron Kennedy, the chairman and entrepreneur founder of Noodles and Company, recalls a huge hiring mistake he attributed to a cultural mismatch. The hire involved a new CEO, and the aftereffects imperiled the entire company. Kennedy quickly removed the new hire and brought in Kevin Reddy, who "[had] all of the right [cultural] values we need.

And he *has a level of professionalism that really took us to the next level as a company.*"[17] That's what the spark of professionalism brings: a competitive advantage for the organization that embraces it. And there's no better place to infuse professionalism than at the top.

SUMMARY

- To what degree is *professional* synonymous with *culture* in your organization?
- Where does your organization rank according to the A, B, and C categories?
- Working in an A culture is often a positive experience, not necessarily because one's self-interests are advanced, but because of the degree of personal satisfaction realized.
- Three words characterize the A culture: collaborative, unity, self-less. They exude energy, optimism, confidence.
- Some positions lend themselves well to a B environment. Individuals who love freedom and independence can flourish in such an environment. "Leave me alone and let me do my work" is often heard.
- B cultures can be characterized by gold stars, mixed values, and flawed processes and practices.
- C cultures are dominated by downtrodden employees who exhibit little accountability and even less initiative. They consistently find ways for things *not* to work.
- The priorities of utmost importance to any organization are driven by the degree of professionalism achieved by leaders, managers, and employees.

CHAPTER **FIFTEEN**

The Great Potential Ahead

There is not one challenge in the world today that will get better if we approach it without confidence in the appeal and the effectiveness of our ideals.

—Condoleezza Rice

In this book we've examined the premise that professional ideals are integral to our success, both individually and organizationally. Given the present troubled times, this message could not be more important or more timely. This final chapter offers a few thoughts about the seven mind-sets of trusted professionals that will put this message in both a national and personal context.

No greater compliment could be given to any of us than to be considered a consummate professional, which is precisely how Gen. Richard B. Myers sees former Secretary of State Condoleezza Rice.[1] So let's begin with her.

Timeless Values, Priceless Benefits

Condoleezza Rice logged over one million air miles during four years as secretary of state. In her role as chief diplomat and ambassador for the

United States, she met with world leaders on every continent and tackled the nation's most difficult diplomatic issues. Despite considerable anti-American hostility abroad and innumerable issues of consequence, consider her reflections on that time:

> I got to see something that, in times like these, hearten me quite a lot and make me optimistic in that way that only Americans are optimistic. I got to see what it is that people really love about the United States. You can come from humble circumstances and do great things. It doesn't matter where you came from; it only matters where you're going. And that's what people admire about America. They may fear our military power. They may resent our economic power. Sometimes they think we're a bit naive and a bit idealistic. But they know one thing for certain. They know that countless people have come to this country and made a life so much better for themselves than they could ever have imagined. And it is why people still seek to come to this country.[2]

The United States has experienced not one but two great migrations, during which tens of millions of immigrants came to this country in pursuit of unfettered opportunities for themselves and their families. Even after many decades, the compelling tug of opportunity is still with us today. A 2005 Duke University study found that immigrants have founded 25 percent of all Silicon Valley technology companies![3] This should not be surprising, because the United States is the most prosperous society in history. And this is due largely to our superior economic system. Free markets can be transformative. The United States has certainly proven that to be a powerful formula.

Yet the optimism that has fueled the nation and the free-market economy has been replaced recently with cynicism and distrust. The nation faces numerous issues of consequence. It's no wonder that we hear so much today about the need to return to homespun values, get back to basics, and remember what made us great as a country. This is particularly true in the private sector. This book is my contribution toward that end.

In part 1 I made the case that professionalism matters in creating a competitive advantage for individuals and for the organizations of which they are a part. Develop professionals and, by default, you build trust. That's why professionalism is especially important now in order to counteract the present era of distrust. In these five chapters, I clarified what it really means to be a professional: the who, what, and why. This material should be a catalyst for many to shift or validate their thinking in important ways. Yet the most important point in part 1 is that most people simply do not view themselves as professionals, at least not on an emotional level. That's a huge gap in our national mind-set, especially when we consider the tremendous power inherent in foundational self-perceptions.

Drummer Carter Beauford of the Dave Matthews Band is a perfect example of this. He had been a member of one of the most successful bands in the business for ten years before he and his bandmates finally viewed themselves as professionals. It refreshed their outlook and changed the way they interacted with each other. As a result, they went on to do their best work. They set future-focused standards and expectations for themselves and chose not to go back to the old ways of doing things.

The Dave Matthews Band experience is surprising because it suggests that so many talented, successful, experienced people do not see themselves as professional.[4] My hope is that, as a result of this book, more people will begin to see themselves as professionals and start taking advantage of their many opportunities. Of course, they need to live up to the ideals associated with being a professional. But as they do, they will begin their own transformation and gain tremendous personal power.

My second hope is that leaders will embrace these professional ideals as the centerpiece of their cultures and instill the seven mind-sets in their people. Certainly chapters 13 and 14 present the case for why it's both important and in their interests to do so. Many leaders do not know what they're missing because they have never worked in an A culture. A professional environment attracts, challenges, and uplifts, but an unprofessional environment repulses, frustrates, and dispirits.

Personal Exceptionalism

Almost two centuries ago, French historian Alexis de Tocqueville toured this country and wrote, "The greatness of America lies not in being more enlightened than any other nation, but rather in her ability to repair her faults." A renaissance of professional ideals is a good place to start. And despite the complex issues we face, there is so much to be optimistic about.

Consider the following perspectives:

- "In ten years time the U.S. will still be a superpower economically as well as politically, militarily, and culturally. This country remains a massive jobs and wealth machine."—David Miliband, British Secretary of State for Foreign and Commonwealth Affairs[5]
- "So, bottom line with the American economy—we have a lot of challenges out there, a lot of problems, but there are very, very fundamental strengths."—Steve Forbes, president and CEO, Forbes Inc.[6]
- "The U.S. economy is resilient, its structure is sound, and its long-term economic fundamentals are healthy. . . . The economy, our economy, will remain a leading engine of global economic growth."—Condoleezza Rice[7]

Secretary Rice is not shy about extolling America's exceptionalism. "I loved representing this great country," she said at the January 2008 World Economic Forum in Davos, Switzerland. At the time there were troubling fluctuations in U.S. markets and concerns over the U.S. economy.[8] The primary issues included trade deficits, budget deficits, income gaps, wealth gaps, mortgage market turmoil, housing turmoil, and the unraveling of the subprime mortgage market.

The annual economic forum at Davos is arguably the most prestigious of its type, and it attracts business leaders, international political leaders, and selected academics and journalists. They discuss the most pressing economic issues facing the world. Given the situation in early 2008, many wondered what the representative from the world's economic superpower would say, especially since that economy had the hiccups.

Conventional wisdom counseled that Secretary Rice would assuage global concerns with flowery platitudes and disingenuous mea culpas. Instead, Rice took the statesmanlike route and chose to speak on "the importance of ideals . . . and . . . the need for optimism in their power."[9] After acknowledging the all-too-real challenges they collectively faced, she said, "I would submit to you . . . that there is not one challenge in the world today that will get better if we approach it without confidence in the appeal and the effectiveness of our [U.S.] ideals—political and economic freedom . . . open markets and free trade . . . human dignity and human rights . . . equal opportunity and the rule of law. Without these principles . . . we may be able to manage global problems for a while, but we will not lay a foundation to solve them."

In a time of darkness and discontent, Secretary Rice provided light and optimism. It was not simply Pollyannaish gibberish, but rather a demonstration of how the principles of U.S. ideals had historically led to success. It was a gutsy move, one that was drawn from conviction. It, indeed, engendered confidence in better days ahead—just as Rice had hoped.

Likewise there is no challenge or opportunity faced today by America's organizations—especially those operating in the private sector—that will get better without confidence in the professional ideals chronicled in this book. Without them we may be able to manage our problems or advance our opportunities for a while, but we will not lay a foundation to solve or advance them.

One Last Observation

I was intrigued at the nation's response to Chesley "Sully" Sullenberger after he successfully ditched a US Airways jet in the Hudson River on January 15, 2009, and managed to save all 155 people on the aircraft. Of course Sully—a consummate professional—is a hero. His skill, level-headedness, and selflessness are admirable beyond words.

At the same time, I believe the national outpouring of adulation for Sully says even more about the nation than it did about the beloved pilot. Ever the reluctant hero, Sully's life was changed forever. The nation could not get enough of him. The problem? America is clamoring for heroes. And when the country finally finds one, we won't let him go.

This lack of heroes is symptomatic of the nation's ills: too much me-first, not enough being part of something bigger than yourself. It's little wonder we desperately seek heroes, someone we can trust, someone to look up to, someone to believe in.

As Dave Ulrich pointed out: "I can't explain why a definitive understanding of professional ideals has languished in the shadows for so long in the world of professional development—but, ironically, it has." Despite the formidable issues we face as a nation and in the business world, I believe in the power of the human spirit and the ideals advanced in this book.

This book is about what's possible. It is an appeal to bring out the very best in people. The seven mind-sets described here do that—I've seen it. People respond. They cannot help but respond, because it's personal! Professionalism is the way; the mind-sets are the means. We need better professionals. We need more Sullys. So much depends on it.

I hope that the ideas shared in these pages have proved or will prove helpful to you. For many, this book has made explicit what they've always known. For others, I hope this book has made clear what's required of all of us as professionals.

To all you trusted professionals out there, I offer my thanks. This book would not have been possible without your legacy. You've taken the road less traveled, and it's made all the difference.[10] It is you whom people think of when fondly recalling the consummate professionals who have shown them the way. Always remember who you are. Your impact has left an indelible mark.

Notes

Preface

1. Phil Rosenzweig, *The Halo Effect: And the Eight Other Business Delusions That Deceive Managers* (New York: Free Press, 2007) essentially makes this same case.
2. John Toland, *The Rising Sun: The Decline and Fall of the Japanese Empire, 1936–1945* (New York: Random House, 1970), xv.
3. Robert J. Samuelson, "Bankrupt Economics: Why the Crisis Will Deepen and Get Harder to Fix," *Newsweek,* September 29, 2008, 31.
4. See Stephen M. R. Covey, "Trust Is a Competency," *Chief Learning Officer,* May 2008. In a related study of fifteen hundred publicly traded companies published in the February 2003 issue of *The Quarterly Journal of Economics,* firms with strong ethics were found to have higher firm value, higher profits, higher sales growth, and lower capital expenditures (see Paul Orfalea and Ann Marsh, *Copy This! Lessons from a Hyperactive Dyslexic Who Turned a Bright Idea into One of America's Best Companies* [New York: Workman Publishing, 2005], 117).
5. See S. A. Rosenthal et al., *National Leadership Index 2009: A National Study of Confidence in Leadership* (Cambridge, MA: Center for Public Leadership, Harvard Kennedy School, Harvard University, 2009), http://content.ksg.harvard.edu/leadership/images/CPLpdf/cpl_nli_2009.pdf.
6. Morality refers to the standards by which a community judges conduct as either right or wrong. For the purposes of this book, all references to morals or morality refer to secular morality.

7. Warren Bennis, *Why Leaders Can't Lead: The Unconscious Conspiracy Continues* (San Francisco: Jossey-Bass, 1989), 40.
8. David Ansen, "The Verdict: A Legend—Paul Newman, 1925–2008, In Memoriam," *Newsweek,* October 6, 2008, 63.
9. John Strausbaugh, *Sissy Nation: How America Became a Culture of Wimps and Stoopits* (New York: Virgin Books, 2007); Diana West, *The Death of the Grown-Up: How America's Arrested Development Is Bringing Down Western Civilization* (New York: St. Martin's, 2007); Mark Bauerlein, *The Dumbest Generation: How the Digital Age Stupefies Young Americans and Jeopardizes Our Future* (New York: Tarcher, 2008).
10. Roger L. Martin, *The Opposable Mind: How Successful Leaders Win Through Integrative Thinking* (Boston: Harvard Business School Press, 2007), 42; see also Dave Ulrich and Norm Smallwood, *Leadership Brand: Developing Customer-Focused Leaders to Drive Performance and Build Lasting Value* (Boston: Harvard Business School Press, 2007), 44.

Chapter 1: The Power Within

1. "A Conversation with the Members of the Dave Matthews Band," Charlic Rose, August 5, 2003, http://www.charlierose.com/view/interview/1858.
2. "Everyday (Dave Matthews Band album)," http://en.wikipedia.org/wiki/Everyday_(Dave_Matthews_Band_album).
3. How someone comes to view him- or herself as a professional may be different for everyone, but it largely involves (1) being treated by others as a professional and (2) holding an aspirational identity of yourself as a professional.
4. Peter Drucker, "What Makes an Effective Executive," *Harvard Business Review,* June 2004, 61.
5. Warren G. Bennis and Robert J. Thomas, *Geeks and Geezers: How Era, Values, and Defining Moments Shape Leaders* (Boston: Harvard Business School Press, 2002), 19.
6. "52 Must Read Quotes from Legendary Investor Warren Buffett," Investing School, http://investing-school.com/history/52-must-read-quotes-from-legendary-investor-warren-buffett/.
7. Frances Hesselbein et al., eds., *The Leader of the Future 2: Visions, Strategies, and Practices for the New Era* (San Francisco: Jossey-Bass, 2006), 146.
8. Hesselbein, *The Leader of the Future 2,* 256.
9. Robert I. Sutton, "The Best Practices Trap," CIO Insight, February 1, 2004, http://www.cioinsight.com/c/a/Past-News/Robert-Sutton-The-BestPractices-Trap/.
10. Robert E. Quinn, "Moments of Greatness: Entering the Fundamental State of Leadership," *Harvard Business Review* (July–August 2005): 75, italics added.

Chapter 2: It's a Bigger Tent than You Realize

1. Ashish Nanda, "Who Is a Professional?" Harvard Business School, March 24, 2005, publication 9-904-047.
2. The process of categorizing job classifications as professional or nonprofessional also contributes to this problem. The federal government typically uses such classifications, as do industrial relations departments in major corporations.
3. Warren G. Bennis and James O'Toole, "How Business Schools Lost Their Way," *Harvard Business Review* 83, no. 5 (May 2005): 96.
4. Kathryn J. Lively, "Occupational Claims to Professionalism: The Case of Paralegals," *Symbolic Interaction* 24 (2001): 343–66.

Chapter 3: The Psychology of Being a Professional

1. See http://en.wikipedia.org/wiki/Carl_Rogers.
2. Jerry Porras, Stewart Emery, and Mark Thompson, "The Cause Has Charisma," *Leader to Leader* 43 (Winter 2007): 26–31.
3. See James Waldroop and Timothy Butler, *The 12 Bad Habits That Hold Good People Back: Behavior Patterns That Keep You from Getting Ahead* (New York: Doubleday, 2000).
4. These suppositions are based on my experience and anecdotal stories from workshop participants.
5. "Elizabeth Vargas Tells Oprah She Wasn't Forced Out," January 23, 2007, 6abc.com, http://abclocal.go.com/wpvi/story?section=news/entertainment&id=4963184.
6. Quoted in John Maxwell, *Becoming a Person of Influence: How to Positively Impact the Lives of Others* (Nashville: Thomas Nelson, 1997), 49.
7. Albert Bandura, "Self-Efficacy," in *Encyclopedia of Mental Health,* ed. H. Friedman (San Diego: Academic Press, 1998), http://www.des.emory.edu/mfp/BanEncy.html.
8. Richard Moore, "Napoleon on War," http://www.napoleonguide.com/maxim_war.htm.
9. *Contra Costa Times,* August 7, 2007.
10. David Dolitch, Peter C. Cairo, and Stephen H. Rhinesmith, *Head, Heart, and Guts: How the World's Best Companies Develop Compete Leaders* (San Francisco: Jossey-Bass, 2006), 84.
11. Marshall Goldsmith, interview with author, July 26, 2007, Napa, California.
12. Dave Ulrich, interview with author, August 2005.
13. Waldroop and Butler, *12 Bad Habits That Hold Good People Back,* 172.
14. See Marshall Goldsmith, "My Dinner with Bono," Bloooomberg Businessweek, April 24, 2007, www.businessweek.com/careers/content/apr2007/ca20070424_499678.htm.

15. Gardiner Morse points out that managers typically underestimate the value of intrinsic motivation in employees. Their view of themselves as professionals is one such example of intrinsic motivation. See Gardiner Morse, "Why We Misread Motives," *Harvard Business Review* 81, no. 1 (January 2003), 18.

Chapter 4: Trust: The One Thing You Have to Get Right

1. CBS/*New York Times* poll, February 16, 2010; 2010 Edelman Trust Barometer: An Annual Global Opinion Leaders Study, February 20, 2010, www.edelman.com/trust/2010.
2. Frances Hesselbein, interview with author, April 14, 2008, New York City.
3. Professor Allan Cohen of Babson College was especially helpful in providing insight into the development of this chapter.
4. The term *emotional glue* is attributed to Noel M. Tichy and Warren G. Bennis, *Judgment: How Winning Leaders Make Great Calls* (New York: Portfolio, 2007).
5. David H. Maister, Charles H. Green, and Robert M. Galford, *The Trusted Advisor* (New York: Free Press, 2000), 12.
6. Tichy and Bennis, *Judgment,* dust jacket.

Chapter 5: The Big Picture

1. Morality refers to the standards by which a community judges the rightness or wrongness of conduct. For the purposes of this book all references to morality refer to secular morality.
2. John C. Bogle, *Enough: True Measures of Money, Business, and Life* (Hoboken, NJ: Wiley, 2009), 75.
3. Stephan Gandel, "The Case Against Goldman Sachs," *Time,* April 22, 2010, 30.
4. My financial advisor, whom I trust, shared this anonymous quote with me.
5. "For the love of money is a root of all kinds of evil. Some people, eager for money, have wandered from the faith and pierced themselves with many griefs" (1 Timothy 6:10, NIV).
6. John C. Bogle, *The Battle for the Soul of Capitalism* (New Haven, CT: Yale University Press, 2005), 1.
7. Bogle, *Battle for the Soul of Capitalism,* 42.
8. Bogle, *Battle for the Soul of Capitalism,* xvi.
9. Bogle, *Battle for the Soul of Capitalism,* xvi.
10. Jeffrey Immelt, "Renewing American Leadership," U.S. Military Academy, West Point, NY, December 9, 2009.
11. Regulatory oversight, while not a subject of this book, has an appropriate role as well.
12. This online query was executed on May 26, 2010.

13. By free, I am not suggesting the absence of regulation but rather a marketplace where goods and services are freely transacted by willing participants. In the literal sense, free markets do not exist in the United States, because some form of regulation impacts virtually all forms of commerce. Often the term *open market* is used synonymously with *free market.*
14. Microcredit is the extension of very small loans to impoverished individuals designed to spur entrepreneurship. It has helped entire villages in third-world environments that have been impoverished for generations to begin to build wealth and escape poverty. Due to the success of this powerful tool, microcredit has gained credibility with many in traditional banking circles. Numerous traditional, mainstream finance organizations are contemplating microcredit projects as a source of future growth.
15. See Catherine Drinker Bowen, *Miracle at Philadelphia: The Story of the Constitutional Convention, May to September, 1787* (Boston: Little, Brown, 1966).
16. See Tom Brokaw, *The Greatest Generation* (New York: Random House, 1998), which is a chronicle of the American men and women who endured the Great Depression and then fought and won the Second World War. Brokaw suggested this was our greatest generation. My father, Rene Wiersma, served in the Sixth Armored Division in the European theater.
17. Just as the quality of a tree is judged by the quality of its fruit, likewise, our national institutions should be judged by what they produce.

Chapter 6: Mind-Set 1: Professionals Have a Bias for Results

1. Stephen M. R. Covey, *The Speed of Trust* (New York: Free Press, 2006), 109.
2. Dave Ulrich, interview with author, August 19, 2009.
3. The story spotlighting George Piro was developed from a compilation of three sources: Piro, interview with author, October 27, 2009; "Saddam's Confessions," *60 Minutes,* CBS, January 27, 2008; and Ronald Kessler, *The Terrorist Watch: Inside the Desperate Race to Stop the Next Attack* (New York: Three Rivers Press, 2007).
4. Katherine Schweit, Special Agent John Perren's representative, e-mail message to author, Feb 5, 2010.
5. Paraphrased from Henry Lee's oration at Washington's funeral.
6. David G. McCullough, September 27, 2007 address, Brigham Young University; see also Paul Johnson, *George Washington: The Founding Father* (New York: HarperCollins, 2005); Joseph J. Ellis, *His Excellency: George Washington* (New York: Knopf, 2004); David G. McCullough, *1776* (New York: Simon and Schuster, 2005); John Buchanan, *The Road to Valley Forge: How Washington Built the Army That Won the Revolution* (Hoboken, NJ: Wiley, 2004); Richard Norton Smith, *Patriarch: George Washington and the New American Nation* (Boston: Houghton Mifflin, 1993).
7. Dave Ulrich, e-mail message to author, August 28, 2009.

Chapter 7: Mind-Set 2: Professionals Realize (and Act Like) They're Part of Something Bigger than Themselves

1. Noel M. Tichy and Warren G. Bennis, *Judgment: How Winning Leaders Make Great Calls* (New York: Portfolio, 2007), 122.
2. Everything attributed to Marshall Goldsmith was obtained during an interview with author, July 26, 2007, Napa, CA.
3. Ronald W. Clark, *Benjamin Franklin: A Biography* (New York: Random House, 1983), 286.
4. See Thomas Fleming, *The Intimate Lives of the Founding Fathers* (New York: Smithsonian, 2009).
5. See Fleming, *The Intimate Lives of the Founding Fathers.*
6. Stephan Gandel, "The Case Against Goldman Sachs," *Time,* April 22, 2010.
7. Bill Moyers, *Report from Philadelphia: The Constitutional Convention of 1787* (New York: Ballantine Books, 1989), August 23, 1787.
8. John C. Bogle, *Enough: True Measures of Money, Business, and Life* (Hoboken, NJ: Wiley, 2009), 123.
9. Keith L. Alexander, "Wizards' Gilbert Arenas Pleads Guilty to Felony Gun Count," *Washington Post,* January 16, 2010, www.washingtonpost.com/wp-dyn/content/article/2010/01/15/AR2010011502656.html.
10. Speech from Jeffrey Immelt (Chairman and CEO, GE) at the U.S. Military Academy, West Point, NY, December 9, 2009.
11. GE and Home Depot both work with American Corporate Partners, which was founded by former investment banker Sidney Goodfriend. American Corporate Partners provides corporate mentoring services for veterans. Goodfriend provided helpful background on this topic during an interview with the author.
12. Gen. Richard B. Myers, interview with author, January 15, 2010.
13. Paraphrased from Theodore Levitt, professor emeritus, Harvard Business School.
14. Elizabeth Weise, "Salmonella Outbreak Linked to Raw Tomatoes Strikes About 150," *USA Today,* June 9, 2008, http://www.usatoday.com/news/health/2008-06-08-tomatoes_N.htm.
15. Jennifer Reingold, "The $79 Billion Handoff," *Fortune,* December 7, 2009, 84.
16. Selena Roberts, "Rodriguez Is a Bauble a Champion Doesn't Need," *New York Times,* October 29, 2007.
17. Quoted in Jerry Porras, Stewart Emery, and Mark Thompson, *Success Built to Last: Creating a Life That Matters* (Upper Saddle River, NJ: Wharton School Publishing, 2007), 68.
18. All content attributed to Gen. Richard B. Myers was obtained during an interview with the author, February 19, 2008, Los Angeles, CA.
19. "Westbrook Helps Seal It—with No TD," *Contra Costa Times,* December 17, 2007.
20. Mike Ditka, *The Tim McCarver Show,* December 3, 2007.

21. Amani Toomer, a wide receiver who played for the University of Michigan and the New York Giants, has described his experience in playing at De La Salle High School in Concord, California, as the epitome of what it really means to be part of a team, to subjugate oneself to "something greater" than self. De La Salle's renowned football program is one of the most successful in the nation.

Chapter 8: Mind-Set 3: Professionals Know *Things* Get Better When *They* Get Better

1. Jim Collins, *Good to Great: Why Some Companies Make the Leap—and Others Don't* (New York: HarperBusiness, 2001), 25.
2. Taking pride in what we do is a very different thing than being prideful (something that creates artificial—and damaging—comparisons between people).
3. David Marcum and Steven Smith have used the term unfinished product in their book *Egonomics: What Makes Ego Our Greatest Asset (or Most Expensive Liability)* (New York: Simon and Schuster, 2007) when referring to people who view themselves as capable but have unrealized potential.
4. Noel M. Tichy and Warren G. Bennis, *Judgment: How Winning Leaders Make Great Calls* (New York: Portfolio, 2007), 241. Tichy, once a GE insider, brings great credibility to this assertion.
5. The perspectives outlined in this section may be hard to implement in a bad economy. As I write this chapter, huge numbers of unemployed professionals are frustrated in trying to find any employment, let alone meaningful employment. That being said, top-notch professionals will always attempt to get a good fit despite the obstacles, even though they may not always be successful.
6. Timothy R. Clark and Conrad A. Gottfredson, "Agile Learning: Thriving in the New Normal," *Chief Learning Officer* (December 2009): 20.
7. Andrew S. Grove, *Only the Paranoid Survive: How to Exploit the Crisis Points That Challenge Every Company and Career* (New York: Currency Doubleday, 1996), preface.
8. See William E. Leuchtenburg, *Herbert Hoover, American Presidents* (New York: Times Books, 2009); and David Burner, *Herbert Hoover: A Public Life* (Newtown, CT: American Political Biography Press, 2006).
9. Quoted from Stephen M. R. Covey, *The Speed of Trust: The One Thing That Changes Everything* (New York: Free Press, 2006), 182.
10. Jeanne Liedtka, Robert Rosen, and Robert Wiltbank, *The Catalyst: How You Can Become an Extraordinary Growth Leader* (New York: Crown Business, 2009).
11. Kathy Ireland and Laura Morton, *Powerful Inspirations: Eight Lessons That Will Change Your Life* (New York: Doubleday, 2002), xxxi.
12. Ireland and Morton, *Powerful Inspirations,* 38–39.
13. Kathy has exceptionally high standards, both personal and professional. Mind-Set 4 (which is all about personal standards and values) could have just as

easily been used to showcase her story. For a number of reasons, I chose to put her story in this chapter.

14. Mabel Jong, "Kathy Ireland: From Supermodel to Supermogul," Bankrate.com, April 13, 2004, www.bankrate.com/brm/news/investing/20040413a2.asp.
15. Kathy Ireland, interview with Maria Bartiromo, September 4, 2008, New York, www.cnbc.com/id/15840232?video=845592030&play=1.
16. Christina Bohnstengel, "The Wide World of Kathy Ireland," *Haute Living,* March 6, 2009, www.hauteliving.com/sections/one-on-one/the-wide-world-of-kathy-ireland.
17. Elisa Ast All, "Kathy Ireland: A Supermodel and Entrepreneur Finding Solutions for Busy Moms," Celebrity Parents: Parenting with the Stars, www.celebrityparents.com/models/kathy-ireland-5847.
18. Ireland and Morton, *Powerful Inspirations,* xviii.
19. Kathy Ireland, interview with Maria Bartiromo, September 4, 2008, New York, www.cnbc.com/id/15840232?video=845592030&play=1.
20. Leaders can traumatize their people, whether by design or by default, by punishing individuals for having dissenting views, disrespecting them by ignoring their feedback, or embarrassing them by making light of their suggestions. Other means exist in addition to these examples.
21. Consultant Sandra Walston has written extensively on the topic of courage; see her *Courage: The Heart and Spirit of Every Woman: Reclaiming the Forgotten Virtue* (New York: Broadway Books, 2001). Texas-based activist Jim Hightower reportedly said, "The opposite for courage is not cowardice, it is conformity. Even a dead fish can go with the flow."
22. Quoted in Tichy and Bennis, *Judgment,* 51.
23. "And So It Goes," words and music by Billy Joel, Columbia, 1983.
24. Stephen Covey wrote extensively about the importance of being proactive in his best-selling book, *The Seven Habits of Highly Effective People: Restoring the Character Ethic* (New York: Simon and Schuster, 1989).
25. Marc Gunther, "Best Buy Wants Your Junk," *Fortune,* December 7, 2009, 97.
26. Roger Martin illustrates this story in greater detail in *The Opposable Mind: How Successful Leaders Win Through Integrative Thinking* (Boston: Harvard Business School Press, 2007), 56.
27. Martin, *The Opposable Mind,* 59.
28. Quoted in Frances Hesselbein and Marshall Goldsmith, eds., *The Leader of the Future 2: Visions, Strategies, and Practices for the New Era* (San Francisco: Jossey-Bass, 2006), 126.
29. Typically these informal conversations were at least eighteen months after the individual was impacted by the change. These anecdotal conversations were informal. No standardized data collection or statistical methods were utilized. Admittedly, most of those conversations occurred before the dramatic decline in the economy during 2008–2010.
30. Gen. Richard B. Myers, interview with author, February 19, 2008, Los Angeles, CA.

31. Madison, however, disdained such laurels. He said that the final document was not "the offspring of a single brain. It ought to be regarded as the work of many heads and many hands" (quoted in David O. Stewart, *The Summer of 1787: The Men Who Invented the Constitution* [New York: Simon and Schuster, 2007], 105).
32. Stewart, *Summer of 1787,* 28.
33. Richard Beeman, *Plain, Honest Men: The Making of the American Constitution* (New York: Random House, 2009), 49.
34. Catherine Drinker Bowen, *Miracle at Philadelphia: The Story of the Constitutional Convention, May to September 1787* (Boston: Little, Brown, 1966), 13.
35. Ralph Ketcham, *James Madison: A Biography* (New York: Macmillan, 1971), 179.
36. Clinton Rossiter, *1787: The Grand Convention* (New York: Macmillan, 1966), 125.
37. Ketcham, *Madison,* 183–84.
38. Rossiter, *1787,* 126.
39. Rossiter, *1787,* 160.
40. Ketcham, *Madison,* 191–92.
41. Richard Labunski, *James Madison and the Struggle for the Bill of Rights* (New York: Oxford University Press, 2006), 22.

Chapter 9: Mind-Set 4: Professionals Have Personal Standards That Often Transcend Organizational Ones

1. "A Conversation with Author David McCullough," *Charlie Rose,* March 21, 2008.
2. John Bogle, *Character Counts: The Creation and Building of the Vanguard Group* (New York: McGraw Hill, 2002), 220.
3. John Bogle, interview with author, February 22, 2010.
4. Rudy Giuliani, *Leadership* (New York: Hyperion, 2002), 70.
5. John Bogle, interview with author, February 22, 2010.
6. John C. Bogle, *Enough* (New Jersey: Wiley, 2009), 99. Note that NFL legend Jerry Rice ran a time-trial 4.6 forty—slow by league standards. On the playing field, however, after he caught the ball, it was rare that anyone could catch him.
7. Attributed to William J. Bernstein, author of *Four Pillars of Investing: Lessons for Building a Winning Portfolio* (New York: McGraw Hill, 2002) and *A Splendid Exchange: How Trade Shaped the Word* (New York: Atlantic Monthly Press, 2008).
8. Taken from Cliff Asness's endorsement of John C. Bogle, *The Battle for the Soul of Capitalism* (New Haven: Yale University Press, 2005).

9. Richard B. Myers, *Eyes on the Horizon: Serving on the Frontlines of National Security* (New York: Threshold, 2009), 117; Gen. Richard B. Myers, interview with author, February 19, 2008, Los Angeles, CA.
10. Peter Peterson, *The Education of an American Dreamer: How a Son of Greek Immigrants Learned His Way from a Nebraska Diner to Washington, Wall Street, and Beyond* (New York: Twelve, 2009), 81.
11. Peterson, *American Dreamer,* 81.
12. Peterson, *American Dreamer,* 81.
13. Peterson, *American Dreamer,* 81–82.
14. Peterson, *American Dreamer,* 83.
15. Peterson, *American Dreamer,* 83.
16. Peter Peterson, *Charlie Rose,* April 2, 2008.
17. Kathy Ireland, interview with author, December 17, 2010
18. Stephen Roseberry, interview with author, December 21, 2010
19. Rocci Ingemi, interview with author, December 21, 2010.
20. Stephen Roseberry, interview with author, December 21, 2010.
21. The following is based on material from David G. McCullough, *John Adams* (New York: Simon and Schuster, 2001); Dumas Malone, *Jefferson the Virginian,* Jefferson and His Time, vol. 1 (Boston: Little, Brown, 1948); and Ronald W. Clark, *Benjamin Franklin: A Biography* (New York: Random House, 1983).
22. Jim Collins, *Good to Great: Why Some Companies Make the Leap—and Others Don't* (New York: HarperBusiness, 2001), 50.
23. Paraphrased from John Bogle.

Chapter 10: Mind-Set 5: Professionals Know That Personal Integrity Is All They Have

1. Gary D'Amato, "Pro Golfer Hayes Penalizes Himself Out of a Job," *Milwaukee Journal Sentinel,* November 18, 2008, www.jsonline.com/sports/golf/34717824.html.
2. This came from the 2007 Harvard study that is broadly alluded to in the preface.
3. Bill George, *Authentic Leadership: Rediscovering the Secrets to Creating Lasting Value* (San Francisco: Jossey-Bass, 2003), 16.
4. Stephen R. Covey has written extensively about the personality ethic.
5. George, *Authentic Leadership,* 12.
6. Ronald Reagan, "Address to the Nation on the Iran Arms and Contra Aid Controversy," March 4, 1987, www.reagan.utexas.edu/archives/speeches/1987/030487h.htm.
7. John W. Gardner, *On Leadership* (New York: Free Press, 1990), 43.
8. Gardner, *On Leadership,* 33.

9. The following is based on David Kirkpatrick, "The Temptation of Facebook," *Fortune,* May 24, 2010, 108–16.
10. Frances Hesselbein, interview with author, April 14, 2008, in New York, NY.
11. This material comes from Jacob Ernest Cooke, *Alexander Hamilton* (New York: Scribner's, 1982); Joseph J. Ellis, *Founding Brothers: The Revolutionary Generation* (New York: Knopf, 2002); Willard Sterne Randall, *Alexander Hamilton: A Life* (New York: HarperCollins, 2003); Robert E. Wright, *Hamilton Unbound: Finance and the Creation of the American Republic* (Westport, CT: Greenwood, 2002).
12. Gen. Richard B. Myers, interview with author, February 19, 2008, Los Angeles, CA.

Chapter 11: Mind-Set 6: Professionals Aspire to Be Masters of Their Emotions, Not Enslaved by Them

1. See Peter M. Senge, *The Fifth Discipline: The Art and Practice of the Learning Organization* (New York: Doubleday/Currency, 1990).
2. I wrote extensively about the relationship between trust and consistency of behavior in chapter 5.
3. C. Terry Warner, *Bonds That Make Us Free: Healing Our Relationships, Coming to Ourselves* (Salt Lake City: Shadow Mountain, 2001).
4. See Bill Wiersma, *The Big AHA! Breakthroughs in Resolving and Preventing Workplace Conflict* (Los Altos, CA: Ravel Media, 2006), 101–15.
5. As noted in *The Big AHA!* 113–14, our emotions are not automatic by-products of our interactions with others. Rather, emotions are our interpretations of events. Thus, we alone assign the meaning our interactions have with others.
6. Seymour Epstein, *Constructive Thinking: The Key to Emotional Intelligence* (Westport, CT: Praeger, 1998).
7. Seymour Epstein, e-mail message to author, April 2, 2010.
8. This example does not imply that the suspect isn't entitled to due process—he is. The example is merely an attempt to point out that the police officer is respecting of the suspect even though she has firsthand knowledge of the suspect's guilt. Despite her emotions, the officer did not respond in kind to the suspect and ultimately treated him better than his crime deserved.
9. Ronald Kessler, *The Terrorist Watch: Inside the Desperate Race to Stop the Next Attack* (New York: Crown, 2007), 157.
10. Wiersma, *The Big AHA!* 111.
11. Wiersma, *The Big AHA!* 8.
12. Jerry Porras, Stewart Emery, and Mark Thompson, *Success Built to Last: Creating a Life That Matters* (Upper Saddle River, NJ: Wharton School Publishing, 2007), 8.

13. Fairness, while an admirable ideal, is difficult to achieve in practice. Interpersonal fairness, which is our focus, is more easily achieved than societal fairness.
14. The original phrase is from Oscar Wilde, *Lady Windermere's Fan,* act 3.
15. George Piro, interview with author, January 22, 2010.
16. George Piro, interview with author, January 22, 2010.
17. Steven Smith and David Marcum, *Egonomics: What Makes Ego Our Greatest Asset (or Most Expensive Liability)* (New York: Simon & Schuster, 2007).
18. Professor James O'Toole notes in a November 2, 2006, e-mail to the author that arrogance may also have as its root cause hurt or anger.
19. Contented ego is discussed in Larry Bossidy and Ram Charan, *Execution: The Discipline of Getting Things Done* (New York: Crown Business, 2002).
20. Michael H. Smith, e-mail message to author, June 16, 2010.
21. The term "worshiping sycophants" is borrowed from James O'Toole, *Leading Change: Overcoming the Ideology of Comfort and the Tyranny of Custom* (San Francisco: Jossey-Bass, 1995), 30.
22. Alexander Hamilton and Thomas Jefferson particularly locked horns.
23. For example, when the Second Continental Congress convened in 1775 to address the military conflict with Great Britain, Washington arrived for the first session in his militia uniform, subtly indicating his desire to lead the army.
24. Marshall Goldsmith, "Succession: Are You Ready?" A draft of the manuscript was supplied to the author prior to its publication in 2009 by Harvard Business School Publishing.
25. O'Toole, *Leading Change,* 189–200.
26. James O'Toole, e-mail message to author, November 2, 2006.
27. O'Toole addresses Deming's experience in greater detail in chapter 9 of *Leading Change,* 189–200.
28. I choose to describe Deming as having an unhealthy ego (inflated, perhaps) rather than use the term hubris, which implies overbearing pride. O'Toole believes that wounded ego (stemming from his rejection in the United States) may have played a significant role in Deming's behavior.
29. James O'Toole, e-mail message to author, November 2, 2006.
30. Smith and Marcum, *Egonomics,* 5.
31. Paul C. Nutt, *Why Decisions Fail: Avoiding the Blunders and Traps That Lead to Debacles* (San Francisco: Berrett-Koehler, 2002).
32. Paraphrased from the well-known catchphrase, "Never mistake acts of kindness for weakness."
33. Luck does not suggest leaving one's success to mere chance or divine providence. However, there are circumstances where events produce unexpectedly positive and unintended outcomes. Post-it notes and the world-renowned Stradivari string instruments are two examples among many.
34. At the time of the book's first printing, Jim Leach was the chairman of the National Endowment for the Arts.

35. Bob Burg, interview with author, March 7, 2008.
36. Marshall Goldsmith writes about this extensively in his bestseller *What Got You Here Won't Get You There: How Successful People Become Even More Successful* (New York: Hyperion, 2007).
37. John Bogle, interview with author, February 22, 2010.
38. Quoted at "The Turtle on the Fence Post," Kent Crockett's Devotionals, http://kentcrockett.blogspot.com/2009/08/turtle-on-fence-post.html.
39. Bill Moyers, *Report from Philadelphia: The Constitutional Convention of 1987* (New York: Ballantine Books, 1987).
40. Catherine Drinker Bowen, *Miracle at Philadelphia: The Story of the Constitutional Convention, May to September 1787* (Boston: Little, Brown, 1966), 54.
41. Moyers, *Report from Philadelphia.*
42. Moyers, *Report from Philadelphia.*
43. Bowen, *Miracle at Philadelphia,* 95.
44. Bowen, *Miracle at Philadelphia,* 96.
45. Roger Martin addresses this topic in detail in *The Opposable Mind: How Successful Leaders Win Through Integrative Thinking* (Boston: Harvard Business School Press, 2007).
46. Paul Orfalea and Ann Marsh, *Copy This! Lessons from a Hyperactive Dyslexic Who Turned a Bright Idea into One of America's Best Companies* (New York: Workman Publishing, 2005), 202.

Chapter 12: Mind-Set 7: Professionals Aspire to Reveal Value in Others

1. Amanda Myers Ellison provided the content for this story, interview with author, July 14, 2009.
2. Paul Orfalea, interview with author, January 25, 2010.
3. Budgets were likewise approached in the same manner, with approval required by three-fourths of the stores.
4. There was a corporate center at Kinko's, and it exerted a centralized influence, but this was far less than other enterprises of the same type.
5. Paul Orfalea and Ann March, *Copy This! How I Turned Dyslexia, ADHD, and 100 Square Feet into a Company Called Kinko's* (New York: Workman, 2007), 51.
6. Orfalea, interview with author, January 25, 2010.
7. Orfalea, *Copy This!* viii.
8. Orfalea, *Copy This!* xix.
9. *Contra Costa Times,* March 1, 2009.
10. John C. Maxwell, "Encouragement Changes Everything," *Success* magazine, www.successmagazine.com/encouragement-changes-everything/PARAMS/article/761.

11. This material comes from Ronald W. Clark, *Benjamin Franklin: A Biography* (New York: Random House, 1983); Walter Isaacson, *Benjamin Franklin: An American Life* (2004); and Benjamin Franklin, *The Autobiography of Benjamin Franklin*, ed. Leonard W. Labaree et al. (New Haven, CT: Yale University Press, 1964).

Chapter 13: Your Competitive Advantage Is Hiding in Plain Sight

1. Noel Tichy, phone interview with author, February 2008.
2. See Dave Ulrich and Norm Smallwood, *Leadership Brand: Developing Customer-Focused Leaders to Drive Performance and Build Lasting Value* (Boston: Harvard Business School Press, 2007).

Chapter 14: Professional Ideals: The Centerpiece of Success

1. David Logan, John King, and Halee Fischer-Wright developed a cultural study based on over twenty-two thousand participants. Their study was not specifically based on professional ideals but on the impact of culture as evidenced by language. Logan is a professor at the University of Southern California, and Fischer-Wright teaches at the University of Colorado Medical School. Their work was published in *Tribal Leadership: Leveraging Natural Groups to Build Thriving Organizations* (New York: HarperCollins, 2008).
2. In my view, this assumption is reasonable and conservative in nature.
3. The reverse is also true. A company with an unhealthy culture can demonstrate success, although typically it proves unsustainable.
4. Logan, King, and Fischer-Wright, *Tribal Leadership*, 117.
5. Daniel Pink, *Drive: The Surprising Truth About What Motivates Us* (New York: Riverhead, 2009).
6. Noble cause language used by Logan, King, and Fischer-Wright. Other related language (vision, future state, big idea, etc.) are first cousins to Logan's description. Both Logan et al. and Seth Godin have written about how groups rally around a particularly compelling idea that is consistent with the values of the members of the group. See Logan, King, and Fischer-Wright, *Tribal Leadership*, and Seth Godin, *Tribes: We Need You to Lead Us* (New York: Portfolio, 2008).
7. See Nucor's company story at http://www.nucor.com/story.
8. Bill Nobles and Judy Redpath, *Market-Based Management: A Key to Nucor's Success* (Fairfax, VA: Center for Market Processes, 1995), http://www.mbminstitute.org/uploads/MBM%20at%20Nucor1.pdf.
9. Teamwork is what the Green Bay Packers teams of the 1960s were all about. They didn't play for individual glory. They did it because they loved one another. Vince Lombardi Quotes, Altius Directory, http://www.altiusdirectory.com/Society/vince-lombardi-quotes.php.

10. Bill Wiersma, *The Big AHA! Breakthroughs in Resolving and Preventing Workplace Conflict* (Los Altos, CA: Ravel Media, 2006), 156.
11. Jennifer Colosi, e-mail message to author, August 13, 2010.
12. How someone comes to emotionally view him- or herself as a professional may be different for everyone, but it largely involves (1) being treated by others as a professional and (2) holding an aspirational identity as a professional.
13. Note that all of these are examples of a work unit that is part of a larger organization. That larger organization has its own overarching culture, but each unit has a subculture as well. The unit's culture is one that clearly impacts people's desire to work there. In Logan, King, and Fischer-Wright, *Tribal Leadership*, Logan refers to these units as tribes. Godin, *Tribes*, has also written extensively about tribes.
14. Geoff Smart and Randy Street, *Who: The A Method for Hiring* (New York: Ballantine Books, 2008), 148.
15. Jim Collins, *Good to Great: Why Some Companies Make the Leap—and Others Don't* (New York: HarperBusiness, 2001), 41.
16. Smart and Street define A players as candidates who have "at least a 90 percent chance of achieving a set of outcomes that only the top 10 percent of possible candidates could achieve" (Smart and Street, *Who*, 12).
17. Smart and Street, *Who*, 37.

Chapter 15: The Great Potential Ahead

1. Richard B. Myers, *Eyes on the Horizon: Serving on the Frontlines of National Security* (New York: Threshold, 2009), 132; Richard B. Myers, interview and e-mail with author, February 2008.
2. Condoleeza Rice, an address given at the Ronald Reagan Presidential Library, Simi Valley, CA, July 16, 2009.
3. Rachel Konrad, "Immigrants Behind 25 Percent of Tech Startups," Associated Press, January 3, 2007, http://www.msnbc.msn.com/id/16459952.
4. How someone comes to emotionally view him- or herself as a professional may be different for everyone, but it largely involves (1) being treated by others as a professional and (2) holding an aspirational identity as a professional.
5. Condoleezza Rice and David Miliband, Policy Talks, Forum at Google, May 22, 2008.
6. Steve Forbes, "The American Economy: Has It Lost Its Way?" Los Angeles World Affairs Council, March 5, 2007, http://www.lawac.org/speech/2006–07/FORBES,%20Steve%202007.pdf. Forbes puts the performance of the economy in perspective over many decades.
7. Condoleezza Rice, Keynote Address, World Economic Forum, Davos, Switzerland, January 23, 2008, www.america.gov/st/texttrans-english/2008/January/20080123183031bpuh0.4350092.html.
8. Both references come from Rice, an address given at the Ronald Reagan Presidential Library, July 16, 2009.

9. Rice, Keynote Address, World Economic Forum, Davos, Switzerland, January 23, 2008.
10. See Robert Frost, "The Road Not Taken," and M. Scott Peck, *The Road Less Traveled: A New Psychology of Love, Traditional Values, and Spiritual Growth* (New York: Simon and Schuster, 1978).

Index

D

G

H

I

J

K

L

S

Hold On . . . *There's More!*

We hope this book has stimulated your thinking—especially for those of you that lead or manage organizations. As importantly, we hope that your new insights and motivation translate into beneficial actions. Certainly there's a great deal from the book that will enable you on your own to become an even better professional and upgrade your organization. However, in the event you'd like some additional help . . .

About Wiersma and Associates

In addition to being an author and speaker, Bill Wiersma is a trusted advisor to executive leadership on senior team development and organizational culture. His work with senior teams is centered on the principles espoused in this book—namely developing people as trusted professionals. When taken collectively this becomes formidable—as power naturally emanates from a culture of professionals. The approach—called revolutionary by some—has as its aims to help individuals reframe who they really are and elevate how they 'show up' at work. Bill's work has high-impact, is results-oriented, and is wonderfully engaging—just like the book.

Bill is the founder and principal of Wiersma and Associates—a management consulting and training firm. His consulting work includes the Fortune 1000 and professional services sector. Media outlets that have covered his work include *The New York Times*, Gannette News Services, Small Business Review and Workwise—a nationally syndicated column.

Beyond The Book

We're envisioning this book being a platform for bigger things. Our expectations are to take the ideas from the book and drive the principles into a variety of industries, vocations, job classifications, as well as within individual organizations. Imagine titles like *The Mind-Set of the Trusted Financial Compliance Professional* (vocation specific), *The Mind-Set of the Trusted IT Professional* (job specific), or *The Mind-Set of the Trusted Professional at ACME* (company specific).

After getting feedback from readers, we're expecting to produce a Fieldbook—something that would especially aide intact teams. We'll also be creating a blog wherein people can weigh-in on issues and get tips from the readership. Higher-education is on our radar screen too.

Ambitious? Certainly! But all of this is possible with a like-minded community of people who not only want to see it happen but are willing to help make it happen. What does 'help' look like? It might be as simple as providing feedback on suggested topics for the Fieldbook, participating in a discussion group, or an expert becoming co-author for one of the new spin-off titles we're considering. Go to our web-site to learn more.

Visit:
http://wiersmaandassociates.com
or call: 925.933.6174
or email: wiersmab@comcast.net